MEMOIRS OF
A WARTIME
ROMANCE

MEMOIRS OF A WARTIME ROMANCE

The Story of Mr. Bops and Miss Boo

Jane Siegel Whitmore
and
Andrea Siegel Feinberg

Order this book online at www.trafford.com
or email orders@trafford.com

Most Trafford titles are also available at major online book retailers.

Printed in the United States of America.

ISBN: 978-1-4669-1196-3 (sc)
ISBN: 978-1-4669-1199-4 (e)

Library of Congress Control Number: 2012901137

Trafford rev. 08/23/2012

 www.trafford.com

North America & international
toll-free: 1 888 232 4444 (USA & Canada)
phone: 250 383 6864 ♦ fax: 812 355 4082

Introduction by the Authors

This is our parents' story. They wanted it told. In September of 1944 Mother wrote to Dad, "Our letters to each other would make a wonderful book and would certainly show people what real love is."

In an initial attempt to have their story written, they met with Gwethalyn Graham, whose book, Earth and High Heaven, was a number one book on The New York Times Best Seller List in 1944. This book was serialized in Collier's; was an important touchstone to our parents; and is mentioned multiple times in the letters. Ms. Graham died before any further discussions occurred. Over the years, we and our children have spoken about who should write their story. After our mother's death (Dad predeceased her by eleven years), we found the letters they exchanged between 1944 and 1945 in Mother's Army trunk.

This is primarily their love story which began on an Army troop ship traveling to an unknown destination during World War II. It is also the story of religious prejudice, as they fought for their relationship over the opposition of Dad's family. This story is central to our family history, as it was a lens through which our parents viewed both their relationship and our extended family. It determined not only where they chose to live, but also our relationships with our grandparents.

Gretchen Boody and Edward Siegel met the evening of January 8, 1942 on the Shawnee, a troop ship, en route to Panama. Her diary, dated January 9 states:

My introduction to Lt. Edward Siegel, of the evening before, culminated into a breakfast date at 8:00 a.m. From then on we spent many happy hours together.

Gretchen was a 2nd Lieutenant, an Army nurse from Hudson, Wisconsin, daughter of farmers, and was raised as a Methodist. Edward was a 1st

Lieutenant, an Army doctor from Poughkeepsie, New York, son of shopkeepers, and was raised as an Orthodox Jew.

They were stationed together in Panama for two years and two months, and had an exclusive relationship during that time. Dad never told his parents about their relationship until March, 1944.

The letters begin when Mother left Panama to return to the States, for home leave, then reassignment. Her letters are typed in italics to differentiate them from Dad's letters and letters from others. We have left their personal misspellings, run-on sentences, grammatical errors, and the punctuation of the time as it was written. We have done our best to logically integrate the letters which was challenging, since Dad dated his, but Mom did not. Where the dates are unknown, we have inserted a "?" in the dateline on the letters, making our best guess based on the content. As you read, keep in mind that it was wartime in Europe and the South Pacific, and prejudice was prevalent and accepted.

No one in the family has any idea where their shared nicknames, variations of "Mr Bops," "Bops" or "Bopsy," came from. Mom first refers to Dad in her diary as "Bopsy" two days after they met writing, "Bopsy played the piano awhile." Mom's other nickname, "Miss Boo," is clearly derived from her maiden name, Boody. These nicknames disappeared from their vocabulary after their marriage.

However, Mr. Bops, a large, stuffed red, white, and blue bear, a gift from Dad to Mom, lives on, awaiting his book tour.

Jane Siegel Whitmore
Andrea Siegel Feinberg

DEDICATION

In 2001, at age 92, Gretchen wrote these reflections about her military service and her country.

It is doubtful many Americans cherish the freedom they have today.

In 1940 only unmarried females were assigned to any of the military services. The American Red Cross was recruiting nurses to sign up for one year with the rank of 2nd Lieutenant in either the Army or Navy. I applied to both and heard from the Army first. The orders came for me to report for duty at Fort Bragg, North Carolina in April, 1941. On December 7th, the attack from the Japanese occurred in Pearl Harbor, and war was declared. This meant that anyone in service would have to stay.

The 210th General Hospital Unit, of which I was part, was mobilized. We reported to the Port of Embarkation; destination unknown. Once on the ship, we were told our destination was the Panama Canal Zone. We built a hospital there from sand hills and empty buildings. It took three years to complete. Most of the casualties were from the South Pacific. During the voyage to Panama, I met Lt. Edward Siegel. We became friends and suddenly felt there was to be a close relationship. We met each day and learned that we were both 28 and single. Ed was a fun companion, and a fine young man, tall, and good-looking.

In May, 1945 we left the United States for Okinawa. The two-month trip on bare decks with no furniture except cots, and with all night black-outs was not easy! We dared not dock safely until the Japanese kamikaze were eliminated. American powers had previously bombed the Island so completely there was no vegetation and many homeless natives. We docked in Naha, Okinawa and set up a tent hospital on an abandoned Japanese airfield. There were rumors that Japan would surrender, which became a reality on September 2, 1945. With our backs against the walls on three fronts, we fought with strength and pride sending the Nazis back to Berlin defeated and chasing the Japanese from every island they had occupied.

Do we appreciate the debt our nation owes our W.W. II veterans and the Americans who supported the war effort back home? Let us not forget the 55,000 ordinary Americans who changed the world forever! Today we are again faced with many new challenges. As individuals we must learn how to ration by carpooling, walking more, and reducing our speed to save gas and oil, and of course, making use of new sources of energy. It is time for our nation's schools to teach more about World War II, and how we became a great and free America. These are my thoughts as we just celebrated the 64th anniversary of D-Day.

I am rich beyond words because of the love of a dear husband and my two daughters and their families.

With her words, we dedicate this book to our parents, and to those who have honored their country through their service.

Gretchen in uniform during World War II and in the same uniform at age 90.

TIMELINE

1941-1943

Gretchen and Edward stationed at Fort Gulick, Canal Zone, Panama

1944

15	February	Gretchen departed Panama for United States
21	March	Gretchen departed from home leave for Camp McCoy, Wisconsin
28	March	Edward's last letter before departing Panama
29	March	Martin Siegel's letter to Gretchen
1	April	Edward arrived in the States
2	April	Edward began home leave
11	April	Edward told Gretchen relationship must end
14	April	Telegram
2	May	Jack Siegel wrote to Gretchen
12	May	Edward arrived Fort Dix, New Jersey
28	May	Telegram; Edward ordered to Camp Blanding, Florida
30	May	Edward departed Fort Dix to drive to Camp Blanding
3	June	Edward arrived Camp Blanding, Florida
6	June	D-Day
	July	Gretchen visited Edward in Florida
Late	Aug-Sept. 8	"Earth and High Heaven" serialized in *Collier's*
20	September	Gretchen ordered to Camp Ellis, Illinois
27	September	Gretchen departed Camp McCoy, Wisconsin for Camp Ellis, Illinois
	October	Gretchen stationed at Camp Ellis
9	October	Gretchen converted to Judaism
18	October	Edward told Gretchen relationship must end

31	October	Edward assigned to Fort McClellan, Alabama
3	November	Edward arrived at Fort McClellan
	November	Edward transferred to Camp Ellis, Illinois
	December	Edward and Gretchen reunited at Camp Ellis, Illinois

1945

6	January	Edward at 375th Station Hospital
12	January	Gretchen's last letter
25	September	Gretchen and Edward married, Chapel of Peace, Okinawa
26	September	Gretchen departed Okinawa for States
23	October	Edward arrived in California
8	November	Edward and Gretchen's civil marriage ceremony

First Meeting aboard the Shawnee

Shawnee departs for Canal Zone

210th General Hospital aboard the Shawnee.
Headed for Canal Zone 1942

17 Feb 1944

My Dear Mr. and Mrs. Boody,

Please forgive my typing this letter but I think you know what my writing is--at least now you will have an even chance of reading what I'm saying.

My major purpose in writing is to tell you that Gretchen sailed on the 15th for the States so please don't worry if you don't hear from her in the next few weeks. There's no way of knowing just how long she will be on the high seas so just be patient and one of these fine days your daughter will come ringing the doorbell and you shall have her home.

I can readily understand just how difficult it must have been for you both not having her home these past two years. The past few weeks have been rather hectic down here wondering just when the big day would come--but come it finally did. Gretchen has done a splendid job down here and she has set a fine example for all nurses and enlisted men to follow. You should be proud of her, I know I am.

Saying good-bye to Gretchen was the most difficult thing I've ever had to do in my life. Knowing her has been the finest thing that ever happened to me and I shall cherish every moment of the past two years. I wanted you both to know that.

Gretchen is a little thin and I told her when she left that you would certainly fatten her up once you got your hands on her. She does everything so well and with so much energy that it is no wonder. But she is really in good health. We all need a little of some Mother love. I know I need it and I'm waiting the day until I get aboard and head for home.

I don't know what the future holds in store for any of us or just how far ahead anyone can plan these days, but I do hope that some day we may all meet. I've heard so much about you that I feel I know you both very well. I know Gretchen's homecoming will indeed be a happy day for you all--I'm only sorry I can't be there to share in it.

My warmest regards to you both--

Ed Siegel

Gretchen in winter dress uniform

Panama
18 Feb 1944

Hello Darling,

Well, here goes my first letter to you. I've been wanting to write since the minute I got back to the post after seeing you off but my thoughts have been anything but coherent. Believe me when I say it was an awful day that I spent Tuesday. I was confused and had the emptiest feeling. You must have felt the same way, poor baby, but it had to be. I have been lost without you and there's really no fun anymore, Bops, no one to run to—but you know all that. I promised I wouldn't write about how tough it is but there's no use kidding you because you feel it the same way. Chin up, darling, it will be easier when we start hearing from each other.

I went up to the Bingo party the other night. Most of the girls had on their shirts and skirts and she made them go home and change into formal beige or OD's. No kidding, Bops, the gals were fit to be tied. Good you weren't here. That would have been the pay-off on top of everything else.

The first bunch is still here sweating it out and there's nothing in sight to get them home. God knows when I'm going to get out and it better be soon because it's no place for me down here without my old Baby to look after me.

Manny had a birthday party last night and I was assed. They are sure trying to keep me from getting lonesome but it doesn't help much. Every drink I had was a toast to you.

My two cross-eyed kids came into the hospital yesterday and I'm going to operate on them to-morrow. I hope they turn out O.K.—keep your fingers crossed.

I finally saw our purple-lidded woodpecker in the show* the other night and he was a riot. The same old bunch still going to the shows. The new bowling alleys open to-day and they are really beautiful. That will give us something to do for a while. Larry is coming into the hospital next week for his work-up. It will be nice having him around for a while.

I sure am spending a lot of time in the hospital these days, you know why. There's nothing to go up to the quarters for. Father Laws finally got his orders and is sweating out a boat. He got hold of me yesterday and

---

*   Editor's note: Woody Woodpecker cartoon

made me go out and play golf with him. I wasn't too bad either after the long lay-off. Went to the ball-game Wednesday and George's team sure beat the hell out of Cristobal.

There have been a few letters for you and they have been forwarded. I hope that this letter is waiting for you when you get home. Have a pleasant time with the family dear and fatten up. I wrote your folks the other day and I told your Mother to fatten you up.

To say that I'm not worrying about you would be a lie. I think of you continually and I know you are worrying about me too but please don't be too unhappy, Miss Boo, none of us know what the future holds in store for us. Let's just see what's going to happen and live from day to day. I still lean on you heavily even though you are thousands of miles away and I'll try and be some sort of pillar for you. Please make the most of your leave and smile. I'll expect a snapshot one of these days showing me a plump Miss Boo—God bless you, my darling.

All my love,

Smack, smack, smack, smack, smack, smack.   _____.

Bops

On the ship from Panama to
US Undated 1 pm

My dearest Bopsy,

You've only been gone a few hours, but already I've looked for you a dozen times to tell you something. Then, the letter—I read it right away & such a comfort it was but my dear in spight of all our big talk about braveness, the future etc. etc. No words can get down to the awful unreality & finalness of it, the knowledge in ones mind still unaccepted by the senses, no I didn't let anyone know my feelings today, but not bragging it was the greatest thing I ever did for I wanted to cry like a baby. I was so lonesome & lost. It's so hard to write to my baby—when we never have written before, but my dear, I'm afraid you can never shake me from your list.

11a.m. <u>censored date</u>

Hi Scruntchy,

You wouldn't be very proud of your sailor honey. I've been sick as a dog. We had been out an hour when my cookies really got tossed. Almost immediately the sea was very rough & everyone took to their bunks. I moved out this a.m. for about an hour but am so unsteady & weak. Think I'll stay here for the duration. Suppose it was the nervousness, excitement & everything all at once & then that horrible let down. The way I feel, they'll bury another sailor at sea.

Baby I thought of you all last night & all today, even when I'm dozing here I keep wondering how you look & what you are saying. It doesn't seem possible anyone could get so into my system so that I don't seem to be one person any more, but part of me is back there with you. (Yah & I wish it were my stomach.)

Gotta rest a bit, you should look upon this unglamorous soul, Doctor—more later.

Hello sweet thing,

Hope you don't mind another little note tonight. It helps so much to chat with you. Golly I'm beginning to feel like Miss Boo again. Kept two meals (little ones under my belt) still lots of other seasick people.

This is a quiet group dear, no one bothers about the other & I'm sure I don't put forth much effort, just not interested. Miss my Bopsy & how I need a smack—so there.

Tom found bed bugs—you can hear him can't you. Ann is doing quite well.

Saw some porpoise this p.m. It's not much fun on deck without you though. So I don't bother.

Must say good night—in my thoughts I just whistled.* Can't wait for my first letter.

Goodnite my dear.

---

*   *Editor's note: When they parted in the evenings to go to their separate quarters, they said a final goodnight with a special whistle.*

Good morning my darling,

This one finds me feeling a little more chipper. Guess I'll live after all. Everything O.K. but where is my Bops. It's like that trip I took. Never really told you I carried on one night & wept but had a return trip to look forward to, but this one is like a bad dream, surely I'll awaken to find myself right back there across the street. Then at noon or in the eve we would be together holding hands in the movie.

The ship is quite peaceful—well behaved crowd. It's such a different trip than we took. No excitement or anticipation. Don't get me wrong dear—it isn't that I am not anxious to go home but I hate it so not to come back to my baby.

This afternoon you will be home, restless, wondering, dissatisfied—& all the time I know what you will be missing. Bops to wash your hair, do your nails & do those little things that we both got such a kick out of just because we were together. Be a brave darling though. Maybe the world has something great in store for us.

9 PM

Tonite I really was homesick. The soldiers had a jam session—piano, clarinet, guitar & they played our piece—yes I sang & reached out to hold your hand, but it wasn't there darling I felt so close to you. Went out to see the stars & let my tears drop in the ocean. Then I realized how little they were in comparison to all that water—it's like you & I in this great big world—lost because of distance & all those intangible things. Must try to sleep & let time help my troubled mind. So good-nite my dear—sleep tight.

Hello my Bopsy

How's my favorite Captain today—by now you are probably stuffing noses & mopping ears. I just called & they said you were busy. Gee darling I wish I could run to a telephone & say hello & then jabber about all those silly little things—believe you even know when I cleaned my toe nails.

Must eat my breakfast & then go see the water. Will tell you more later.

Baby,

It's been a lonesome little gal that wandered this boat all day, keep thinking when we land you will be there to meet me. How I need a big bear hug & some delicious yum yums. Honey I have tried so hard to be brave. Tom & Ann say I'm a real soldier—but they don't know what goes on within. They have been very nice to me.

Funny thing today I met a Captain who is a shirttail relation. His uncle & my uncle are brothers. (My dad's sister's husband). In other words my first cousins are his second cousins. He is from Iowa & a nice person.

Our meals have been excellent. The two times of the day that I want to be finished quick is dinner & supper cause then I will see my Bopsy. That's the way it has always been & it's a hard habit to break.

Honey I may not get to write tomorrow but will mail this as soon as possible. Hope you understand that this all has been such a great help to me & after you read it, probably it will sound silly, but my dear it has been my every thought & feeling these past few days. Will be waiting so anxiously for a letter & perhaps my next letter to you will be more sensible. I've been so mixed up. Good-nite baby dear. Keep your mind at ease cause I'm being brave & am well. Am realizing more & more each day how we depended on each other. I loved it that way.

Be sure to tell me all that is going on—give my best to Sam, Mac, the kids in the clinic & everyone. Hope it won't be long before they can all be with their families.

Keep the chin up sweet thing & always remember to love

Your baby.

20 Feb 1944

Good Morning, Miss Boo,

This is Mr Bops and it's such a pretty morning out that I thought I'd just sit me down and talk to you for awhile. I'm going up and listen to the lottery numbers after awhile and maybe I'll be sending you a check for $500. One of these days. Ho-Hum!

Went up to the Club last night and they sure did have a crowd. I think every officer on the Isthmus was there and it sure was some party. Needless to say, a great many were wondering where you were and when I told them you had gone back they all felt badly because they had seen us to-gether so much. I didn't stay very late.

I'm going to the ball-game to-day and I'll be cheering for the team as if you were there also. We sure had a pretty good time that last game, didn't we? Old Bops keeping score and getting a kick out of it.

I bet you must be freezing up there now but when it gets too cold just picture yourself wrapped up in a big hug of mine and I know you'll feel warm, you sweet old thing!

That's all for now. Makes me feel better when I just sit down and dash off a quick note to you like this.

I love you,
-*Bops*-

2/26/44

Hello Darling,

I thought that I would have heard from you before this but so far no letter. I suppose that I shall get one Monday. I would have written more letters than the other two but I just was waiting to hear from you—you know how it is!

Before I go any further, I'm putting in a call to speak to you this Sunday, 5th, in the morning some time. I don't know anything that would make me happier than to just hear your voice if only for a few minutes. I assume that you are home.

I've been thinking of us so much, darling, that I find it practically impossible to sleep at night, Remember I told you that I do all my thinking at night? You sure did look after me, didn't you, Baby? The thing that stands out about you time and time again is how good and fine you are way down deep inside. I can't but repeat that you are the finest lady I have ever known, you old sweetheart! The idea of not seeing you again is just too much for me to contemplate and therefore I hope (in spite of you wanting to go to the West Coast) that you are assigned near the East somewhere. Maybe you can fix it!

There must be some answer to you and I somewhere in this world and when I get back to the States I intend to find out. So please keep your chin up darling and don't be forlorn—I love you with all my heart and I know in my heart that there may be a silver lining somewhere.

The first bunch haven't gone yet and where that leaves me you know—right behind the 8-ball. We're a bunch of maniacs right now just waiting.

I haunt the mail-box regularly now and Joe Silverman is just as anxious for you to write as I am so I'll quit bothering him.

So long, for now, darling, and I hope the call comes through Sunday.

Your old baby,
"*Bops*"

Gretchen's undated 1st Letter from U.S., censored

My darling—

Baby, baby we're here, in good old United States, its wonderful, glorious, heaven. The only thing missing is my Bopsy to enjoy it with me.

We had a fine trip dear, the usual hurry & wait, but its been worth all the trouble.

Honey we screamed with joy to go down the street, to see Woolworths lighted signs, real store windows, bright shining head-lights. They brought us out to <u>censored</u> in trucks so to date we have seen <u>censored</u> through the back end of a 2 ton, but its good just the same. The air is brisk & smells so good—already I feel refreshed.

Last night we had supper, late, had physical exams & are now stationed in the barracks, its very nice, but the bed was too soft to sleep. We went to the officers club for a Coke, the club is charming, but very quiet. Most of the girls went in town. Ann & I stayed here, must keep my resistance up & not be too worn out when I arrive home. Bopsy dear it's hard to realize we are really here, it seems I should be able to run to the phone & tell you all about everything. Miss you so terriably much & how I hope your turn will come sooner than you expect. How I would love to meet you on arrival we would have so much to catch up on. My thoughts are always with you my darling. I've prayed for two years it would never end like this. I belong with my baby don't I?

We are awaiting further orders. Will write you very soon again. Will be expecting a letter home with all the news.

Bea good darling, have fun & remember

Bops loves you.

My Bopsy dear—

Such a mix up all the time, doubt if even this letter will be straight, but just want to let you know I'm still in one piece.

Four of we girls went to the movie last night, silly but I almost held Lydia's hand, she was sitting at my left. The picture was fair "Phantom Lady." The short was best "Red Hot Riding Hood"—terriably funny. We couldn't leave the post & to-day is the same so it doesn't look like we will see the city at all.

Am going to give you a few tips—first if you have to bring that helmet & gas mask, get rid of it. Second send all your foot lockers home by mail & keep just your hand luggage & as little of that as possible. We have done nothing but chase, turn in, load & unload & check and double check.

Hope you receive the cable I sent. Know your serial # is wrong, but I sort of guessed. Also I've sent 2 letters previous to this.

We met Dotty Fuller in q.m.* this a.m. She is still at <u>censored</u> awaiting papers. She arrived only a few days ahead of us. Malo—huh? She was fine and very excited to see us all.

Bring what liquor you want. You'll need a pick up in confinement. All seems very lenient.

Miss my old manager so much darling—a million times I've needed you for advice sweet thing.

It's hot. Am glad for my summer suit, we got our heavy coats today. They are nice, so certainly I should be warm enough.

Bops, are you well? How's the cold? Be a good boy, have fun & miss—your baby—

---

*   *Quartermaster*

My darling

True to form, that sweet thing had a letter waiting me on arrival-was I thrilled, but you sounded kind of lonesome-poor dear, your baby shouldn't have left. I realize more each day how vitally important you are in my life. Knew in my mind that I had to leave, maybe we did what we were supposed to but on my part it has been without courage. Bopsy your letter was so wonderful & it made me want so to see you. It will be some easier now that we can write, but even that is a poor substitute for my Bopsy. We had such fun, were so happy & everything happened just for us.

Well dear I'm home. You can't imagine how perfectly wonderful it is. Mom & dad are in heaven & their soldier rules the roost. Neither of them were feeling too well on my arrival-hard colds-but believe I've fixed them up so both are feeling much better. My poor daddy has to work, well or not. So I put on my coveralls & was a real farmerette. It's really fun. The farm is beautiful, so well kept up. They are in the midst of redoing our living room, walls, floors, new rugs etc. So I'm in my glory puttering & advising. Tomorrow we are going to St Paul to get the carpeting-expect I'll have a fight to help with that but must do something for them.

To-nite I am at my sisters. We were here to dinner. Edward you should see these youngsters, they are priceless. Virginia is 4 mo. So I've helped feed her, it is so odd holding a tiny baby, but its fun. Margaret is cute as a bug, she loves her auntie & I gave her "Mr. Bops" & that is just what she calls him. Of course he has changed appearance a bit-minus his whiskers. Charles is all boy—talks like a child of 8-he says he must go to the farm to help grandpa with the chores because he is so busy and needs help. I've laughed so much at him. We have had a real rough house & such a tease-maybe he takes after me.

Edward you just must get home soon. Your mom & dad will be thrilled to pieces. They all have so much love for us & now I really appreciate their feelings. Mother keeps saying how much they want to meet you & baby I've told them all-it makes no difference as I told you. I know that anyone I love they love too. Parents are really wonderful people.

A little about the last part of my trip. Our last nite we were all taken sick on the train with food poisoning. I was really miserable-diarrhea etc. The whole bunch were up all nite. We think it was pork so when we arrived at Sheridan we were all in. (about 5 went to the hospital.) It took just four hours to sign in & out, get our orders & leaves & be on our way. That is the most efficient post I've ever seen. Took the train to Milwaukee & the sleeper to St. Paul. By morning I was much better. Got in St. Paul at 7:40 & in Hudson at 9. Was so glad to end that trip.

Baby if you could only smell the air, wonderful weather, no snow, but cool & crisp. It just makes me sleepy but I'm sort of tired. Got on the scale last night 104 but with the eggs, milk & cream mother is pouring down me that will be past history soon.

Oh yes mom & dad appreciated your letter so much, mother has written I think.

Guess you will be weary with this long letter, but have been waiting to find time & quiet. So much excitement you know.

Hope the cross-eyed kids turn out o.k. have my fingers crossed for you dear & I have great faith in your ability.

Am glad you are getting out a bit, just don't forget to keep the chin up. Will be waiting for more & more letters sweet thing-in spight of all the wonderful things here, I miss my Bops every minute.

So just keep on loving Your baby.

My darling—

How disappointed I am to-nite. Came back from the city at 5 & Dot's husband told me that I had a call from New York. Of course I was so excited. Couldn't eat my dinner but they had to have the call deferred & I know the set up so please try again dear. Will undoubtedly hang near the telephone until it comes through. Bopsy I just can't wait to hear your voice. Am so homesick for you.

Took Mom over to St. Paul to-day & we really splurged. We got the rug—had a chair reupholstered—Mother a new coat & it was really fun. Mom said to tell you she wishes you were here for the grand opening of the new room. I believe the room will be lovely & that sort of thing is right up my alley.

What's new down there by now. Just keep thinking how much you would enjoy being home, It has taken me days to think of all the unusual things that happened which we thought were everyday occurrences. Mom was so proud to see me return a salute today. Was amazed though at the scarcity of uniforms in St. Paul & Minneapolis.

Have you been bowling in the new alleys—how are they?

My trunk arrived to-day—must trace the blue one it went astray between here & Harahan—it wasn't in the baggage car when I arrived at Sheridan.

Oh Bops the call just came saying you would call March 5th so I will be right at the phone. Right now my heart is beating so fast can hardly write you. Just can't imagine darling what is going to be like to even wait that long. I love you so sweet thing. Hate to seal you up in a letter & say goodnite.

Write so often dear—all my love—Gretchen.

Darling, darling, darling,

Finally received your first two letters to-day evidently sent from New Orleans. They were both censored and the only thing cut out was the date on one of the notes you wrote from day to day.

I can see my poor baby being lonesome and crying on the ship and I shared every tear that you shed. I know, I know how hard it has been for you but as you say, perhaps there's something grand in store for us, who knows. During the past few days I've had the funniest feeling that maybe this isn't the end for us and it has made me feel much better. One thing I am sure of and that is that I shall see you sometime when I get back if it is humanly possible. How's that? I only hope that you aren't stationed too far away from the East.

I went down to Tropical Radio this morning to place your call and when I told the gray-haired lady with whom I wanted to speak (you remember her) she wrote down Lt. Gretchen Siegel and I then corrected her and she said, "You mean, not yet." Darling it sure was a funny feeling hearing your name and mine. Please God that it were. Who knows? I don't know whether you'll get this letter before or after I talk to you or whether you'll be at home or not. If you're not home yet I'll postpone the call a week and we'll speak on the 12th.

I'll bet it was a swell feeling hitting the States and I know that you will have a good time at home just taking it easy. You didn't say whether you were cold or not, I expect that you were.

It does help, doesn't it, to sit down and write all about everything. Makes you feel closer. I'm about to go up and take in the "Falcon" our old pal, remember. Yesterday George, Mae, Johnnie and Alphy and Me went over to the other side to see George play ball and we all had a swell time. We came back to George's and had cold turkey sandwiches and coffee. Old Bops should have been there. Last Thursday I was over to George's for fried chicken and made a pig out of myself. Mae said being in love certainly hasn't hurt my appetite and I said when there's fried chicken in front of me I'm not in love, just hungry. Heh! Heh! Some joke—

Enough for now, my old baby, and consider yourself scruntched, hugged, tickled, slided and—oh well! That will have to wait—I slapped my hand—I'm a bad boy.

Anyway, I love you, so there—

"Bops"

Barracks in Canal Zone

Officer s Mess Hall, Canal Zone

210th General Hospital Building, Panama

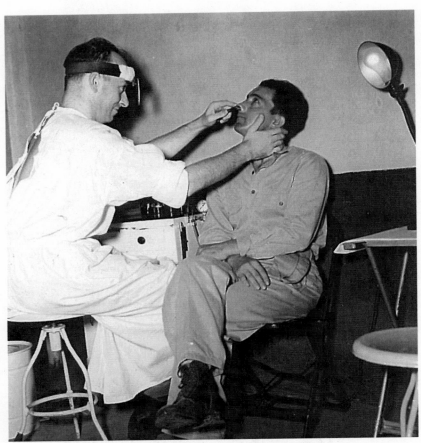

Ed at work in Eye, Ear, Nose and Throat Clinic

Gretchen in Clinic

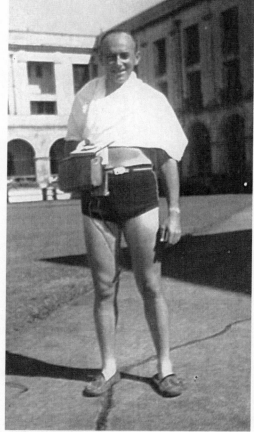

Ed at Hotel Washington pool, Colon

My dearest Bops

Its way past my bedtime & the eyes are droopy but must get a short note off to my scruntchy. My favorite auntie came to visit me to-nite & we had to stay up a little later than usual. I still get sleepy at 9:30 dear. All they can say is "my you are so thin"—well anyway I've gained one pound of the eight I lost on my trip-so signs are good anyway.

Spent a quiet day at home. Mom & I really can putter around. The rug comes to-morrow then we will be all settled. Think the room will be lovely.

Had a short note from Del*—she is so thrilled at my homecoming. Wish I could see her. Of course she hopes I will be sent near her but for my sake-hope it isn't south.

Its been cold to-day & I really noticed it, needed a big bear hug from my Bops. Golly how Gunboat misses that and the guy who gives them. Bopsy can't we be together ever again? Sometimes you seem so close. I almost reach out to slip my hand in your pocket. Weren't those happy times darling? Wasn't all of it good. I'm glad it all happened to both of us. So we can be closer just remembering.

Am looking for a letter—only 2 so far. Have all 6 of mine arrived? Did you get the cable? Can hardly wait until Sunday-won't it be wonderful dear. Will probably just blubber.

Tell me all the news; excuse the scribble I'm in my nice big fat bed all cozy like we talked about except for—oh well you know.

Enough kisses to keep you warm

Your baby

---

* Del (Delma) was Gretchen's former roommate from nurses' training. She re-appears in future letters when she and her husband are stationed in Jacksonville, Florida.

Good morning, darling—

How's my sweet old Baby, this morning? I'm fine although yesterday I had one of my rare hang-overs. They had a Leap-Year dance at the club night before last and all the girls were cutting in on the fellows and taking them up to the bar and buying them drinks. It was pretty nice and your old Bops is still a pretty popular fellow. But, I didn't have any idea of how to make small talk. Every drink I had was drunk to you and you were with me constantly. It sure was funny the way all the girls were watching over me and making sure that I remained faithful to you. Sis Porter was the funniest. She watched me like a hawk all night. She said, if I didn't stay true to my baby, that she would never believe in anything again. She needn't have worried because all women are shabby compared to you darling! And I'm sure that they will always suffer in comparison with you.

I hear that there is mucho snow in the Midwest right now. While playing bridge with Kenny and Evie last night we heard it over the radio and we could all picture you bundled up in twenty coats trying to keep warm at home. We (Murph and I) were over for chop-suey supper and bridge and Murph and I swamped them by over 4,000 points. Only trouble was that I couldn't play with Bop's toes!! We have been bowling practically every afternoon and the alleys are swell. I'm enclosing the pictures of you and I thought you'd like a shot of the alleys to show your friends. There's also a picture of the Eye Ear Nose and Throat (EENT) Staff I thought you'd like to have. Right?

I've received 4 letters from you to date and they have all been censored, cutting out all mention of New Orleans evidently, etc. However, the important stuff is there to read that you love me and that's all that matters and that you are well. Please put on some weight and don't forget to send me some pictures.

It's sure tough down here, Bops, just waiting. I'm happy that you found the States nice. I understand of course about the attitude of most of the people back home but I guess Americans only learn the hard way about how tough this war really is and only those suffering casualties actually suffer.

Chaplain Pincus was in the other day and we had quite a long talk about things especially you and me. He's very fond of you and wishes to be remembered.

We talked over a few angles that I wasn't familiar with but I'm not up enough on things to let you know anything more definitely as yet. I'll let you know more about our talks at a later date.

Enough chatter for now and I love every bit of "Gretchen Talk." Please keep it up. I love you darling. Hope to talk to you Sunday.

Bops

My Darling,

Received both your letters dated the 28th. And at last my baby is home. I'm so happy that at last you are with the family and that they are looking after you. Good to be with people that love you, isn't it? Well you went from one love straight to another, darling, and that's the way it should always be. You should never be without those that love you. I heard from your Mother and she mentioned that she had just spoken to you over the phone from Milwaukee and that you were quite ill. It wasn't very clear and hearing from you this A.M. cleared the whole thing up. I was scared sick that my old Bops was ill and I wasn't there to look after her and give her the old pep talk.

I shall be talking to you before you get this letter and our conversation will probably sound very silly to anyone but us. But there are a few things I insist upon in case I don't make myself clear over the phone and they are: 1) You must gain at least 10 pounds before you go to your new post. 2) You must not feel forlorn and heartsick about us because I intend to see you when and if I get out of this place in the course of the next month or two, just make believe that this is a furlough and we shall see each other again soon. Please be happy darling, you're home again and I shall soon be home and perhaps something will turn up or other after I get back. Don't build up a lot of castles in the air and hope for too much but where there is life there's hope and maybe parents are really as wonderful as you say. So let's just sweat out the next few months and see what it brings us. Please, please, please don't be unhappy. I know it's tough but I'm always close to you darling and never fear of anything. But, I DO WANT YOU TO PUT ON SOME WEIGHT AND BE THE BOPS THAT I USED TO KNOW ON THE SHAWNEE, you rascal, imagine picking me up like that !!! Don't hit me!

I'm O.D.* to-day and have nothing to do but sit here and pound away at the machine writing to you, and it's the most fun I can possibly imagine unless it would be saying these things to you myself. This was a real shock to Larry and myself but someone I know was admitted here yesterday for observation as a homosexual. The kid's really broken up

---

* Officer of the Day

and he will probably be given the chance to resign from the army. That's the way it goes.

It's funny Bops, but before I used to hate writing letters and never could think of anything to write about but there's so much to write you that I could just go on and on. I could just jabber on and on from now until then. Fun writing, isn't it. I can imagine how excited you were when you found out I was going to call. Did you think that I might? I bet you did and were really expecting it all along, you rascal.

The dental replacements have arrived and you can imagine how excited they all are. They moved Sammie's replacement in with us and he's a young 2nd Lt. It's not the same old place anymore. I had to kick him out of the bathroom this morning and send him downstairs where 2nd Lts. belong. Boy, oh, boy, am I the rough-neck but he doesn't belong in our house, does he? There are so many memories of you that linger and linger. Just yesterday I found one of your hair ribbons and I almost ate it up.

The kids sure must be fun back home and if I was a kid I'd want to have an Auntie just like Bops. I'd sit on her lap all day long and at night I'd well—sit on her lap some more—!

I think I'll take in the "Man from Down Under" with Charles Laughton to-night. It's playing here at the hospital.

Oh yes—I played poker last night and cleaned up a few bucks. I snuck a few glances over to the radio but Bops wasn't there although I know she'd like to be, Right?

You may take it from me, a very truthful and impeccable young man, that I shall not stop loving you—

"Bops"

My darling

What a wonderful tonic to hear your voice this morning dear. Couldn't sleep last night just to terriably excited. So sorry you weren't able to hear me better. Your voice was so clear & natural. Did you hear me give you a big smack baby? Yes my chin is up. I'm gaining weight, but most of all I'm waiting for my Bops to come home. Really had lots to tell you over the phone, but it was rather useless since you couldn't hear, so will write a big fat letter instead. How's that?

Last night Mother had a wonderful chicken dinner for me. Dot & her family & the Dorwins were here. There were twelve of us. After dinner we had home movies & really a lovely time. Honey when we had dessert I kept thinking how my Bops would love it. Angel food cake with strawberries & whipped cream.

To-day dear we have a big fat Sunday paper, it's cold outside but cozy & warm in, so soon as I've finished your letter. I'm going to curl up on the davenport & read. Now doesn't that make you homesick?

Sorry to discourage you but there were no replacements that we knew of or saw in New Orleans. It's hard to tell though they may have been there without anyone knowing it. Can't figure out just how they run things in that dept. It's a crime to keep people there so long.

Plan to go to Madison to-morrow. Mrs. McWilliams called me & was so thrilled. She is planning a party & wanted to know what girls I wanted. Will return home Fri. Expect to have a lovely time. Nevertheless I'll write while there, to keep my baby smiling. Will wish all the time that you were there to have fun too.

About my reassignment baby. No news yet, but am fast changing my mind about wanting to go too far west. All I want now is to be sent close to my Bops. It's so horribly lonesome being away from my sweet thing. Am sure too dear there is something for us to-gether in the world. It isn't right for us to be apart is it darling?

How are the movies Bops. Have seen all the ones that are showing here. We thought we might go to-nite but think some of the young people will be in for the eve. I have a cousin & his wife, Dot & Harold & a couple who are friends of theirs. Secret darling—I'd be happier just going to bed. Rest & quiet is so necessary to me.

Mother & I have our living room all fixed, it looks lovely. She is happy. My arrival was just at the time she needed an opinion on the rug.

Bops you probably cuss at this long letter, but I have to jabber & tell all about everything.

Be a good sweetheart, don't worry about me, and here are oodles of smacks for my scruntchy.

All my love baby
Your old Bops

Must tell you again how thrilled I was with your call this morning dear. Could you call again sometime?

Bops loves you so much dear.

Dearest—

Here I am again, writing my darling about everything and anything I can find to write about. Am I being a good boy in writing? I try to write every day and I have so far. I've been receiving your letters regularly and a great comfort they are, my darling.

The more and more that I think of us darling, the more I realize just what it was that we had. As you once said and I now agree, it's something that very few people ever get in a lifetime and I know I shall never again experience that love for anyone else as long as I live. Of one thing I am certain, and that is, that I'm going to speak to the family about us when I get home. I know that is going to make you feel better, isn't it? I've always felt so ashamed when you asked me if I had ever told the folks about us and I now realize how terrible it must have made you feel. I have already written to my Uncle and Aunt from Philly.*

I've told him all about us darling, how much I love you, how much you mean to me and all that goes with it. I've been on the verge of writing the family but inasmuch as I'm going to be home in a short while I hope, I felt I could talk to them better. It's tough to discuss anything in a letter so I'll just wait until I get home.** Darling, you know that there is nothing I'd rather have in this world than you, to live with you, make love to you, do all the little things in the world for you. The thought of you and I ever having a child (a boy, of course,) is enough to make me take on the world single handed. From all of this you may gather that I'm going to do my level best to have all this work out for us both. Well darling, what do you think?

I only hope that when I get back, my old baby, we can get to-gether. I'm waiting expectantly to hear where you are going to be reassigned. I hope it's in a large town and accessible, for me, but I shall find you again wherever you are.

So they all think that you are thin. Well, I could fix that up in no time if I had my way. I could tell them why you're thin—thinking, thinking, fretting, wondering why this has to be and why that has to be, isn't it—?

---

*   *Uncle Murray and Aunt Sally LeVine.*

** *They had been dating and together for two years at this point. He had never told his parents.*

But, as I said in my last letter, please carry on these next few months, if only for me. Will you, Baby?

Remember the afternoon in the house we were practicing meeting each other, well—that wasn't for nothing and I don't want any slips for the reunion embrace. We're better than the movies anyway, aren't we Bops?

Everyone asks for you day after day. Mac keeps hounding me as to what I'm going to do with you. The gals watch out that I behave myself. I don't have a chance to sneak in even a little Blue Moon. It's funny Bops but when I go to the movies I compare you with everyone I see on the screen, I picture you with all sorts of nice clothes, oh, Bops you know what I mean—I shouldn't be saying all these things because it makes it tough but the way I feel to-day I could take on the world and if I know my old Bops she's just as tough as I am.

I love you, so there!

My darling,

Well at last, I think that letter came by dog sled—but it was so good to hear from you Bopsy dear. Had only the two & when nothing came was thinking all sorts of nice things, that your orders had come etc.

Can't imagine why none of my letters have arrived. I believe I have written eight. In fact as soon as I hit good old U.S. I mailed the one I had written on the boat & wrote another. Also sent the cable which will probably arrive next month. Anyway sweet thing. You haven't been neglected for a minute—Bops thinks about you constantly & just can't help but worry cause she knows how lost her baby is without "Tag."

Edward the states are wonderful, this good clean fresh air is worth millions. I really feel wonderful, pretty frisky. Open my window wide at nite & sleep like a baby. Am not like you, do my worrying & thinking in the daytime. Poor baby—try to get your rest & hope when you get home the answer to all this will be found. You know how I feel & my families reaction so there is no problem here darling.

Mom is feeding me real cream, fresh strawberries & all kinds of good things. She said to tell you it's hard to put fat on a trotting horse, but she is doing her best. She is glad for a little help. I'm pretty good at K.P. with my past experience.

Charles is staying out here. He is grandpa's boy & really is a riot. He's such a handsome youngster & a big tease. Wish he were mine.

Expect to go to Madison Tuesday & return Friday. Must find out what Dr. Williams has for me. Also see about my fur coat. It will be nice to see all the folks.

Only two more days before I can give my Bops a big smack. Oh goodie. It will be so wonderful hearing your voice.

Can honestly say dear I've seen very few changes in Hudson since I left. Not many young men around, but the people certainly aren't suffering. Never saw so much merchandise in my life as the other day when we went into Woolworths.

Baby, take good care of you for me. Go to all the ball games & movies & don't forget to play poker. How yah doing without the kibitzer?

Bops loves you to pieces dear so don't forget to write & love

Your Baby

Give my best to the gang & pray so that you all can come home soon. Do you want an emergency Bobs? ha

3/8/44

Dearest, Gunny, Grootchy, Bops, my baby—

To date I have received 1 cablegram and eight letters from you. To-day I received the one dated March 3. I've been receiving your letters regularly and I don't know where you got the impression that I hadn't heard from you but I have. Darling, hearing from you is the only thing I look forward to each day. I think that you aren't receiving my mail as you should because I write you every day right after lunch. That's my ritual and I enjoy every minute of it.

Your description of the air in Wisconsin made my nose quiver and when Bops's nose quivers that practically amounts to an earthquake. If you had my nose full of nickels, we could retire. I'm so happy that you are feeling well. Darling, to know that you are feeling well means so much to me. You know what a worry wart I am. Even when you get a little ache or pain it drove me crazy. I'll never forget the day you got bit and had that rash on your leg. I wouldn't let on to you but I was so damn scared I didn't know what to do. I bet you knew it too didn't you rascal.

More and more that you are away do I realize just what my Bops was to me. It scares me sometimes to think of how two people can become. If I can't marry you darling, I know I shall never marry anyone. You used to say that and I'd try and talk you out of it. What makes you so smart, anyway? I guess I knew it all along too. The thought of anyone else ever holding you in his arms makes me want to eat nails. You're my baby, aren't you?

Last night I sat down at 9 o'clock and wrote all about us and how we met. I wrote the letter in long-hand, then revised it, edited it and when I got through it was long after 2. If I'm not out of here in a few weeks, it's going to the folks. I've fooled around long enough and my old Bops had to leave me before I got any sense. Darling, don't you have the feeling that things are going to turn out all-right for us? I do. Please be patient, Baby, old Bops will look after you.

Bops, do you think that they will still send you to West Coast because you signed up for it when you were here. I sure hope they don't. Have you written your friend in Washington yet? If wonder if she knows where you will be reassigned. Bops, I'm so happy you're away from all this bickering and pettiness.

Baby, my baby, take care of yourself and please be happy. There are great things in store for us, I am sure, I just have to get you in my arms for a great big hug and smack pretty soon or I'll bust wide open.

I'll write again to-morrow so until then sleep tight and dream of me, just a little, will yuh? I love you—

Have some strawberries and cream for me—

Edward—that's me!

My darling,

No air-mail today so I haven't heard from my baby. How are you darling and what are you thinking about these days? I hope it's mostly about me.

We saw the Bob Hope show* last night and darling, it sure was wonderful. He sure is a funny man and the boys all went crazy about him. He's supposed to come over to the hospital to-day and see the patients. Maybe I'll get a close look at him and his gang. You would have loved it.

Baby, it's awful just waiting and waiting here to get home. No kidding if I don't get out of here in a month or so I'm afraid I'll just have to have an emergency to get home. Everybody is leaving me, now is that nice?

They had Monte Carlo night at the Club last night and they sure aren't like the parties we used to give. I won $16 at the roulette table lucky me and then I went in and tried to get the jack pot on the quarter machine and lost it all. I'm a bad boy. You know that machine near the bar hasn't given a jack pot in over 3 months.

I guess that your trip to Madison is about over by now and you'll be home again. Tell me, how do you feel about going back on duty again? I bet you are really wondering where they send you. I know I am.

Bops, are you going to take some pictures and send them to me. You know I don't have a really good portrait picture of you. I know when I get home I'll send you one of me. I think I have a few left. Would you like that?

Bops, I keep wondering what you look like and whether your wearing your rats** or not and how you used to wash your hair, you stringy, straggly thing you—. I guess I love my old Baby, don't I?

Darling, remember my writing you about my talk with Chaplain Pincus and that there was something he told me that I would write you about? Well, I thought that I could explain it all to you better when I see you again but after thinking it over I think it would be better if I tell you about it now. The sum and substance of what we talked about is that it is possible for a Non-Jew to become a Jewess. The reason for doing something like that would be that children would then be Jewish. The

---

* USO Show with Bob Hope, Frances Langford, Jerry Colonna, Vera Vague

** "Rats" were masses of hair used to create more volume. Very popular.

procedure is very simple and consists of the person taking instructions in the history of the religion, etc and after about a month or two, the person becomes Baptized and from then one is a Jew. I guess it is just like a Protestant becoming a Catholic, and vice versa. Darling, I realize just what it is I am asking you about and what such a step means. After all, I know of no two people who believe in the same things as we do. When we are to-gether everything is so simple and easy. There's my Bops and there I am. My religion is very simple darling, there is no fanfare, no demands, all that it amounts to is the following of the Golden Rule. But, when I think how wonderful it would be if you and I were to becoming that much closer and how much easier it would be when there were children. After all, Baby, a child needs some sort of religion to start him on his way. He can't be a mixture. He must be one or another. Darling, I'm not asking you to do anything right now but I think that we should at least think about it. If I could tell the folks, that here is a lovely lady who loves me so much that she is willing to be what I am and worship as I do. I know how you feel way down deep in your heart darling and I know that you would never marry me if you thought that you would be coming between me and the folks. And when the day comes that I tell the family it will be Mother who will write you just as your family wrote me. Darling, I feel that everything is going to turn out all-right. All I want you to do now is just think about this for a while and let me know just how you feel about it. Baby, when I think of all the sacrifices that you are willing to make and how understanding and wonderful you are, I wonder that I am worthy of a person such as you. I never knew that there were such people such as you and your folks and I pray and pray that if this turns out all-right that I may be allowed the privilege of worshipping you and making it up to you for the rest of your life.

Well, I guess you have enough to think about for awhile now. I know you will have loads of questions to ask so please ask them and I'll try and answer them if I can.

I love you, my sweetheart—may the Good Lord get me out of here as quickly as possible so I can gather you in my arms and make the world right again for us both.

Edward "the Bops"

Dearest Bopsie—

Received your letter of the 5th this morning in which you had just spoken to me over the phone. I'm so happy that you enjoyed the call and when you go to your new post I'll call again.

I am quite the local hero and big-shot today. Yesterday Bob Hope was here to see the patients and give them a show and when he was through he said he had something wrong with his eye and ear. Well, your old Bops took him down in the clinic and examined him. Bops he sure is a great fellow. You know that he was in bed for 6 days with an otitis media and they told him he shouldn't make the trip but he insisted because he said he promised and didn't want to disappoint the boys in Panama. While I was examining him he was cracking jokes all the time and he said, "Just think Doc, now when you hear them kidding me over the radio and the movies about my nose, you'll be able to say you know more about it than anyone else and that you looked up it." We sure did get a kick out of them. Besides that Vera Vague couldn't sleep at night and I had to give her some luminal. Then Wendell Niles, the radio announcer for the Pepsodent show said his throat was sore and I examined his throat and told Bob that the best treatment for his announcer was for him to keep his mouth shut for a few days. Bob thought that was funny and I wouldn't be surprised if he made some sort of crack about it over the radio one of these days. To top it all off, Jerry Colonna had something in his eye and I took it out. You should have seen the clinic. There were about a million people around. Brass hats watching, etc. The only one I didn't get to examine was Frances Langford. Yum. Yum—! It sure was a hectic day and the boys are all kidding me about being personal physician to Bob Hope. He's a swell guy and thanked me profusely including a word to look him up if I ever get to the Coast. Nice, eh?

I just finished lunch and I sure could use some of that angel cake and strawberries. Bops, it sure sounds so wonderful. And the big fat Sunday papers. I want to be there with you so we can both curl up and read them to-gether. (This typewriter is getting worse every day.)

I received a swell letter from my pal in St. Louis, the one who works at the Central Institute for the Deaf and he has a new contract with the Surgeon General working on hearing aids for the veterans. He's the boy who married a Gentile gal and they are very happily married, have a little daughter, etc.

Schwartz just called me up and he wants to play a little tennis. I think I'll go up and clean up the court with the little man.

I'm so happy darling that you are feeling fine and putting on weight and that things are a little clearer now. I too feel that this is all going to be all-right darling and in the next month or two we'll know just where we stand. I love you darling and although I miss you terribly my pain is a little easier now that I know we are both going to fight for what we want. Sweet, sweet, sweet, sweet, hmmmmmmmmmm!

Take it easy and if I hear about you going around with any other fellows (except to see how much nicer I am) I'll come up and skin you alive, so there! So long until to-morrow, my baby—

Edward

My darling,

My hands are so cold I doubt if I will be able to make my pen go straight but here goes.

Honey all I can think of is that you should be with me enjoying the wonderful time I'm having. Was fortunate in getting a ride all the way to Madison, & drove in the most beautiful snow storm I've ever seen. Think it snowed just for me as it has been disappointing so far not to see any. We didn't get into Madison until 9:30 & I couldn't help but compare the evening—moonlight on fresh snow & the trees were just sparkling—some difference between that & moonlight and palm trees.

This afternoon we are going out to Truax to get my pay. Will also have my hair done as my leaving a day earlier sort of upset my plans.

Honey I believe I am going to lose this other tooth. Remember how black it looked. Will have Dr. xray all of them & that one is bothering me. It makes me sick (shiver gosh I'm cold)

So far there is no news of my reassignment. Mom will call me if she hears anything.

Baby I keep thinking of you. How good it was hearing that million dollar voice last Sunday. If you would only hurry home. Have decided not to ask for an extension on my leave so I am anywhere near when you do come it will be possible for me to have some time off. My Bops of course is the only one or the only thing at 837 that I miss & that is a whole big bunch.

It is lunch time dear & maybe some warm food will warm me up, however I can think of a big hug I'd like better.

Be a good sweetheart, chin up & remember to love

Your Baby

Smack, smack, smack sweet thing

Dearly Beloved, (a new one)

Here's the old, bald-headed doctor again. Time for my daily epistle. I received your letter dated the 7th this morning and darling, your letters sound so happy and you are having such a wonderful time that I'm getting a little jealous. Whatsa idea of having so much fun without me, you rascal. I'm kidding of course, if you knew how happy it makes me baby, to learn that you are having a good time and are happy about being home. I get just as much fun out of all the things you are doing that you do and when you write me about them, I share in them too. Keep it up!

I'm sorry to hear about that tooth and I hope you don't have to lose it. Doggone that dentist, I'm so damn mad that if he were down here I'd knock his block off.

I'm glad that you aren't taking an extension of your leave because I want to be able to take a few days leave when I get back. We are going to have our little tour of New York come hell or high water, families or no families, regulations or anything else that you can figure out. Right? You are hereby invited to see the sights of New York as soon as this young man gets home. How about it? Bops you'll love it. Jeepers I can hardly wait!

This morning I came into the clinic and in front of my office was a great big sign with Bob Hope's picture and big letter saying, "Capt E Siegel, personal physician to Bob Hope." These kids sure are something. I'd like to take them all home with me when the war is over.

I sent home another foot-locker to-day and as soon as I know I'm really leaving I'll send home the other one. Then I'll only have hand-luggage to carry with me. I'm following your advice, about time, isn't it?

I bowled 8 games yesterday and averaged 178, I sure was hot. Murphy was hot too and he averaged 184. We sure were knocking the wood over. Those alleys are a God send and the boys sure are using them.

You haven't mentioned how much you are weighing these days and I want to know and no fibs.

Be a happy Baby, darling, I love you and I'm looking forward to your reaction to my last letter although I know exactly what you will say.

Close your eyes, lift your head up, put your arms around me, snuggle close,—SMACK! Good wasn't it?

"Bops"

3/8/44

My darling

Its terriably late for me to still be up-but can't help it. Must tell you a few highlights & get it off in the a.m.

First of all baby how are you. This is my concern. Are you near as lonesome for somebody as I am? In spight of all the terrific excitement underneath it all I keep thinking of my Bops that is all that is missing to make all of this entirely perfect.

We just finished a beautiful dinner party. 12 of my closest girlfriends from Madison were all guests of Mrs McWilliams. It couldn't have been more perfect to have such a large group of my friends all to-gether—you can imagine how we chattered & laughed. It was something. Most of them brought a gift & of course it made me feel terriably special. This noon I had lunch with Dr & to-morrow my calendar is loaded, lunch, afternoon, dinner & evening all at different places.

In the midst of our dinner party mom called long distance. My reassignment—what excitement. The orders read (well really darling I hate to tell you. Am afraid it will be as upsetting as it was to me-cause after your call & letters I want to stay close by you)—well here it is Ft. Lewis Washington. Golly what will we do-I'm at wits end. Bopsy you have to try now to be near me or don't you want to. I'm really upset.

It's a funny world darling. We wish for things, change our minds & everything goes into turmoil. So what will we do. Bopsy I just have to see you some way somehow, some place. This living without my Bops is just too big for me & that is from the bottom of my heart.

Guess there isn't much use saying more. Will be on pins & needles waiting for your letter. Could wish for a call if I knew we could discuss it but it's out of the question. Mom said there are no other letters for me but am praying 4 or 5 will be there Friday.

Will write Friday or Sat fear to-morrow will be all I can handle & still be able to sleep by bedtime. My friends are so wonderful to me dear they can't do enough. If you could only be here to see these receptions.

Good-nite sweet baby-sleep tight & I'll be praying for us.

My greatest love
Your baby

My darling

Guess what time it is? Ha—2 AM & I'm still poking around. But your fooled sweet thing has no date-so there. This is it. Left Madison at noon & arrived home at 8:30 & when I walked in-here was a big surprise party. Well it was perfectly lovely. About 25 of our old friends & neighbors. We played cards. I showed them all my lovely things—(especially a few from my baby). Mother served a beautiful lunch—it was one before we knew it (except my eyes) I was terriably thrilled & excited Darling everyone has been so wonderful to me.

Not until after all had left did Mom give me my mail & just think two letters from my Bopsy, & such wonderful letters dear. Honey I eat all your pictures up-look at them every day. To-night you just got talked to while I was looking, could you hear me saying all my pet names & hoping the picture would come alive—gee whiz.

The graciousness of all my friends down there overwhelmed me—& I'm one proud gal darling to have real friends.

Darling I'm on pins wondering how you will accept my new assignment. I'm really upset—course I'm so afraid you won't get out to see me—I'll die if you can't—honey I love you so. We just mustn't be apart. Please God that we don't have to. Honey what are you going to tell your folks & how will it turn out. Remember this though, have great confidence in us & in me & my acceptance of whatever comes. I'm praying day & night darling for it to be what we want.

So glad to hear about replacements but can't see some stranger in my house with my baby. It must be so hard darling.

Hangover-what's that? Gee Bops we had very few & usually one or the other of us took care of the sufferer-but it was good darling that you had fun-I'm so happy-cause scruntchy you just must be happy & Bops thinks of you as much as you think of Bops—(hope the censor can figure out the relationship of Bops & Bops).

Honey if you can't read this scribble I'm sorry-am all curled up in bed. Not sleepy but its almost 2:45. Hate to send you up in an envelope-but guess it must be.

Keep well my darling. Write so often. Keep smiling & remember to love your

Baby

Let me know more about your talk with the Chaplain Pincus-do you have confidence in his advice? Darling can it be-oh how I hope he says yes.

Good-night again sweet thing-& smack smack smack & bushels more

Tag.

3/11/44

I think of witty things to say,
I'd be considered bright
Except I always think of them
*In the middle of the night**

My darling—

Two more letters today from gunboat old sweet thing. I really wear them out dear. Over & over & even between the lines I read-so there. Think darling you are beginning to have an idea how upset I've been for two years just expecting our parting. Its terrible isn't it dear-but your Bops has known it would be—(womens intuition) Honey I feel so strongly that all will be well but for you I'm not building castles, but having a wonderful time making the plans. Bad girl huh? Well Bops-when a person is as deeply in love as I am those things are bound to happen. Got my little ring out of the safe & it even sparkles like a diamond—guess your baby is hopeless & won't give up.

You asked me what I think dear & of course we hold no secrets so here is one of the poems I've cherished & wouldn't let you read-but they are the way I feel (Enclosed) For us to have a little boy is just what I want darling-to-gether we could conquer anything. In fact baby my mom said to tell you that from all they know and hear of you, they would be proud to have you for a son.

Bops I bought a big fat rat for my hair & it is done up the way you like-also have an overseas cap which makes me look much better. Honey do you miss poking in my hair for those two little rats? Ha

How truly wonderful dear that you intend speaking to your family—am sure they will understand & give us their blessing like my family. We must have that though dear-because I want them to love me as a daughter or else we could not be truly happy darling. You may believe my dear that you & your mom & dad would be my greatest concern & I would never fail you darling believe me. Am getting so impatient about your return. So need my Bops & his great great love.

Sweet thing we are invited to dinner at the Dorwins & I must get dressed. They all are trying to get me fat. Ha ha. I'd like Bopsy's way better. Slap my hand I'm a naughty girl.

Be a sweet heart & here is all my love for my own scrunchy.

Your baby

Tell the gals I'm not wondering at all about your faithfulness. I have too much confidence and trust in my Bops.

---

* Popular poem, author unknown

My darling,

Its late again. Seems it always is when I get through with you-but we have much better talks when its quiet & I have you all to myself.

How was the ball game to-day. Who played? Funny how your old gunboat got to like the game better & better. That's what I like about us dear. Our interests were so common & cause one liked something the other always did his or her part to make it mutual. Nobody like us huh, Bops?

Busy as usual-dinner with the Dorwins last night. We played bridge & I stayed with Peg. We didn't get up until eleven & honey I really rested & slept. Guess I'm finally relaxing. Have spent the day with Dot & family. Auntie spoils the baby though. She is so cute & cuddly—just like I had to spoil my Bops. Couldn't resist buying the kiddies some cute clothes in Madison & Margaret was cute as a button in her new red jumper with white blouse. She really strutted to show it off. She is so adorable & good.

Mom & I are going to Minneapolis tomorrow want to go out to Snelling & then make my reservation on the Empire Builder for the 21st. Honey I dread leaving—it will be so lonesome seems Bops should be there to meet me. Darling something will have to happen. I'm a big girl & being sensible about everything but life without my baby isn't fun & nice. At home it is tolerable because of the family but alone-way out west. Gee. No dear not self pity—but we had so much & it has to go on doesn't it dear. Would you consider asking for the west-suppose not. Then what?

Bops I keep wanting to whistle across the street at bedtime & wait for my answer-but whats the use its too far to Panama for you to hear. I'm terriably lonesome to-nite darling—but my chin is up. Just keep going on & on about us—but we both feel the same so you understand.

Darling there are so many things I want to ask you, talk about & do for you. Sometimes I think so hard that off guard I turn around to say something-& then I can hear myself laugh-the absurdity of it all. My Bops is miles & miles away. Have thought so many times it would be hard leaving but hadn't fully realized how empty the world would be without you. Nothing seems the same.

My sweet sweet Bops. I love you-it hasn't changed & never will even if—oh no that can't happenI know.

It's sleepy time really. I keep praying for you & for us-so good-nite my dear. We'll be to-gether in my sleepyland. All my love

Your baby

My darling,

Uncle Sam is giving me wonderful service on my letters. The one written & mailed the 10th arrived today. Isn't that super?

Well you rascal. Now taking care of the movie stars. How nice for you to have the opportunity of meeting them that close. Can just imagine your firing wise cracks back at Bob Hope. Sweet thing. Frances Langford huh-would the competition be so great? Anyhow you can't scare me celebrity or no celebrity-so there.

Darling I'm feeling wonderful-am almost 110 but my face looks so much better-even mom says so. Yes dear I dread terriably going back to work-would rather go to work for my Bops. Its just going to be too far away for me for one thing-but will be a brave soldier & hold out in these difficult months.

Edward I'm beginning to get the receipts for my bonds, two have arrived all ready. My sum total of bonds is 19-good girl huh? Then too the bank account is swelling. Proud old thing I am. Did I tell you I insisted on letting my dad use some. He fought like mad but finally consented. Told him he could pay me any time and he gave me a note for $300. Honey, I'd do anything for my dad & he is doing so well getting the farm paid for. Wanted to help him just a little. In spight of that have close to 500 again.

Mother & I had fun this afternoon. We had a sleigh ride to the timber. Daddy wanted to get some wood for the fireplace. I even helped saw down a tree. Keep warm doing that believe me. It is nicer today not quite as cold. Baby you would love it on this lovely place. Part of it will be mine some day, or ours, we hope.

About the picture darling, of course I want one of you-the portrait-have always wanted one, but hesitated to ask for it. You know why. When I am located again I will have a nice one made for you. Am waiting purposely to put on a tiny bit of weight. OK? We have taken a few snaps but the roll isn't complete. Will hurry up though.

Florence sent me a lovely formal that was too small for her-it is gorgeous white & dotted with rhinestones. Doubt if I will ever wear it until we have our next dress-up date-you'll like it Bops.

About my going out with fellows—that's a laugh—honey—I needn't go with anyone to see how nice you are. Anyway I just couldn't be bothered-it wouldn't be fun & I will read & sew & dream about us. Want no one to cross my very private threshold of thought. Bops I miss you more every day, its *accumulative like some horrid medicine, but we have a world of new things to look forward to my old sweet thing haven't we?*

Hope above hope that your call comes through to-night. Just have to give you a smack & hear my Bopsy's voice. That will be better than any present in the world.

Aren't I a jabber face? Can't help it we have so much to talk about. My greatest love darling all for you from your Baby

3/14/44

My Darling,

Well, for once the army gave you what you wanted only now we don't want it any more. I've felt all along that this was going to happen but never for one moment thought that the army would for once give someone what they wanted. All the girls have gotten just what they asked for. We both thought we were being smart. I don't know just what there is to do now Baby. In yesterday's letter I said that you should get in touch with the Service Command at Fort Sheridan but they probably won't be able to help you. The only thing I can suggest darling is that if there is still time before you go I would telephone your friend in Washington, D. C. and she could probably get your orders changed for you. You might tell them that because of certain conditions at home it would be better if you could be stationed somewhere near home or at least in the mid-west somewhere. No kidding, darling, I feel as upset as you do about the whole thing, but it's something we all have to face in this day and age. I guess the best thing to do darling after all is said and done is to go ahead and go there. After all, I don't know just where I am going to be assigned and maybe fate will again take a hand and send me your way. Again, you will probably be able to transfer after awhile after I know where I am going to be. Also, as long as I'm still down here it doesn't make much difference where you are stationed. I don't know how long I'll be down here and when I do get back to the States and find out where I'll be then we can make further arrangements. At least you will be at a beautiful post and I know you will be better off there as far as well-being and comfort goes. Of one thing I am sure and that is that our love will stand up against anything they throw at us, won't it baby?

I'm going down to Tropical Radio this A.M. and try and put in a call for you for tomorrow night. I hope it goes through.

I'm rushing this off in the hopes that you at least get this before you leave. One thing you should do regardless and that is get in touch somehow with your friend in Washington either by telephone or letter and ask her advice, etc. about your chances for getting transferred at a later date, etc. Don't be upset darling, I love you and I always shall. We will see this thing through somehow and I know everything is going to be all-right. Be a good soldier darling and have faith, all this can't go on forever. My Baby. I love you, I love you, I love you.

Bops

My Darling,

Baby, this has been a hectic two days for both of us I know. I was down to Tropical Radio last night from 7 until past 10 trying to get a call to you but the connections just weren't any good. I sent you a radiogram telling you what I think you should do. I've changed my mind from my past two letters about what you should do and I hope we can get your orders changed. I'm quite sure that they will let you remain in your corps area. Darling, Ft. Lewis is just too far away and I want you as near to me as possible. Your home corps area is just right no matter where they send me and you'll be within striking distance of not only me but also your family. The next month or two are going to be important ones darling and we should be as close to each other as possible. I don't know what I was thinking of when I wrote yesterday that you should go to Lewis and I hope that this letter still finds you in the Mid-West. If the phone call doesn't go through tonight I shall send another radiogram. I know the Nursing officer in Washington will give you what you want if you just tell them that for certain domestic and personal reasons you must remain in your own corps area. After all, they want to send you where you wanted to go or else they wouldn't have given you orders to Lewis. I'm sure it will all turn out all-right. We have so much to talk over darling and when I get home I intend to spend at least 4-5 days of my leave with you and if you're in the Mid-west it will be so much easier. I'm so damn mad at myself for not anticipating the possibility sooner of you getting orders to Lewis and telling you to write for a change sooner. It just never occurred to me that the Army was going to give you gals what you asked for a change. At any rate, I'm afraid to think of you and I ever not being to-gether. I sit in my little room at night and think of how fine you are darling and how deep my love for you is and I pray that it will all work out for us. I just have to get out of here before long and get us straightened out don't I, baby?

If the call doesn't come through to-night I'm going to try again every night until I get you. Be brave darling, and warm yourself with the thought that I think of you constantly and one of these days I'll be there with you.

Your baby,
Bops

My dear dear darling

Your old baby is so nervous & excited, can hardly write. Really Bopsy I can hardly believe it all. Naturally your families reaction has me worried-simply can't wait to hear, so we will know for sure. It's a dream darling-a dream just can't realize such wonderful things could happen to one little girl. Even before I talked to you to-nite Mother made me take a sedative to quiet me—isn't that awful-but baby I know you too are just as nervous & excited. We would probably eat each other up if we were to-gether.

That Bopsy's voice to-night was so wonderful to hear. So very clear except for that one minute. Honey your rascal is expensive isn't she? Just think how much you would save could you take me to a movie every night.

No letter to-day-but expect one to-morrow. Darling when are you coming home. Is there anything of encouragement in sight? Have Manny write me if you leave like you wrote mother.

Sent a night letter to Col Blanchfield right after you called. My only hesitation in sending it early this afternoon was that if your mom & dad would say no-I would want to go far away-but darling they won't will they? This is the letter I sent:

"At my request permanent change of station is to be Ft. Lewis Washington. Last day of leave March 21st. Due to unforeseen circumstances on my arrival home would greatly appreciate consideration of a request for transfer to home corp area. Wire immediately collect." Is that ok dear? They can't any more than say no & if the change can't be made I can always come back. I too couldn't bear to think of going so far away.

Darling my family is so wonderful about it all. Mother asked me to-night if we would be married by a rabbi, and I said yes. Expected them to be grand & understanding but they are even more so than I expected.

Dot & children were here to-day. That Charles is a brick-he said he wanted to stay & say hello to Edward-instead he found this picture & said here Auntie I bet this is like Edward. He is just too smart for 4½ years.

Honey it would please you so to see my cheeks—they are full of color & actually look like a squirrels—can hardly believe it myself—but say sweet thing—why are you losing. Miss your old Bops don't you?

My baby I'm just too excited to write more-think of you constantly-no one else enters my mind. Can't possibly think what I'd do darling if your folks don't approve. Aren't I the old worry wart—but Edward our dreams, hopes & plans just can't crack now can they?

Will go to bed now & dream our dreams. Keep well my sweetheart, chin up, be brave & keep busy.

All the love in the world

From your lonesome
Bops.

My darling,

Darling, when I got finished talking with you last night I guess I was just about the happiest guy that ever lived. Before the call went through I was worried, upset, jittery, I was down in the dumps all day I guess because the previous call didn't go through but I heard you so clearly last night and I felt that you were so close to me. Jeepers, what a wonderful person you are darling and how good you make me feel when I'm blue. You know before we talked the censor asked me if I knew the regulations I told him I did. There is a regulation that radiograms and messages aren't supposed to be mentioned but I told him that I was an army captain and you were a lt. nurse and that I just had to ask you all about everything and he said, OK say anything you want. It sure was nice of him.

I don't know as yet whether they will grant your request or not but I feel that they will. If they don't it will be simple for you to transfer later on to where I am. I feel just as you do darling, that one of these days all this will iron itself out and I'll be able to ask you the question I've wanted to all these years. I'm an incurable romantic you know and I want to ask the question just like they do in books. I guess I'm really a baby, aren't I? I'm writing to the family this week-end, so we just have to wait and see.

I just received your two letters telling me about your Madison trip and all your parties. Your $100 gift was truly wonderful darling, only there isn't enough money in the world to put a price on your sincerity, thoughtfulness and fidelity. You really have some swell friends and I'm happy about the whole thing. How could anyone help but loving you darling, I don't know. You'll love my friends too. Just think of the fun it will all be darling meeting each other's friends. Jeepers when I think of the happiness that we both could have to-gether I don't know what to do. It's great to be young and in love isn't it? Our time is coming and when it does get here, watch our smoke.

Thanks for the pine needles. They sure smell good. I almost ate them. The poem is really beautiful darling and I appreciate why you didn't want me to read it at the time. I think I could write a better one though, don't you? With that old Gunboat as inspiration I could write anything.

Couldn't I?

I shall write your friend asking her to send me some candy. Sounds funny doesn't it? Dear so and so, please send me some candy. Hah! Hah!

I'm enclosing a toast which was in Winchell's column the other day and I thought you should add it to your list of toasts. You know Bops, when we are both in good shape we sure run the parties don't we?

I just have to say again darling how wonderful it was talking to you. I love you, baby, and the thought of seeing you again and holding you in my arms is what really makes me go on day after day without you. Be happy, darling, and trust in me—I'll look after you always.

Bops

My Bops darling—

Another day—a slow one. Apparently due to my anxiety about lots of things. No letter from my Scruntchy either, but guess I should be satisfied since we had that wonderful talk last night.

Honey you should see the country to-day. Mother Nature shook her featherbed & has made a fairyland. The evergreens are heavy with new clean snow & it is simply beautiful. Mother says this is the most winter they have had so am egotistical & say it is all for me to see & enjoy. Since my galoshes are in the last trunk I can't go out—rubbers aren't enough—but perhaps I could go up in moms attic & dig out my snow boots.

Mother is at the beauty parlor this afternoon-so am staying home alone-waiting for that wire. Since I can't mail this until to-morrow—will leave it unsealed & see if any word comes. Daddy & I had a long talk this noon. He, too, is so happy for me & is most anxious to meet my Bops. Right now he is debating about a milking machine. His work is just too heavy, but he hates to give up any of his bossies cause they are paying so well. He certainly is a business man even if he owns a farm.

Baby I keep wondering what you are doing, saying, thinking. Its funny how much easier it is writing then I thought. How is the tan dear, everyone has remarked how tan I am isn't that funny? Are you eating well, getting your rest. How is the sand flea situation?

Going to a party at Dorothy's to-morrow night & a dinner party at my aunties on Sat. Monday if my change comes through-will have to go to Snelling to turn my ticket in & see the transportation officer. Dad wants to go to Minneapolis anyway.

Bopsy darling I love you—never never forget that dear. Miss you more each day.

Your Baby

My darling—

Well sweet thing—your wire is off bearing good news. Aren't we the lucky people. Honey, Camp McCoy is about 150 miles from home & about that far from Madison-convenient to Chicago & certainly a much better location for our future plans. Am terribly thrilled dear & now only one thing left to find out isn't there? Know you will be pleased about the consideration I was shown. The message said to await orders to expect them in a few days. From here Bopsy I will be able to go most anyplace won't I?

Dad & I are going to Minneapolis Mon. to turn my ticket in. Someday you & I will make the trip to Washington, but it will be a lot more fun with my Bopsy anyway.

Honey one of these days you will be coming home—how excited I am. You must go home first & make your plans from there. Wonder where they will send you dear—any idea?

Am having a problem about white uniforms have tried all over Minneapolis—will just wait until I get to McCoy. They may have some in Q.M. Otherwise I'll wear my seersuckers until some are available.

Charles saw me writing to you so he had to also. Notice it is already in the envelope so maybe you can decipher the message. He is such a rascal darling—makes me want more than ever to have a son of our own.

Mother said there is a letter from you. She will bring it in to me to-nite. Will finish this after I've read yours.

8:30. Just got your letter Bops dear-as usual it was super-you old sweet thing.

Sounds like all is going wonderfully well. Guess we miss each other huh? You have no idea my darling how I'm looking forward to our New York trip—and I shall not take a speck more leave until you come home baby. What all is going to happen—tell me everything dear—sometimes I Wonder if I have been expecting or planning too much. Please dear tell me. Cause so far everything I've done has been for you & around our dreams.

Darling, guests are arriving so will give you a million smacks & a big bear hug with lots of snuggles.

Things are quieting down I'm getting more lonesome every day. Love you so much dear

Don't forget to love
Your baby

My Darling,

As soon as I heard from you this morning about your reassignment I immediately sat down and wrote you what first came into my head about what I thought you should do. I then went down and put in a call to speak to you Tuesday night and this letter is being written Monday night. I, of course, don't know what you may have to tell me then but in case there is nothing new this letter is a follow up on what I have in mind telling you about going to Washington for your new job.

I've talked this over with Kay Callahan and one or two others and we all think it best that you do go to Ft. Lewis even if you did have the opportunity to change. You see darling, I don't know just how long I shall be down here and in the second place I don't know where I am going to be sent. There's no telling just where they may send me and I may end up around the West Coast, who knows? Besides they tell me that it is relatively simple for nurses to transfer from one post to another. Besides, I think it best that we save asking your friend in Washington a favor unless we really have to. I know it's far away darling but it's better that you are there until I get settled and know where I shall be definitely and then pending how things turn out we can make our plans.

Darling, my darling, be a brave soldier and I know that everything is going to be fine all around. We are having a tough job of it right now but the fruits of all this will be sweeter in the months to come.

I hope that our conversation, if it comes through all-right and I can hear this time will help us both.

It's funny I just had my atlas out and I found Ft. Lewis in it after a while. I studied the air routes and everything, it sure looks beautiful on the map. It's halfway between Seattle and Olympia and near Mt. Ranier National Park and everyone says how fortunate you are to be at such a beautiful post. Have faith darling, and I'm sure that everything turns out for the best, you know our motto!

I don't have to tell you, baby, how much I miss you and how lonesome I get at times. Right now, I know how you must need me and how much I need you. But, I know we'll be all-right and that our love will see this thing through. Above all, please be happy in your own mind darling, and don't fret. You've got to be my beautiful Bops when I do see you and it'll take more than a few thousand miles and priorities to keep me from you.

<u>Your baby,</u>
Bops

My dear bald headed sweet thing,

I love every inch of hair that isn't there any way. So there.

Its very late 12:45 & gee whiz that's late for this 10 o'clock girl, but the party was very nice. Dotty is a lovely hostess.

Darling I couldn't go to sleep before having another little chat. It makes me feel so much better just thinking after I hurriedly rushed that note off to you to-night—what a selfish girl I'm being. Baby maybe your naughty rascal has been worrying you because of my fretting in the last few letters. It must be so hard for your dear, even harder than for me because your problem is so much greater. Darling I'm sorry if I have been too insistant in knowing—guess its just because our future is so on the pendalum. But there I go when we agreed to live from day to day these next few months. Know in my heart that everything will be all right because I have such trust & faith in your every act. Have you any idea my baby what this all means to me-we had said good-bye & we're being so brave & then my darling you too are willing to make great sacrifices. Edward I am so terriably happy & proud of you—want everyone to know & love you my darling. Its so awful without my Bopsy. We have had heaven for two years & it will continue if it is in my power. Be brave my darling have faith, & I pray that any decision you make you will never, never be sorry for.

Bopsy I get so mixed up in my thoughts. You know what they are. Will Edwards folks like me—will they say no, will they find it hard to give their son to one little girl & oh just everything. Suppose dear every person goes through a thing like this—but you see this all has been such a great great thing in my life-because I thought you were reconciled to the fact that we could part & forget. Darling you bad rascal knew it couldn't be that way—it scares me to think what would happen had you not been brave and thought of your life too. It's so hard to say or tell anyone, it's a fight each person has with himself. That's why darling what you asked me to do was an easy decision & one that I am proud to make. Please dear, tell me all I'm supposed to do. I know one thing-be patient until we know for sure-isn't that right?

Can't think to-night Bopsy dear, but had this on my mind, knew I wouldn't sleep.

Just wanted you to know I fully realize what you are doing for me & for us. You are in my every prayer.

This was a special little letter since I wrote one to-day. Will write a long one to-morrow, & be a good girl & not fret any more. Just want you here to talk to & to love, we have missed a whole month, good night my darling. I worship you.

All my love,
Your baby

Let me know how fast a free letter comes. Will send the next that way for you.

Mornin' Darling,

Sunday morning and I'm hungry, I wish you'd run over and get me some breakfast. Hurry up, Bops, I'm impatient.

The place is lousy with rumors again most of which aren't worth repeating but there is some news bound to break here one of these days and when it does I'll tell you, baby. I was speaking with Charlotte to-day and I hear that some of the girls have already been reassigned in many of the places that they asked for. Jeepers Baby, I don't want you all the way over on the coast somewhere. I'm quite sure that if you are you may be able to change it but we'll just have to wait and see. After all, I have no way of knowing just where I'll be going but the chances are that I'll be in a hospital somewhere around the East. I expect that by the time you get this letter you will already have been given your assignment. I'm sure waiting to hear where it is.

Well there's a double header this afternoon and I'll be out there yelling for the old home team. If it wasn't for the game on Wednesday and Sunday I don't know what I'd be doing with myself. I just hang around, in bed every night early, getting plenty of rest. Gee Whiz, Bops, I'm just no good without my "old pair of shoes" around. Remember that little spat we had. I'll never forget it because it was just the only one we ever had. You know Bops every time I think of the way I used to mope around and act the first few months we were down here I get surprised all over again that you put up with me. I sure was a nasty man on one or two occasions, wasn't I?

Bops I was up a good part of the night worrying about that tooth of yours of all things. What a guy, I bet I'd worry about a hang-nail if it was bothering you. Sweet thing!

For once I hope the army doesn't give you what you want. You know what I mean. Bops if you do get sent out the Coast before you go why don't you go down to Sheridan and see just what you can do about it. I'm quite sure that they will change your orders before you go if you decide you'd rather stay in the mid-west or the East. I guess we'll just have to wait and see.

Bops I've been looking around for something to send you, you know me, and there hasn't been anything worthwhile. Is there anything that you need that I can send you. Make sure so I'll be able to get it.

I hope that one of these days I'll be able to tell you that I got a home run in a ballgame—but there's nothing new right now.

So long darling, I love you and every time I think of how you love me I feel so wonderful and happy that anyone so lovely would love an old thing such as I am.

Your "Bops"

My darling,

Well, the die is cast. I wrote to the folks today and for 4 single-spaced typewritten sheets I poured out my heart and story to them about us, darling. I don't know how they can say or do anything but what we want baby, now all we have to do is wait. I expect that their first reaction will be one of hurt darling—not so much hurt as surprise but I'm sure that they will come around and see us through. Don't worry, I'll let you know as soon as I hear. Jeepers, I sure feel better now that I've written. Every time I think of all the time that we wasted I get so damn mad at myself. You knew all along didn't you darling. You women are really smarter than men about these things aren't you?

I heard from my Aunt and Uncle today darling and they told me that the important thing was whether we were in love. It was a swell letter and they said that no matter what I did they were with us 100%. They mentioned the deep religious upbringing of my parents, etc. and told me of the things we might encounter in a "small town" but they also said that the important thing was that we loved each other. It was a swell letter and made me feel better. I then sat down and wrote the folks. Uncle Murray is going to speak to the folks about us.

I guess I'm anxious awaiting hearing from the family to write coherently about anything. All I care to say to you over and over again is that I love you baby and know somehow or another we are going to get what we want. If the family ever saw the way I look at you and the way you look at me. They'd know, wouldn't they, baby?

I still can't get over that swell phone call we had. It was really swell. I guess you're what the doctor ordered, you old sweet thing.

Waiting for that wire about where you'll be. Boy, we sure do spend our time waiting for messages, letters and stuff don't we? The anticipation is terrible!

By for now darling, and I think tonight I'll go to bed and just think and think about you . . . (for a change)

I love you—

Bops

My darling

Mother is ironing until she comes to my shirts & my auntie is here from Minneapolis & is doing a little fixing for me so will take a few quiet moments to write to my sweet thing. Mom came after me this morning & now I'm back on this quiet lovely farm. If my Bops were here-all would be perfect.

Received your two letters this noon written the 12th & 13th by the sound my letters must be taking a dog sled to reach you. Many of the things I've told you-you haven't received. Honey your letters are so perfect & my medicine for the day-can hardly wait for that mail man. Be sure to send my mail from now on to Camp McCoy. Baby every time I think what a wonderful break we got-just know we have a guardian angel watching over us. Am so happy we didn't wait too long.

Promised a better letter to-day. Will try to make some sense this time. Your bad rascal gets so lonesome for the only man in the world-sort of forget the promise of "chin up."

About the tooth. It is O.K. Dr Mac took pictures. He was mad as hops, the black as I told you was a piece of amalgam. Smart gal, huh? Have a little work to be done, but I'll have it taken care of soon. Nothing serious.

Baby I'm so spoiled-keep thinking about that telephone call Sunday. Bops & his silver toned voice. Remember when we first went to-gether how you called me in the barracks & pretended you were someone else. You know my darling I have always been in love with you & even at that early date wouldn't have considered going with anyone else. Bopsy I'll always forever & ever be true & again if our plans don't go through I don't want anyone else. Couldn't bear to think of anyone trying to take my sweet old things place.

How are the ball games going-it's a Godsend that you have that interest besides bowling.

When Mom & I get to St Paul Mon. have made up my mind to have a picture taken for you. Think my face looks so rested & plump. Oh yes I weigh 109-it is staying right there & certainly now that I'm in real fresh air again will gain more in the next couple months. The only thing is if I gain too much it will be tough on the clothes situation huh? You better stop comparing me to movie actresses but will always try to keep you proud of me. Think we both love clothes, wouldn't we have a glorious time in New York getting dolled up. Am dying to get in a civilian dress. Did I tell you when my sis got a hat the other day I went with her & put on all the saucy little ones I could find. What a thrill.

Darling you asked me what you could send me—well the same thing I've been saying every birthday & Christmas—you my sweetheart—you.

Am awaiting anxiously your reaction on everything—never a dull moment in our lives is there dear.

Don't get too lonesome-when you do just remember your baby loves you bushels & bushels.

Until to-morrow Scruntchy
All my love
Gretchen

Dearest Darling, Gunboat, Bops,

I got your wire yesterday and I was so happy about the whole thing. Just think you are between your own home town and Madison. You shall be near your family and your friends and I shall know that you will be near those who love you for the next few months. We must have been crazy at the time when you signed up for Washington. Jeepers, just think baby, all the way out there by yourself, no friends, I'm sure happy we wired for the change. This way I can get to see you darling when I finally get home on leave. I know you and your family are just as pleased as I am. The Nurse Corps sure didn't waste any time in giving you what you wanted did they?

Well darling, I guess the only big thing that's holding us back now is waiting to hear from my family. I should hear from them by the end of the coming week. I have no doubt at all but that it is going to be all right, sweetheart. They shall probably be upset at first but when they know that I've made up my mind and finally meet my baby, I know they'll love you just as I do. You sweet, old thing!

Baby, I went to Jewish services Friday night and I enjoyed them so much and all along I kept feeling you at my side when the day would come when we shall be going to them together. I've been reading the history of Judaism and our book of Laws, known as the Talmud, and no where in it is there anything that says I can't marry you. It's a beautiful religion and is based on only the equality of man, tolerance and love. There is no fan-fare or pageantry. The main rule of our religion and I know you will love it as yours is the Golden Rule. The services are simple and understanding. Golly, darling, when I think of the happiness in store for us I just can't wait a moment longer.

Darling, I think the time has come when I would like you to write to the folks. I'm sure if they heard from you and were able to understand how fine and wonderful you are all this will work out easier. You can use your own judgment as to whether you want them to write first or whether you care to. I'll leave it up to you. As soon as I hear from them I shall write to your folks.

I've felt more content than I have in a long time. I've explored my religion and have found that there is no reason why we shouldn't marry. I can truthfully look my family in the eye with the deep-seated knowledge that what I am doing is right and that there is no reason for them not to accept our love.

We're starting to get the breaks my darling, your reassignment change was the first and I think that from now on it will all be O.K. All I want you to do now is sit tight, be happy, feed yourself well, and walk around with a look of happiness and anticipation in your eyes. No more heart-ache for my baby, you've had enough. It's time for happiness in this day and age. Any little bit we can find.

I just can't tell you how happy I am that you are at McCoy and where your friends and loved ones can be near you in the next few hectic months.

I love you.

I sure would love to have that great big new rat in my hands right now. I'd really poke around and mess you up!

Bops

My Darling,

When I arrived home to-night dad said to me, "Edward called, we had a long chat, he asked me all about the cows & the farm." The rascal—but anyway dear I was so disappointed not to be here. Why is it we get all mixed up & I'm away when you call. Darling do you know what it means to me to have you think that much of your Baby—its worth the whole war debt. Am hoping above hope that we can make connections to-morrow night like daddy told the operator. Your just a blessed sweetheart.

Mom & I went to Minneapolis—over to Snelling & got my ticket & reservations—imagine dear $15.65 for 1ˢᵗ class & my Pullman-nearly fainted-so believe you me honey when you come home somebody is really going to travel to get to her Bops-or else you must come part way to meet me. Darn this war. If you were only here now. We visited a couple of my aunties and started home at 8-but it was misting & freezing. Tough driving. By the way dear you didn't know I was a good driver. Well my mom trusts me—she wouldn't think of driving when I'm along & she drives well. Its wonderful to get in a car & drive. Got 5 gal of gas for my furlough but it goes a long way.

Bops just think that good mailman had 3 letters awaiting me when I got home. They were all so wonderful—just about devoured then—but since I read all your letters 4 or 5 times—held my appetite. Those letters are perfect dear, full of news & love & so good & long. I never will grow tired of writing my Bops & its so easy—cause we can just ramble on & say anything we want & in any manner.

Honey the big question which you are awaiting answer on-is no problem to me-so will answer it & ask a question or two. Edward you know that I will do anything in the world that will assure you happiness & help make our happiness complete. I see nothing difficult in learning more of your religion, rather ours because it is all fundamentally the same. Could I continue believing in my beliefs along with yours dear? I mean it would be difficult not to-you see my dear Protestants have just gone on a little further but we still believe just as you do-and as long as we all believe in God that is the main thing. Yes darling we must have all this straight first so our children will have an easier path. The main thing is to have them believe in God & any family is lost without a mutual religion. Baby I know too your mind is uneasy as to the advanced beliefs of Protestants. Mine is too, but we can't help but be better men & women by knowing & trusting in the Golden Rule

& that has been my religion already since childhood. Yes darling I will be anything for my Bops for we must be to-gether in all things.

Edward dear I haven't had to think this out or ponder at all—its so simple because I lost 20 pounds thinking & now I know the answer. My Edward to cherish & to have the rest of my life, otherwise no one. It is as easy as that & darling I know down deep in my heart that it is all going to be the way we want it. Your family just won't say no dear. I simply have asked God for two years for them to understand. Darling its people like you & I, unselfish, unafraid & with love so great nothing is to much to face that will make the things for which we are fighting for as Americans come true. Bopsy after all we are all Americans & we are fighting to prevent racial discrimination aren't we?

Am curled up in my bed trying to keep warm, its beastly out-but aren't we having a lovely talk?

Good for the U.S.O.—at last they came through bet the Bob Hope Show was a real treat. The only thing wrong was that we couldn't enjoy it to-gether.

My darling Bopsy. What will we do with you at the east & me at the west end of the U.S. Oh well distance makes no difference in our love even if we have to wait. While in Washington I might even be able to take my lessons in Judaism, then if mom & dad say "yes"—well mountains & plains could never keep us apart. Could they?

Have oodles more to write, but will wait until tomorrow cause your eyes will be tired.

God bless you my own sweetheart. I'll be waiting to talk to you-yummy-good nite & I'll dream of us—your own baby.

I love you—surprised?

My darling,

Just think darling, you've been gone since the 15th of last month and it seems just like a million years. The time really drags now that we are apart but when I look at the calendar it doesn't seem possible that it's March 20 and I'm still here but I suppose that one of these days I'll be getting out and then up to see my baby.

I wrote the family yesterday that you were going to write them and I hope you will but as I said before you may use your own judgment. Jeepers Baby, it's going to be all right, isn't it? I just happened to remember that you are an Eastern Star and so is Mother. Isn't there something in your ritual that says something about there being only one God. I think there is. Darling, I know that my prayers and yours too will be answered and that we shall be together one day. We're sure sweating it out though aren't we? Well, the fruits of our anguish now will be so much the sweeter later on.

Darling, I've written three letters to the family in the past three days and I really poured out my heart to them in it. If they go unheeded, well they're just not the parents I think they are. Enough for that now.

It looks as if all the nurses will be leaving here shortly. The hospital is going to be reorganized shortly and there sure will be a lot of changes going on. Hope that one of them is to get me out of here. I'll keep you posted on all developments.

Remember last week when we were doing all out telephoning? Well, I just realized the other night that I hadn't been to the Post Theater in almost 10 days. Just think about that Bops. I started going again last night now that I finally have you settled in your new post. I haven't played golf in almost two months because I like to sit down and write my Baby after lunch each day and before I know it, it's too late to go anywhere and who cares as long as I'm writing to Bops.

All the medical officers down here have been working on a medical problem which requires us going into the jungle a few nights a week and taking blood smears on all the Puerto Rican troops. The other night I got back at 4 in the morning and you can imagine the bitching that's been going on from the officers. Oh well, if it isn't one thing, it's another.

Will you be able to get home for a week-end or the day now that you are so close to home. Are the hours tough and tell me all about everything, won't you Baby? I bet you haven't even thought about your promotion since you've been back, there's been so much else to think about, hasn't there? Shows to go you, how things will wear off and no longer seem important when there are other things to consider.

We are expecting some ships one of these days and I hope that maybe there'll be an eye man or two on them. Gosh, how I want to get back home and see you and the folks. I know that when they see me coming home after 2 ½ years they will feel happy and the world will be ours.

We just had to vacate all the dental offices across from the clinic and my new office is now in the clerk's office. It's a little crowded but here I am just the same. I don't care anymore what they do. We are all too damn fed up and unhappy about being down here to care much one way or the other.

Signing off, now baby, until tomorrow. Baby, baby, we need thousands of smacks and hugs don't we? I love you—

Bops

My darling,

I'm on one little wee corner of this big davenport dear, have a lovely fire in the fireplace & mom is popping some corn. Won't you drop in & keep me company? Honey it would be so perfect & I miss my old sweet thing more & more.

Am spending to-night being quiet & lazy-to-morrow we go to Minneapolis, will do the remainder of my packing & leave Tues A.M. Dad & mom will take me to St. Paul to go down on the Milwaukee train. It is about three hours ride to camp. So Tues. eve I'll be writing from there.

Bopsy it is going to be hard to go to a strange place-at every corner I'll be lookin for that rascal of mine. It will be terriably lonesome dear without you, but imagine that hospital is busy so that will help. One consolation is my being able to write to my darling-that is a special hour in my life each day now. Its such a great privilege dear to have someone so wonderful to have a special interest in.

Edward have I answered all your questions about everything? Are there any things you want to know further about my family, their attitude & anything? Guess the only thing to do now is just to await orders from my darling. Whatever you want me to do dear, please don't hesitate.

I am yours to command. Keep wondering dear if this is a dream or if my Bops is really coming back to me. The whole world circles around you dear.

It has been a beautiful day here-only ten below this morning-its putting roses into my cheeks and I've almost stopped shoveling, but its been a pleasure to shovel to get back to the U.S.

Was just thinking when we had lunch to-night what a relief it was to have crisp crackers. Every day I note things that were so common place before, but are a real treat now.

Saturday night Edward one of my aunties had a lovely dinner party in my honor—such luscious food. We had aged T-bone steaks, fresh garden salad, French fries, fresh rolls, fresh strawberry sundaes. I thought of you dear & how you would have loved it. Yes I've had a wonderful furlough & can hardly wait for you to be home & have a wonderful time too. Its great darling.

How was the ball game to-day & what movie did you see to-night? See I know exactly what's going on don't I. A—ha. Two things I haven't done on my furlough—have a date or see a movie—isn't that something? Darling I don't even want to have a date until its with you.

This is awfully good pop-corn baby—but am getting your letter all messy. Maybe I'd better be quiet anyway. So will turn off the record.

All the love in the world for my sweet thing—Here's an extra big smack-like we both love

Your baby.

My Darling,

Here's the old newsman again bringing you choice tidbits from the land of the Trade Winds and the Southern Cross.

I just received your letter of the 13th in which you stated your views about my big question. I guess down deep in my heart I knew just how you would answer my questions. Darling, you're so good and honest and broad-minded and every little thing that you do shows me how deeply you love me. I appreciate again why my baby was losing weight in the past two years and I knew the reason all along, didn't I but did nothing about it. I owe you so much darling, that I hope I am given the privilege of dedicating the rest of my life repaying you. Yes, dear, the moment that we get the green light from the family and I pray to God that it will come, we can make arrangements for my darling to start being one of "God's Chosen people." As for what the Jew believes in, it's very simple, its basis is the equality and brotherhood of man and we also believe in a hereafter. The greatest Rabbis since time began have said and said again that the main theme of the Jewish religion is the "Golden Rule" and I know how you have always followed it. You're so good inside darling, I always come back to that. You're an angel only I'm glad you don't have wings or else you'd be too high for me to reach.

I haven't as yet heard from the family darling, and I suppose there will be several correspondences between us until things work out but as you and I feel that it will be all-right.

There's no sense keeping secrets from you Baby so I must tell you that I am going through some very trying moments right now. Knowing my family as I do and the fierce pride with which they have always conducted themselves and expected me to, I know that their first reaction is going to be a very great shock to them. Not a shock in the fact that they won't love you once they know you but a shock in the fact that suddenly I have asked their permission for something which they never thought that I would do. But, the big factor is that I down deep in my heart know that what I want to do is not wrong in the eyes of God and my own religion. I read in your letters of your love for me and I remember the look in your eyes during the past two years and I ask God if such a love as this could be wrong and I know that it can't be wrong and that it is right. All we have to do is show them we are right and I am more than sure, yes I know, it will be all-right. So be patient darling, and we shall see this through. As I said in my last letter darling, I think if you sat down and wrote Dad and Mother just what this means to us, your love for me and how you want to even become a Jewess for me, I'm sure that they would imbibe some of the feeling that we really have for each other.

You must realize darling, that it will be a little rough at first, we can understand that because of human nature but with a little time and love and one look at that sweet Gunboat, I'm not worried. It's hard darling, to throw over an idea of what they think is right in just one minute and it will take them a little longer. Let's understand them a little and if things do not suddenly blossom out into a perfect understanding, I know they will eventually. I know my Father and darling he'll love you the minute he knows you.

I hope that you are getting settled at your new post and I can only say again how wonderful it is that you are so near home. I think God is starting to look after us a little, darling, isn't he?

Keep praying darling, that it will be all-right. I love you so much, baby, it hurts, please God—help us!

Bops (crossed out Eddie) (tsk! tsk!)

My Sweet thing—

Am so rich today-3 letters from my Bops. You should hear daddy kid me. He says he can remember when he felt the same so he knows how it is. What a riot that guy is. I'm his pet you know. Both mom & dad are so anxious to meet you dear, they already love you cause your so good to me.

To-day darling I had the mug photographed for you. Have one in uniform & one without which will it be? The latter no doubt that is what I planned. Will get the proofs Thur. imagine. Will be awaiting my baby's picture with open arms. These little snaps just aren't enough are they?

Went to Snelling & had my ticket redeemed did a little shopping & home at 4. Mom & I really waste no time on our trips. Got everything I need except an alarm clock & there isn't such an animal in the states. Maybe you will have to come to my rescue on that item. Have they any at the PX dear?

Must tell you some good news-went down to see our old family Dr. to say hello-got on his scale in uniform without my coat & tipped it at 114-isn't that super. Maybe you'll be sorry if I get too fat-huh? Honey I'm feeling wonderful-my face especially feels full, all my wrinkles are gone. Now you'll have a little more to squeeze. Mother is so pleased and says I look so much better. See I followed the Doctor Bops & his orders, he's a super guy-do you know him?

Thank you dear for the little toast-it was cute & of course I think you can make up a better poem than anybody. Mine that you wrote is still in my purse-its so beautiful.

Just finished my packing a few minutes ago-leave at 7:20 in the morning. Will be there before noon, so that is really an easy trip.

So our little house is all torn up-my poor darling living in a bare place. Remember how much fun we had fixing it up Bops, those were happy days, but our whole two years was just one happiness after another. Such old love birds.

Guess it won't be long before you will be receiving that all important answer. I'm so excited honey—but not terriably worried for I know it will be all right. Bopsy are you really goin to get down on bended knee-ha ha, but honest my darling I want it to be like a story book. Our whole romance has been that way.

I love you my sweet thing & to know that you love me so much too is what keeps me a brave soldier

Faithfully & forever
Your baby

My darling

Well your soldier gal is at her new post & from all outward appearances & hearsay-think it is going to be most enjoyable. Left Hudson at 7:20 this A.M. & arrived here at 11. My trunk won't be in until to-morrow so will have an extra day of rest. Had to catch the sniffles the last day of my leave, so now I will have a chance to get over them.

Everything has gone very well so far, the only thing I missed to-day was your letter & oh that is such a lot to miss dear. Again you're spoiling me darling-but I love to be spoiled. Expect my mail to be straightened out in a day or so-can hardly wait for your letters.

Know you are anxious to hear about a few things so here goes.

Our Chief Nurse is Maj. McGovern, the girls are wild about her & say she grants your every request. She gave me a lovely room, corner, N.E. with the words "I think you deserve it." Most of the rooms are double deckers & cots, but I have a nice fat mattress & am by myself.

The majority of the girls here are taking basic training, from that they are assigned to units & reassigned, all new in the Army-2 weeks etc. Am pretty sure none of this will affect me as I'm assigned to Station Hosp. These girls taking basic are not on floor duty at all.

Was happily surprised to meet one of the Drs. Assistants I used to know in Madison, Marian Smith, a charming motherly person. She is a lab Tech here, so has told me heaps of things & it is so good to know at least one person. She was in to-nite & visited for two hours & now I don't feel quite so alone. Isn't that nice dear? One of the chief's assistants told Marion they hadn't decided where they would put me, but that they felt I deserved more than ward work. Apparently time & rank means something here.

Honey I know I'm going to get the right breaks, just feel it. The post is large, but beautifully located among the pines. Its really lovely. Theatre about 2 blocks away-Px, store, tailor shop, library etc right in the Hosp. So convenient. Food excellant. $30 per month, all the fresh milk & fruit we want etc. You will really see an old healthy Bops on your return darling.

Honey I miss you so terriably. There is so much I want to talk to you about. Its going to be heaven to get into your arms & snuggle again-so baby dear keep the chin up-smile for Bops-brush your teeth every day-hurry home to that gal that loves you so much.

Need some digs, scruntches, slides & all our funny definitions for things, most of all some smacks. But here are bushels anyway.
Good night my darling. I keep praying for you & for us.

Your baby

My darling

This has been a long lonesome day-but before going to sleep will have my little chat with that sweet thing, then all will be well again.

My trunk didn't come until late this P.M. so spent most of the day reading & whiling away the hours. Took a lovely long walk about 4-breathing deep of this fresh luscious Wis. Air & thinking how fortunate I am in being in the homeland again. Its really beautiful around here dear & the girls say its like a summer resort in the summertime.

Got 6 new white uniforms to-day-issued so was pleased about that. It seems new regulations allow 12 & I had only gotten 6 so it's a good thing none were available for purchase in the Cities.

Will go on duty in the AM-believe on septic surgery—so have my white uniform all ready & the alarm set for 6. Dread these first few days dear, but have come to the conclusion that I've had more service than most of the nurses here-so am more confident in that respect. One other girl & myself are the only two in camp that have seen foreign service so we both are greatly respected. Its quite a thrill after all the pettiness down there. It will probably take awhile to prove myself worthy of promotion but feel dear it will come in the not too distant future.

Was invited to a social club this eve, helped me get acquainted, majority of the 15 members are 1st Lts. So felt quite honored.

Darling all I want now is good news. Have counted the days & will keep counting them until you return-it just didn't seem right without my Bops.

No mail of course for me to-day. It will probably be awhile before mine catches up to me & consequently I've felt very neglected not hearing from my Bopsy. Know by this time that you must have an answer one way or the other & honey I'm petrified really. Whatever shall we do if the answer is no—it scares me to pieces.

Be a good angel face-but never forget your "Tag" loves you more than anything in the wide world.

To-night I need you to talk to & confide in. Will be a brave soldier though baby just living for our day.

Good-night my darling smack smack

Your baby

My Darling,

Jeepers, I received 6 letters from you today. I was reading and reading them just like a book. They sounded so happy that it made me feel happy. I pray to God that you shall always be happy darling.

Darling, your letters sound so wonderfully happy and you are making so many plans for us that if anything went wrong with them I really don't know what I'd do. I think it would kill me if all this didn't work out. I think so much of your happiness and your well-being that the thought of this not working out as we want it is a great, overwhelming hideous thought. I suppose that I am making a mountain out of a molehill but I must be frank with you—but the past few days have been a nightmare for me. I keep thinking of the family saying no, I keep thinking of whether they'll be too hurt or not, I keep thinking all sorts of things. If I didn't feel that down deep in my heart this is the right thing for me to do you know I wouldn't do it. But the only thing I see before me is our love and the knowledge that we belong to each other and that we are right and everyone else is wrong. Don't for one moment think Darling, that I'm sorry I'm not. I wouldn't change anything in the world for what we are to each other and I know, I just know that this present mood of mine will pass and the folks will be all-right and we will laugh about it afterwards. You mentioned in one of the letters I just got that you think I must know something that I haven't told you or else I wouldn't have written you to change your orders, etc. I don't know anything you don't darling. The thought of you going away out there by yourself and my not being able to see you was just too much.

In a time like this you must be near your own folks and I also wanted you as near to me as possible because I've never needed anyone as I need you right now, family or no family. I know that being away from you is making this a whole lot worse than if we had been here together and sweating it out. I know that all I need is for you to hold me in your arms and tell me everything is all-right darling.

Gee Whiz, what a gloomy Bopsy I'm being but it's the way I felt darling, and I have to tell you don't I?

I hope that you have written to my family and told them all about us. I know that when they meet my old Baby, they'll love her as much as I do.

Mrs. Roosevelt was at the hospital today and she saw all the patients and I think that the nurses had their picture taken with her. I just had a little peek at her because the officers were not supposed to be anywhere around.

I'm so impatient to get back to the States darling and see everyone. When, oh when is it going to be? Get a Ouija Board and find out for me will you?

Darling please don't worry about me although I know this letter sounds down in the dumps. There's so much to think about I just had to write it all down. I suppose that I shall be hearing from the family any day now and when I do you shall hear from me immediately.

Your letters have been beautiful darling and they are helping me. I cherish your love more than anything I know, it is a Gibtralta I am leaning heavily on. Thanks for all of it—I love you.

Your Baby
The pictures were cute!!

3/23/44

My sweet thing—

Honey if they don't get this mail situation straightened out soon—I'm going to call you. None since Monday & its about to upset me. Its just the fact that it has to be readdressed from home-but golly one would think I'm a thousand miles from home. Surely there will be some to-morrow.

How is my old lonesome baby anyway. That's two of us-naturally I expected this let down, a new camp is always tough but darn, I want my Bops—oh so bad. Did you get your hair washed all right this week & gee whiz no manicure for so long-you know darling I loved to do that job just to get a chance to hold your hand. That's one reason I've seen no movies, fraid it would make me too homesick & anyway whats fun without that baby. Would rather stay in and read & dream.

The girls in this barracks are swell, my room is full all the time, it seems so strange-but they are cute kids & just came in the Army. Naturally I feel like a mother hen & her flock. One girl across the hall is a riot enjoy her company especially.

Went on duty to-day. On Septic surgery for 2 hours then specialled a gun shot wound until 2 PM. To-morrow I will have charge of a ward of my own-almost certain its ENT. Darling if it was only your ward how happy I'd be. Know it will be impossible to keep my hands off the phone to keep from calling every few hours to see what your doing. Darling no one could have told me that one person could have crawled into my heart & soul to this extent. Guess its incurable.

Went to an orientation film this P.M. on Tunisia, in Technicolor & excellent, perhaps it has been there.

You haven't told me who all has left there-how are the new girls making out & how many have been making eyes at that sweet thing of mine. They better keep hands off huh? Or else they'll have a blonde blizzard on their necks.

My proofs came to-day. They aren't bad-will send them back in the A.M. Do you think when it is finished that I should send it there or to Poughkeepsie. Maybe it wouldn't catch up to you—or am I planning too far in advance?

Your baby is drowsy—if I could only have a good night smack, even a wee one all would be well. Next would come our whistles & then I'd go right to sleep. Instead I must stay awake for awhile with my memories of all those things.

Good-nite my darling-God bless you-& always be mine forever—

Your Bops.

3/24/44

Dearest Beloved,

I skipped writing you yesterday and I am a bad boy but I got tied up with some patients and before I knew it I was OD and kept busy. Forgive your old Baby, will you?

I haven't heard from the family and I don't expect to hear until next week and I'll let you know as soon as I do. Now that the time is getting closer to knowing I become surer and surer of one thing and that is my darling, that no matter what they say or do about us I know that my life and destiny lies with you and you alone and if they deny me this I'll never forgive them. You are the first real thing that has come into my life, darling, and I'll fight anyone that says I can't have you. You haven't heard me speak like that before have you baby? It's just that I feel so lonesome and I know you love me so and I just have to be near you soon. I guess I sound like an old sissy, but it's the way I feel.

It looks as if all the nurses will be going back shortly. They have so many they don't know what to do with them and they're going to get rid of them. About time, I say!

Darling, I wish that you would write me the best way to get in touch with you by phone in case I get a chance to call you at your new post. There's talk of the 2nd group getting out with the first and perhaps I'll be home sooner than we think. Please the Lord, I hope so!

Haven't been doing much of anything lately. It's so good to hear from you darling, and I know how important my letters are to you. I especially appreciated the letter you wrote (the extra-special one) about my speaking to the family and deciding to do what I want to. I fully understand about your wanting to know so quickly but please don't be too impatient. The way I have it figured out, the family's first reaction will probably be for me to come first and talk it over. I can understand that darling, can't you? Not that there is anything to talk over as far as I am concerned but they probably will feel that they want to see me first. If they feel that way, don't be too impatient, my darling, we've waited two years and we'll have to wait a few weeks more. Be strong and brave with me darling, I lean on you heavily right now just as you lean heavily on me. I know down deep in my heart that there is happiness for us somewhere and we shall find it together. Right?

Just think I haven't played golf since the last time I played while you were here. I just don't feel like it I guess. I've been sticking around the office writing letters and thinking of you all the while darling. I can't think of anything pleasanter to do, can you?

I shall probably hear all about your new post in a few days and it should be interesting. I'm still happy over your reassignment near home. That sure was a break.

Glad that your tooth is going to be all right and that the Doctor is looking after you.

Until tomorrow, my darling, sleep tight in the thought that I cherish and adore you and shall forever—just like you, if it can't be you, it's no one else.

Bops

Smack, smack sweet thing-hello

Hows that for a different beginning? Anyway your still my darling.

Well Bops this has been a much better day, first & most important your letter of the 18th arrived—golly I've really sweated that one out—2nd I'm in charge of a very nice ward. You know how interesting it is getting things straightened out to suit ones fancy. 3rd a letter from home. 4th another bond came. 5th a big piece of cake at a birthday party & 6th writing to the one I love. Summary in a nutshell-huh?

How perfectly wonderful dear that your auntie & uncle are with us, already I feel better. Yes dear. I've considered, thought & dreamed all angles—they still are no barriers, and there is no doubt at all about our being in love is there? They ought to see these love sick puppies. Edward as soon as I feel in just the right mood to write a difficult letter, will do so-it will be a great pleasure & thank you dear for your confidence in me. Bopsy this is all so hard for you-keep thinking about that & hoping so that we will find out very soon about everything. It will be a great load from our shoulders. Don't worry my darling I shall never fail you.

It was good getting my teeth into some work to-day. You know me & my cleaning streaks & having things just so. The ward officer is very pleased to have an experienced girl. He is an older man & it will be nice working with him I'm sure. Even have a W.A.C. Ward boy or girl-Pvt. Meredity. My ward master is a SGT (a fellow) and very competent. The little WAC is a good worker, but it's a new experience this war business. Ask the boys how they like them. Thought of working with Pvt & Cpls (women) Can hear them holler. The ward is nasopharyngitis or rather U.R. S.—no surgery. My hours are alternate day on 7-9 or 2-7 next day 7-2. ½ day a week & a week-end once a month. Night duty for 2 weeks every 3 mo. So it isn't half bad. Tell the kids their crazy if they don't want to come back. The U.S. is wonderful.

To-night one of the girls had a birthday so the whole barracks had devils food cake & Cokes in the front room. It was fun & I am certainly more satisfied living in the barracks. Of course it would be different if my baby were here, but this keeps me from being so lonesome.

Did some pressing & reading this PM & to-night I have written some thank you letters & a little knitting. Am making a sweater for Zee & Larry's cherub to be. Is that all right from us dear?

The air is so wonderful I sleep like sixty & get up so full of pep-it would take a team to hold me down. Honey you will have the old Bops back again when you come home.

Knew there was something I wanted to tell before ending this (do you mind 2 pages?) One of the nurses who is married just received news to-day that her husband is being transferred-Our Chief Nurse took the trouble of finding out where he was going & got a transfer to the same post for her. This nurse hadn't even asked her to do it, but Bops it shows you that there is one real Chief Nurse in the Army. Think I am so very fortunate & it will make it easier for us dear.

Darling if my letters are too long & jabbery please tell me, just get started talking to you & forget to stop.

Dear darling—

Had dreaded this day thinking what a long lonesome one it would be, but Uncle Sam even worked on Sunday to give me three choice pieces of reading—your letters. Honey they are truly wonderful-each one has so much in its contents-especially of your great devotion & love. It makes me so terriably proud dear.

Worked this morning-was alone but got along fine. The Capt. has said so many nice things Bops which has shown me that my work is most satisfactory. Am really trying to do my best, even though it seemed hopeless when I left there, to even try any more, but this place is so utterly different & extremely pleasant. Yes darling I've forgotten completely all the pettiness, the promotions & bickering of 837. The only thing I haven't forgotten is my Bops—& loving you is what makes me go on with courage.

This afternoon I will do some ironing & then dear the difficult task will be tackled, that is writing to your family. Thank you again darling for your confidence in me. Will try not to fail in any way. The only thing I can tell them is just how I feel & what my understanding of all this is. After all my baby we parted thinking we could be stronger than our love & Bopsy since you never promised me a thing about our future to-gether it has given me such great trust & faith in you. That too has been what makes me love you so & your fairness & truthfulness.

My baby I fully realize how terriably hard this is for you. If I could only be with you to give you courage & comfort. Perhaps I'm not worth this great devotion darling, but feel we both are beyond reproach as to our conduct attitude & reactions in our love for each other. Baby we not only have been true romantics, but buddies, pals, friends, companions & all the things that are so necessary for a successful & happy life together. Just remember to keep that chin up & some day we will know how worthwhile it is to travel the bumps first & the smooth road till the end of our journey.

Edward please don't fret or explain or worry about our religion. There is only one God & He will see us through. It is utterly important that we both believe in that one thing. All or most of civilized religions believe in one God & the only difference is that some add more to interpretation of it. The Golden Rule as I said before has been taught to me since childhood also the Ten Commandments, the Lords Prayer & the 23rd Psalm. They all offer to everyone all the things worthwhile in the world to lead a pure and *wholesome life. Being a Jewess my darling is just another part of our love which will make it more perfect & our understanding of each other more profound. Did not explain the last step to mother & dad because they offered no adversities to our union. All they are interested in is my happiness & your true love for me. So unless they ask it won't be necessary to explain, they are truly wonderful people dear.*

My sweet-sweet thing, of course this love of ours isn't wrong, I have known that for two years, & that's why I kept saying, "why, why, why." Then too darling I never gave you up even though you gave me no encouragement, because you are so fine & good & felt that my prayers some day would be answered in that you would come back to me & seek an understanding & the reasons of why we couldn't be together. Thought it best for you to fight that battle alone-wasn't I a naughty girl?

My darling please don't worry about my having patience with your family. I know it is hard for them, but Bopsy just have faith in them & their love for you as their son.

3/26/44

My Darling,

Received two lovely letters from you yesterday and I was so happy to learn that my old baby is getting to be a regular Fat old thing. Gee whiz, I can hardly wait until I see you and it may be sooner than you think.

Guess what? I was playing softball to-day and I GOT A HOME RUN! No kidding, I sure was excited and I know you know what I mean!! I guess I was pretty lucky because the others didn't even get a hit.

It looks as if I won't be here to get the answer that we are both waiting for but at least now I'll be able to plead our cause in person and that should make it a lot easier, I hope. I think that I'll have time to only write about one more letter, darling, so please be patient for a while if you think the mailman is disappointing you. I'll make up for it all in person as soon as I can, you understand, don't you?

Darling, to be perfectly truthful I'm too excited to write much and I've been running around getting things settled. I've lost a little weight in the past few weeks but I'm sure I'll put it on again when I get a little home cooking just like you did.

There sure are great changes going on down here but I'm glad that you are away from it all. Your descriptions of your leave were wonderful and believe me I enjoyed every moment of it with you.

Well, baby, the next month or two will probably answer a lot of questions for both of us, and I'm glad that I'll be able to get the answers to some of them myself and then be able to tell you myself. Better that way! In answer to your questions about if there is anything more that I want you to do or any questions there are I want answered, there are none. You have done everything possible darling, more than your share, and from now on the show is mine and I'll carry the ball the best I know how. Above all, my dearest, don't be too impatient and please don't lose faith. We are both going to have to be brave, and wearing your love as my shield, I know we shall win out. Gather my love around you darling and wear it as a protection. It shall always be with you because I love you, my darling, your intelligence, your virtue, your dignity.

If I don't have time for any more letters, I'll wire you when I get home and make arrangements to call you up.

Chin up, baby pray for both of us and little side prayer I don't get seasick.

Your baby,

Bops

Dear darling—

Is everything all right, are you feeling better? Poor sweetheart. Just make believe I'm holding you tight & saying "Don't worry Bopsy dear. All will be well, & the main thing anyway is that we love each other." That gloomy letter just didn't sound like my sweet thing at all-but you know how you are feeling & I'm sharing it. Remember dear I've had days like that too in our two years, it's just the uncertainty. My thoughts were always "oh am I going to lose my baby." Its horrible baby, but if it's to be it will be & it takes days & hours like these to make us realize what we're fighting for. Nothing would be worthwhile if it was just handed on a silver platter.

Darling all I hope & pray is that you are not sorry—that's all that matters, to know you care enough to face some hours & days of discomfort. Please baby-for me-chin up?

Know you will be glad to know that I wrote your family last night, a very simple letter, just telling facts & how fully I realize what anguish they are going through. Hope it was O.K.

Old man winter came again. We had a gorgeous snow storm. About 4 inches. It was so clean & white. It won't last long though—too close to spring.

Tell Dee I sent her powder & also that she owes me a letter.

Finally struggled out last night & went to a movie with the girls. It was wonderful don't miss it "Up in Arms." This Danny Kaye is the funniest character I've seen in ages. In fact I liked the songs & antics so well that we all decided to see it again to-night so I just got home. It's late & I'm weary as I worked until 7:00.

Bops if you could only have some of this wonderful food. It is the best Army food I've ever tasted. It would do your heart good to see me stow it away. Milk 3 times a day. Salads, good desserts & we have 2 large meals one at noon & one at night. The patients' food is excellent too, they all get a pint of milk at every meal & all the real fruit juice, undiluted that they want. There are so many things I like about this hospital—its so very well organized, the wards are consistent as to their bookkeeping, procedures & duties—& little or no griping or bickering. It's a real pleasure to work & we don't work hard—just keep busy. Hope you do as well at your next post darling.

So you had a distinguished visitor. Think she better stay home & conserve gas.

Baby you should see me strut with my ribbons—it is amazing with all these girls to be so all alone in that I've had foreign duty. People just look & ask questions. Its my only distinguishing mark from being classified & just getting basic training. Some stuff huh? All our trials & tribulations aren't for nothing after all.

Your old tag along is a real jabberer isn't she-just hope to keep my darling happy. We both are such faithful writers. Again I say-there's nobody like us Bops.

All will be well my sweetheart-no matter what happens, just be brave, don't worry about me & I'll always be waiting. Am still counting the days-but you must go home first even as badly as I hate waiting. There is a silver lining behind these dark clouds.

Tell me all the gossip dear & remember Bops loves you from head to toe, inside, outside or upside down.

Here's a big bear hug & bushels of smacks to keep you warm & happy.

Your baby

3/28/44

My darling,

Received both your lovely letters from your new post and it really sounds wonderful. I'm so happy that it is what we both expected and I know that before long you'll be a 1st Lt.

I'm writing this letter with practically one foot on the gang-plank because I wanted to get this off before I left. I heard from Dad this morning and his letter was just as I expected. He and Mother were both very upset and the immediate reaction wasn't very good, darling, but as I told you before we both expected that they would react that way at first, didn't we? However, it isn't all that bad because I called home this morning and spoke to Dad and told him I would be home in about a couple of weeks and that all I wanted was for us to sit down and talk it out and he agreed to that. As I wrote in a letter or two back, darling, we're going to have to fight for this but I'm sure that when I get home and see the folks and talk to them they will see the light. In the meantime there's nothing for us to do but wait until I get back and as soon as I hit the States I'll call or wire. All right? So much has happened in the past few days that I'm really in a dither. There is so much for us to talk about that I can hardly wait until I get home and hold you in my arms and we can just sit down and talk. Please don't feel upset about the family's immediate reaction darling, I expected it to be this way and I know you did but they are sensible enough to want to talk it over so that's where it stands at present.

Believe me, dearest, I know what you are going through right now and how deep your anguish is but I'm going through it too, darling, and your love for me and my love for you drives me forward fighting for what is right, and I know down deep in my heart that this is right! So far our prayers have been answered—First I realized that I had to be with you—second, we got you reassigned, thirdly, I go and get orders to go home suddenly, and I feel that when I get home and talk to them, it will be all-right. Don't think about what we will do if they insist on saying no. We'll cross that bridge if it presents itself. Let's be thankful that so far things are moving along.

Baby, my baby, I love you so much and I need you so badly. I know you need me too. Please sit tight and continue being fat and lovely as I know you to be. Are you getting those lovely curves back, darling, that you had when you first came down. Yum—Yum—Yum!

Well darling, that's all from your old Baby until I hit the Estados Unidos. You know how those trips are and we have no way of knowing where, how, and when so just sit tight, keep saying your prayers, don't stop loving me, keep those curves in tack, and start practicing up on your smacks (on yourself, you rascal) because the Old Bops will be around for 1,000,000,000,000,000 of them before long.

I love you—
Your Baby

My darling darling Bops

Honey I'm quite beside myself to-night. Am about frantic really. No mail again to-day. Its awful-not knowing or hearing from you. Is anything wrong. Oh I hope not. My imagination keeps running away with me. Of course in this particular mood—nothing good.

If it weren't for this cheerful bunch of girls here dear-it would be even worse. They just were in for our evening gab session but my darling in my heart I'm so lonesome and need my Bops worse every day. We both are going through pure unadulterated agony, but its worth every moment for our love, isn't it? Keep thinking how I cheer you up & then comes a letter cheering me up-what guys we are-just belong to each other like bees to honey.

Can't think straight to-night-my nerves are so on edge-keep saying over & over "It will be all right" but darling I can't help but worry for you & for us until we know. My darling I love you so, that's the reason.

We're having a real Wis. blizzard all last night—day & to-night—it's beautiful out but cold. The icicles hang thick on the eaves, my first real winter in 3 yrs. Really enjoy it dear but am looking for spring to get me thawed out. A better warmer-upper would be your arms Scruntchy—please hurry home.

Am going to write to your auntie & uncle to-night. What shall I tell them? They probably will think me brazen do you suppose, but Bopsy I so want to do the right thing.

Last night you were so plain in my dream-we were in a car-trying to sneak a smack going down a street. Laughed this morning when I thought of it.

You know something Bops. Never did before in my life but am saving your letters & cause there were none for 2 days I read the last few over again to-nite. They are so beautiful my darling, can I keep them & tie with a blue ribbon someday—Can I huh? Grootch is a bad girl isn't she—but gee sometimes I can't help it.

Baby please, please wire or call or something soon-can't rest darling. I want to see & hold you & have you hold me tight. This love of ours is too great for me to take calmly.

Oh yes to-day I got weighed in my duty uniform—111—that's good don't you think?

Darling I mustn't ramble on. Anyway this isn't a cheerful letter, but we have to let each other know don't we?

I love you sweet, sweet thing—miss you, our whistle & oh so many things

Your old baby

My darling,

The mail-man just isn't good to me these days—thought surely to-day there would be some mail from my sweet thing-but none came. Can only think of three things 1. You have had bad news 2. mail service is held up and 3. you have left there. Honey I'm beside myself to know. Its just more than I can do to sit here, be calm & patient—am so worried about my old baby. Can't even think straight.

Its funny darling how distinct you have been in my dreams. Can remember every detail. Last night we were at my home. You were taking a nap. Guess its because you are on my mind so much, day & night.

Old Man Winter has really blown it, it is still snowing to-nite. That makes 2 days & 2 nights. Maybe we'll be snowbound or something.

Have been staying in my room constantly thinking some message may come. Anyway darling I haven't the heart to do anything—just want to think & write to you.

Guess I'm all caught up on my letters, now. What else should I do? Have written your folks—on the 26th & to your auntie & uncle yesterday. Certainly by this time you have gotten a letter from home. Darling please have courage & patience. Maybe it will take a little time on their part-but feel so definitely that I could make them love me as belonging to you. Bopsy dear I need & want you so terriably—and that has been always—you know that to-night again I am awfully alone & lonesome—but for some odd reason just this afternoon I experienced a wave of contentment & inside I feel a little calmer. Feel sure it must be because everything is going our way—why would such a feeling be dear—maybe I'm psychic or psycho—one.

Baby dear I can't think straight-my letters are terriable I'm sure, forgive me but perhaps after I hear from you all will be more clear & then can write coherently.

Good night my sweet darling-Bopsy loves & misses you. Oh so much. Please God make it all right for us.

Your baby
Smack smack

Letter from Dad's brother, Martin Siegel   Wednesday March 29, 1944

Dear Gretchen;

I am answering your letter to the family; and hope that you don't mind, please. They are too heavy hearted, and all thru life we have all shared in all our problems to-gether so please feel as if they are writing to you as we are all one united family.

Let me tell you that we all at home, Mother, Dad and myself, feel for you and Edward and understand deeply the pangs and suffering you have and are going thru. We also realize that perhaps your future happiness is at stake; we love Edward and would do anything in the world for him. We also feel certain that you are a wonderful girl, even tho we have never met, and that you must be all and perhaps more than Ed has told us; as he could not fall in love with no one else but a fine person. With all this Gretchen, we cannot consent to his marrying you, since we firmly do not believe in intermarriage. It is nothing personal, as you can understand, since we do not know you, but intermarriage does not work Gretchen, the world is cruel; people would not respect Ed or you or your children. In our town there are two intermarriages of Doctors, they are not accepted either in Christian or Jewish circles; their children are ridiculed; I do not say this is right; it is very wrong but we are living in a practical cruel world, not in a theoretical utopia. I pray to God that there should be only one religion then things like this would never cause heartaches for all concerned; but since we must face practical facts, there is this horrible realization; and cannot possibly consent to this marriage, for both your future happiness; as there could never be any for you both.

If you could know and understand our heritage and background then perhaps things would be lighter for you to know why we feel like this. Ed and I come from a background of orthodox family and tradition, of Rabbis, Religious teachers; and although we are broadminded and modern, intermarriages are just out of our reason and understanding, and will never work out from many points of view. This came as a tremendous shock to us that Mother had a complete breakdown; Dad is completely a nervous wreck as Ed of all people, even more fond in Dad's heart than I am, is simply stunned about the whole thing. It is something that the family would never forgive, never forget, and literally Mother would never live through it. These things I tell you as not emotional but cool plain facts.

So in all, please understand; we are all sick at heart and frankly, Absolutely do not give our consent and hope that you will find your happiness in someone of your own faith; someday you will know that what I am saying is the perfect truth. There is no further chance of changing our feeling, it is definite, it is final, we cannot consent to this and hope that you will understand all I have tried to say and make you see the light, for your personal welfare as well as for Ed's.

God bless you,
Martin

Jack and Ida Siegel, 1941

Ida Siegel, Ed's mother, selling War Bonds

APRIL, 1944

My dear darling

Oh my Edward I am so glad you are home, safe & well. You are the most important person in the whole world right now in your families eyes & in mine, and darling I am praying every minute that we all haven't ruined your homecoming. Know your mental anguish has made that hard trip even more difficult & darling you must stay strong & think straight & be brave.

Am not going to burden you with my feelings my darling, only to say that if we hadn't been for that great pillar, our love couldn't have kept on. Its difficult to write, just want to be held in your arms so I can tell you everything. Even forgot to be brave baby the day Martin's letter arrived, held to-gether long enough to call your folks. I was nearly frantic, thinking what I had done to them. Then just this morning I had to turn to someone. Rabbi Schwartz came to me, he knew I was sincere & in great distress & darling the past few days he has been my strength to-gether with your love.

Edward you must know I'm not better, for we both have expected this & I fully understand perhaps it's just being alone without you that caused my loss of control. You must come darling as soon as you feel able to make the trip. Will keep on thinking only of our love, our future & you & with that keep brave.

Darling I won't stop fighting for something that is right. You taught me that—so please my dear sweetheart see it through & remember I'm with you now & forever & will never forsake or let you down. No matter what others think or say or do to us.

My baby is everything going to be all right. What can I do or say to help. We can't be wrong Edward-we just can't be when our love is so pure & beautiful. We have our lives to live too that's why we have been in the war to-gether.

Darling please give your family my sincere hope & wish for their return to better health & happiness now that you are home. Tell them that I didn't mean to cause them unhappiness but that I can't help my love for you, that you are my life & my strength.

May God keep you strong my darling & remember this, that this first blow has changed nothing. Am ready & willing to take up Judaism & whatever comes, good or bad my baby I want to share it with you.

All the love in my heart & soul is for my Bopsy. Am waiting & needing you desperately.

Your baby

My darling

Another long weary day of waiting has just past—they are endless Bopsy not hearing from you makes it so hard. That telephone just must ring for me soon—however I realize if you are restricted in New Orleans like we were, it is almost impossible to get a message out. So I'm using reason & heaps of will power.

Darling I want you to know I'm being very brave, & your good soldier, couldn't bare to think of letting you down. Am so confident of your ability in doing the right & the best thing. Have held up my chin in the past day or so knowing that our love for each other will see us through.

Rabbi Schwartz has kept in touch with me constantly dear, think he is doing a lot of praying for us, he's a fine person. He also told me that he had written your family. Wonder what their reaction will be to that. Edward I have been so worried & concerned for I don't want them to hate me because I love you so.

Work is just work. It's best to keep working and it helps me to keep from fretting all those hours. I've had a terriable time trying to wear a smile for the public. Haven't told anyone anything except the chaplain consequently I'm fighting this alone, but knowing you are too so again we are to-gether.

There is so little to write darling, the world is dark & empty. My enthusiasm & joy are no more until I see you. Keep trying to eat, sleep & work because I have to. Bopsy dear I want you to have a good hard spanking ready for me cause I've upset & worried you so—guess this is a bad Gretchen after all.

Perhaps I shouldn't write any more, your family may dislike it—but darling I've just got to. It's the only consolation all day long.

Be a brave sweetheart. Just keep remembering that nothing in the world counts except you & our love. Bopsy my baby I am so positive I can make you happy & keep you that way. Please hurry to me so we can talk & talk. Yes I will keep brushing the thought out of my mind if your family persists in saying no—that is a horrible, unreal thought. For darling its you & you alone that must be totally happy.

I love you my baby-its too great to ever change. Here are millions of smacks & hugs to give you courage & warmth.

Your own baby

April 5, 1944

Dear Gretchen:

It was nice indeed for you to take the initiative in writing to us, for we have known from Eddie about your deep feelings for each other. We wish you weren't so far away, so that we could get to know you, since you are to be a part of the family.

I wish too, that you hadn't encountered any complications, for it is a fine thing when two people find each other, as apparently you and Eddie have done—But I suppose you know that life doesn't run along without difficulties, and overcoming them only brings out our strengths—and tests our true feelings. We understand Eddie is on his way home, and we are anxiously awaiting word of what happens there—My husband knows of the fact in that he is Eddie's mother's brother, is caught in between his feelings, while I suppose I can be more objective because my environment and culture were different and we learned our values of life with a different emphasis. I hope it will work out for you both, with as little pain as possible, for heaven knows there is too much pain in the world already.

Gretchen, I hope you understand how much we want everything to work out happily for you and Eddie, and for Eddie's parents.

We have plenty of reason to hope for an early ending of the war, and the return to normalcy, which is so necessary for all these young people.

Our best wishes for a Happy Easter with the promise of true happiness ahead—

Aunt Sally—

WESTERN UNION

1201

A. N. WILLIAMS
PRESIDENT

The filing time shown in the date line on telegrams and day letters is STANDARD TIME at point of origin.   Time of receipt is STANDARD TIME at point of destination

R20 NL=TDN ELMHURST NY APR 9 1944

LT GRETCHEN L BOODY=

STATION HOSPITAL CAMPMCCOY WIS=

ARRIVED NEW YORK TODAY WILL CALL YOU IN TWO DAYS

LOVE AND KISSES=

EDWARD.

NY WILL APPRECIATE SUGGESTIONS FROM ITS PATRONS CONCERNING ITS SERVICE

My darling, my darling,

I am finally come darling to my home after 28 months and believe me I never thought it could be like this. Mother has been ill for over a year even before she knew about us and my dearest Gretchen, I took one look at them both and my heart almost stopped. She had missed me so much and had been worried about me so much that she had worried herself into a wreck and on top of that all, her hypertension has been mounting readily. And then when she heard about us she had a complete relapse. Baby, my baby, what can I say? My love for my family, my love for you are in one great big muddle and it's our battle and ours alone. Why is it that people that love each other so much hurt each other so much. Darling, of one thing you must understand, Mother understands us both and realizes how much we mean to each other, she knows you are wonderful or else I wouldn't love you and darling, she just stopped crying in my arms because you and I are so unhappy and that how tough it will be for us to part. And she's honest enough to admit that she doesn't have an answer as to why things should be this way but that's the way they are. Baby, do you remember how I used to explain to you why we couldn't get married, do you remember all the reasons I gave. If we were all alone in the world and didn't have to worry about anyone but ourselves it would be simple but we must think of the years to come if we were married and if anyone said or did anything to hurt you I would never forgive myself for putting you in that position. Darling, you know down deep in your heart that we love each other. Our love is so great that I'm thinking of you and I know that you are thinking of me. My own father and mother think the same way—they are heartbroken that you and I are unhappy but they know that we cannot take the chance of risking our happiness for the rest of our lives. Darling I got a letter from Gordon today and I told him about us. Baby he is so unhappy that I hate to tell you about what he wrote. His folks were heart-broken, baby, not that they didn't like the girl or that she wasn't fine, but just the idea that they thought they had failed in raising their child to do what they thought was right for him. He told me that although his father and mother now accept her as Gordon's wife yet they all feel an invisible barrier that try as they might, something is lacking. Darling, my darling, if you think that I would expose you to anything like that for one minute, well, just picture, baby, how you would feel if you knew that the folks resented our being together. You would be heart-broken, I would be heart-broken to see you unhappy and the whole thing would go up in one great heartbreak. Darling you and I know, we could be happy away from the world but what would happen to our love if discontent and doubt began to creep in. Darling, we both know what we have to do. I knew it when you went away and I was brave. Then when you were gone I was lonesome because I was left with all the things around me to remind me of you constantly. I just couldn't carry my burden alone and I had to write the folks if not out of fairness to myself but also out of fairness to you. Now you know that I have done all that. I can do without wrecking our lives completely.

Dear heart, dear heart, I know the deep anguish you and I are going through, my family is afraid that I will remain bitter towards them. Believe me they are sharing our misery with us and Mother's heart is breaking that I have to write you this letter but you and I must part darling. We did it once and it was tough and we'll have to do it again. I'm going to speak to you tonight on the phone and that's the reason I'm writing this letter before. You will want me to come out and see you darling, but what are we going to say to each other. We would be tearing each other's heart out, crying, pleading, and what would be gained when it is all over. No darling, please be brave and strong with me in this final ordeal. Sweetheart, my love, I know it's going to be tough for the next few weeks and months but if we love each other, please let's not hurt each other anymore than we have to. For the little time that we were with each other (2 years) I know we shall carry with us to our dying day. You have given me so much and I know I have given you a lot. I know that in everything I shall do you will be a part of my success or failure, you shall be with me in my heart forever as I shall be in yours.

Go ahead and cry darling, go home and speak to your folks, they above all will understand. Above all baby, don't carry this to yourself too much, speak to your family about it they will comfort you, that is why I'm so glad that you are near home. If you had been out in Washington by yourself it would have been awful for you all alone. Of one thing, you must be sure, and that is that don't ever feel badly about the way the family took this and don't think that you are in any way responsible for Mother's illness. Believe me darling, Mother understands and feels for us both. She insisted that I be sure and tell you that she has nothing but love and respect in her heart for you and that she is truly sorry that things couldn't work out. I know you are saying that we didn't have a chance, but dear heart, what Mother is afraid of and I am too is that supposing that something should happen that would spoil our love. It's better now when we are both young and can look to other worlds than to wait until after we were married and saw everything come tumbling down. You feel right now that you could make me happy no matter what and I feel that I could tackle the world too, but darling it's not that simple. There's a doctor here who married a Non-Jew and darling they are still in love with each other but his boy came from school the other day and said to his father, "Daddy, why do they call me a Jew, I don't want to be one that's laughed at, etc." Oh my darling, can you imagine anything like that happening to you and me. No, no.

My darling, I can't leave Poughkeepsie and start anywhere else, you know that. For what have my parents worked for all these years, they've given me money, a beautiful office. Baby you and I know what it would do to them if I left it to go elsewhere to start out because of one thing is certain, I could not remain in Poughkeepsie if I married you baby. I know all you are thinking, and you are wondering why. I don't know darling, Mother and Father told me that they didn't know, no more than they or God tells us why millions of boys have to be killed in war. If God and man can't answer that how can they answer our one problem.

My baby, what else is there for me to say. Our love is, and I know will be beautiful. It may seem hard to say darling and your heart will deny it but although the world is black for us both right now, I know and you must believe me darling, that the reason we give each other up physically is because of our great love. I'd rather this love of ours remain strong and beautiful to guide us than for us to do anything that will spoil in the long years to come because whether we believe it or not darling, there are laughter, and smiles and happiness ahead for both of us somewhere. Have I ever lied to you baby?

Please believe and trust in me now. Give the future a chance, my love, and the time will come when we shall look back on our love and friendship with nothing but kindness and fond memories.

The best although the most brutal way for us darling, is to stop writing all together. I'll leave that up to you but if we must write the letters must not be full of heartache because how could we write to each other without professing our love and by doing that each word would drop like a dagger on our hearts.

I'm leaving home for a few days to go away and see if I can't straighten myself out. If I know that you are being a brave soldier as you always have been it will be so much easier for me. I know why you lost all your weight and I gave you a sign of hope for us and you gained it all back. Baby, you are near home, let your friends comfort you, don't become a recluse—above all darling don't feel any self-pity for yourself. Give yourself a chance and some day we shall both be able to perhaps talk about it when we meet in the future. Darling, we must both be sensible. I've cried to myself for days and I shall probably cry after I speak to you tonight but we must both face the future with courage and confidence. I don't have to say that if you ever need anything, please darling turn to me, I may not be able to give you what you want most but all the material resources I have in the world are yours for the asking. I know it sounds silly saying the last but oh baby, I want you to have the best and someday I know you will.

No good-bye darling, in our own ways we shall love each other forever, you shall live forever in my heart and for every little tear you have shed for me, I won't say I'm sorry because I have shed one for you. I love you, my darling, and all I can say is that let us both pray that the future will find some answer for not only people like you and me but for the whole world.

All my love,
Your Baby

My Baby,

Gretchen, my darling, I'm writing this letter the a.m. after our call last night. Darling, what can I say to you? What words of comfort, what magic words can I say that will blow away this cloud of torment and misery that engulfs us both. God know you and I can stand so much but how much more can we stand of this self-torture that we are heaping on each other. Darling, darling, I know you want to see me and I want to see you but what will we accomplish when we do see each other. I'll hold you close and we'll both cry and each moment will bring added torture to us because we shall only have to part again and we'll be back where we started from. Darling, you said last night that you don't know what to do if you can't see me anymore. Don't I know how you feel baby, darling, we've got to help each other right now. Do you think it's easy for me being here when I know how you feel and if I thought a visit to you would accomplish anything, believe me, baby, I'd be there right now but one of us has to make the break and try and be strong and I guess it is me. Darling, please try and think clearly just as I am trying to do. You left me at Panama and you had hopes that perhaps I would see the light when you were gone and would miss you so much that I'd do my damndest to try and get us together. Well, that is what happened darling and believe me, I don't have to tell you how I tried and tried. You asked me again last night to speak to the folks and I did but darling, we all had another scene, not a hateful one, but just like we had when we came home. Baby, I love you and I love my family. How, oh how, I ask you could we be happy knowing the way that they feel. Darling, I must remain in Poughkeepsie when and if the war is over. Baby, you know way down deep in your heart that I am right.

I just received your telegram saying that you are going home for a few days emergency leave. That's right, darling, go home and be with the folks. I know that they will comfort and guide you. I think that they also know down deep in their hearts that all this will pass some day.

"Dearly Beloved" remember the picture with Bette Davis and Paul Henreid, the one with the two cigarettes and how you and I appreciated it so much. They loved each other but he had certain honor-bound obligations to meet and they both knew he had to meet them. Darling, you know what he said, "We've had the stars, why reach for the moon?"

Darling, right or wrong, I know that I have a definite role here at home and that there could never be any happiness, real lasting happiness, as long as the family feels as they do and they can't change, they would try, but down deep there would be the lasting hurt and you would never be able to overcome it.

Darling, show my letters to your Mother. She will understand. Darling, I just can't go out and see you. You must believe that it is the best for the both of us and your Mother will tell you that also. We would hurt each other so much more.

Darling, let's not hurt each other anymore. It's going to be tough to reconcile ourselves but please try darling, don't become an emotionally unstable girl. You must be brave and strong even though it's tough. Darling, search your heart for an answer and you will know that marriage to be a success must have love and help to be a success. We can't build a barrier around ourselves and keep the world out. Darling, if I said the hell with my family you know you wouldn't even do anything yourself. That's why you love me because I am thinking of not only myself but you and my family when I say, Baby, get a hold of yourself and don't let this thing get you sick. Don't you see that the sooner we each start getting mentally well and alert and the sooner that I know you are taking this in stride, the sooner we shall all be happier.

A final plea darling, chin up, the world isn't as bad as it seems right now and I am with you each moment knowing what you are going through. Please fight it out, please for our love, for our future.

Your Baby

My dear darling

 What to say, where to begin I just don't know. Just this-hearing your voice last night was so wonderful baby how I love you only God knows how much. Couldn't be brave, just couldn't, it was more than I could take.

 Left McCoy last night at 12. Arrived home at 7 this morning, darling I couldn't face it alone-trying to carry on & working. Mother & dad are so wonderful, fully understand & are with both of us in our great trouble. Mother says it must be that God willed it this way & for me to try to be brave, think straight & be understanding. They also tell me that we don't know what the future has for either of us—but certainly it can't be all heartbreak & sorrow.

 Baby dear I can't tell you how dreadfully sorry I am to have your furlough ruined, it is so awfully hard for you, torn between two great loves. Always remember, even in the darkest moments that your Bops has her arms around you & saying "Darling its all right no one can ever take our love away, what it's meant & is." Be so brave dear heart I'll never let you down, even though we can't be together.

 Bopsy please console your family, tell them I have no bitterness in their decision. Perhaps in years to come we will understand their attitude better. We must pray for strength though during these dark days.

 My darling darling I need & want to see you so terriably. What shall we do. Will it be easier not seeing each other? My baby I can't bear the thought of that though. Don't want to be selfish or cruel because you have gone through so much. But my own Bopsy—we must meet again-sometime, some place, if not right now, then a little later. Can't face this life without talking & loving you once more. Our hearts are broken aren't they. Will they ever mend?

 Edward dear more than anything in the world I want you to be happy the rest of your life-even though this all is killing us, we just have to not let it ruin our lives. You have so much to go home to after the war. The hardest part of all is my having to even see you belong to anyone but me. My memories of our joy & happiness to-gether. Why why why baby must these things happen. I was so sure you would come back to me after I left, that's why I left saying not too much. Was so confident that it would all straighten out. Am afraid my darling that I can never have faith & trust & loyalty for anyone else. It will be utterly impossible to face people without thinking I'll be hurt again & darling I just can't take any more.

It's tragic darling that this beautiful chapter in our lives must end this way. The world is cruel & hard—but again I'll say darling I'd go through anything for you, but I understand so well what your folks mean about the future, have thought it out over & over.

Keep writing me darling don't ever stop until we decide to-gether one way or the other. Please send me your picture. I must have something to cling to.

My darling I love you more than life itself—but for you & you alone will I be brave & try to go on.

Keep brave my blessed sweetheart, give your family hope & courage. This is no ones fault & something we may never find the answer to except that we love one another.

Rest, eat & keep well & remember you always have my love to keep you warm. I have your love & that adorable sweater. Thank you my darling for your faith in me & all you have done materially & spiritually for me.

Your own & always
Baby

EDWARD SIEGEL, M. D.
TWENTY-SEVEN CANNON STREET
POUGHKEEPSIE, N. Y.

12 April 1944

Dear Mrs. Boody,

By this time Gretchen is home with you for a
few days and I can't tell you how miserable I am about this whole
state of affairs. I need not go into details about us but I don't
know what to say 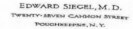 for bringing this heartache and misery to
Gretchen. God knows I love her and worship her but I am appealing
to you as a Mother of children to help her see the light and
show her that what I am doing is right. You of all people should
know the love my own parents have for me. Believe me when I say
that they are a heart-broken over this just as much for Gretchen
as they are for me. They know we are both suffering but they feel
down deep in their hearts that they just couldn't accept Gretchen
whole-heartedly, the way they would want to accept her and the way
Gretchen herself would want to be accepted. You must understand that
my future belongs in Poughkeepsie and that for me to pull up stakes
and leave home and seek a home somewhere else would just about break
their hearts. My Mother has been sick for over a year with
worry and grief for me just because I have been away from home and
they never told me. They didn't want me to feel badly about it.
If I had known how ill she was I wouldn't have sprung this on them, but
my love was so intense and I was so lonesome I had to tell them
about it and I did. Mrs. Boody, please tryand convince Gretchen that
she is not to blame for Mother being ill. My own Mother is so heart-
broken that Gretchen and I are unhappy. Believe me, theirs isn't
an unforgivable attitude but we both know they are right.

Gretchen feels that she can overcome any obstacle
that the world can offer but it's not as easy as that. You can't
overcome some invisible barrier and the cruel world who will insist
on making known to her thatbshe is a Gentile and I am a Jew.

You must understand that I give Gretchen up because
I love her so much andwant to avoid hunting her in the future.

Can you picture us being married and something coming up that will show us our differences as J w and Non-Jew. It's easy to speak of the brotherhood of man and the Golden Rule but the world is different.

I blame myself for all this and Ihumbly beg four forgiveness for the anguish I have heaped on darling Gretchen. She wants me to come and see her but Mrs. Boody, what will we accomplish? We'll cry and go through this all over again. For her sake and her s ke alone I must not see her, am I not right?

I have never met you but may I write you again some time and find out how Gretchen is? Thanks God that she had her orders changed and could be with you in the next few trying days.

If you can find it in your heart to forgive me, please do, I love Gretchen and I know she loves me. We shall carry that love in each other's hearts for years to come but I know that there is s mething in this world for both of us and you and her friends must help her now as she has never had help before. I can't do it because each time she hears my voice or reads a letter from me she will feel badly all over again.

Above all, please make her understand that my family does not hate her, on the contrary they feel for her and are heart-broken but they feel that we are all saving each other a lot of grief by this happening now and not later.

I can't find the answers to all these questions more than if I ask God why there has to be war and millions of boys get killed. Maybe there aren't any answers but the world goes on.

I want to know how Gretchen is please, I shall be home for a couple of weeks but mail at the above address is my office and will always reach me.

God Bless you and your husband and I know you'll take care of our Gretchen. Ixxshall be hers eternally in my heart.

4/12/44 Home at night

My dear darling

    Have been trying for hours to go to sleep but just can't—keep thinking & thinking. Maybe if we have a little chat it will ease my mind & yours my baby.

    This has been a horrible day-really exhausted to-night, but mother made me stay in bed & I did sleep some. We all have had a good talk & they have comforted me as much as possible. We all feel my sweet darling that you have proven yourself a real man worthy of any parents pride & admiration as a son. There are so few now days who think of anyone but themselves. It makes me so terriably proud my darling to have had you as a loved one, a friend, pal & companion. Darling we will always be friends, that word is so cold though, for we are and will be more than that the rest of our lives won't we?

    My dear Edward am beginning to believe along with mom & dad that we better not tackle the job of meeting at this time. It would kill both of us. Time will help heal our hearts. I have felt that from their letter they neither trust nor admire me for my courage & love. My darling I don't want to be hated by them as a trouble maker. Don't they understand that real love can't be turned on & off like a faucet?

    My baby over & over in my life I will probably turn to you for advice & council. You see you are the only one who will be truthful & know how I think & feel. You shall always be my pillar & guiding star. No one in the world can be or could be what you are to me darling. Do you understand?

    We both must be brave soldiers & oh if we could only be in each others arms right now-everything would be so different.

    Bopsy dear please please don't blame yourself for all this—only God can explain love. We both know now what it really is.

    Tell me everything my darling-you still love me don't you. Nothing can change that can it?

    God bless & keep you my darling heart

Your baby

Western Union telegram:

BY DIRECT WIRE FROM
WESTERN UNION
A. N. WILLIAMS
PRESIDENT

CLASS OF SERVICE
This is a full-rate Telegram or Cablegram unless its deferred character is indicated by a suitable symbol above or preceding the address.

1223

SYMBOLS
DL=Day Letter
NL=Night Letter
LC=Deferred Cable
NLT=Cable Night Letter
Ship Radiogram

The filing time shown in the date line on telegrams and day letters is STANDARD TIME at point of origin. Time of receipt is STANDARD TIME at point of destination

PR201 18=OR JACKSON HEIGHTS NY APRIL 14 735P=

= LT GRETCHEN L BOODY= A N C

STATION HOSPITAL CAMPMCCOY WIS=

CHIN UP DARLING WRITING YOU TOMORROW WHEN I RETURN HOME
PLEASE DONT WORRY AND FRET ALL MY LOVE.

EDWARD....706P

My dear darling,

Your letter arrived to-day dear & what a great comfort & joy it was to my soul. I've read each line a dozen times & between the lines. My darling there is nothing in this world that you don't think of and reason out it makes things so much easier & I am able to see everything so much more clearly.

Let me assure you baby that the sudden blow is passing. I've prayed for strength & guidance these past few days & for God to make you strong in bearing all of our trouble so bravely. My darling you are the Rock of Gibralter & may you let this all pass without bitterness & regret.

Edward my darling I don't want to hurt you any more, you know darling that I've never had a selfish instinct where you are concerned. This all is the hardest thing in my life to face & it is for you too. However in giving each other up we only mean giving up for your family & the world, not for ourselves. That can never be, for our love is far too deep & pure & loyal for that. My darling I shall always worship, adore & respect you & wherever you are whatever you do my thoughts & prayers will be with the only one I love. Please dear heart believe in that won't you?

Baby as you say we could never stand people making a difference between our religions, in our eyes to-gether there is none, but we have a cruel world to live in. Anything that hurt you would kill me-because I love you so. My darling therefore we are making this supreme sacrifice, without courage of course but because we know it has to be.

Edward please don't think I misunderstand about your not wanting to forsake your family. I would never never let you do that. We could never be happy were that so. You see my dear I really down deep in my head believed that they would understand & because it would be your happiness that they would accept me. Perhaps darling I really don't understand, but I remember how many times you tried to explain.

I love you my darling—don't ever forget that, if I didn't darling I could never come out of this brave & strong.

Baby for me make the rest of your furlough as happy as possible, try to go on with joy in your heart the way you thought your home coming would be.

I know you are feeling better darling because your worry has been much over me & darling I'm going to conquer this thing.

All the love I possess is for my Edward—Yours forever

Gretchen

Hudson, Wis.
April 14-1944

Capt Edward Siegel
Poughkeepsie, N.Y.

Dear Friend:

I appreciated your letter that arrived on the noon mail, explaining the difficulty you and Gretchen have run into. I do feel very sorry for both of you. But am also glad that it has not gone beyond the drastic stage.

It was very kind of you to think of us, and how we may feel about it too.

I know you are every inch a very dear boy, and am proud of you to take your dear parents into consideration. For there are millions of young people who during this war are getting married thinking not ahead of what the outcome will, or could be.

And marriage is too sacred a thing to take lightly, and it is just a misfortune that you and Gretchen are not both of the same faith and I feel no one is to blame. Please believe me. I know Gretchen has been heart sick, and so very upset, but she is a brave Christian girl and will make the very best of it all.

I have tried to console her, by saying only God knows, and it no doubt was meant to be their way, and that it is for the best.

She has had nothing but the best of words for you, and I am sorry we did not meet you. But it is as you say, only making things worse to see her. I am sure you are right about that.

We are indeed very glad she was so close to home, and had the confidence in her parents, that she could come home for moral and spiritual support, and I hope we have helped her.

I was sorry to hear of your mother's illness, and no doubt there are millions of other mothers going thru just what she is doing. But if we trust in our God I am sure things will right themselves.

I hope wherever you are sent, you will have the good fortune to be returned to your loved ones, and wish you the best of luck.

We do not feel bitter towards you at all, and all I can say that it is just one of those things that comes to just a lot of good young people on this old wicked world.

We will be glad to hear from you whenever you find time, and care to write.

I wrote you while Gretchen was home on her furlough, but I suppose you left before it arrived. It no doubt will catch up with you before long.

We are glad Gretchen likes her work, and hope she will stay there until things are over, over there, she has gained a little weight, but the past two weeks have been a bit trying for her.

But I know she will look at it all in a very sensible way, and I am sure will want to be a good friend to you always.

I am yours truly
Mrs. R. H. Boody

Dear Edward,

Just a few lines in answer to your letter. Surely appreciated your thoughtfulness in writing to us. I never have gone through what you, and Gretchen are going through. On the other hand we have had about 35 years of most enjoyable married life, and suppose it is hard to realize just what it is. It sure grieves me to see our Baby feel the way she does, and know you must feel the same.

It seems you young folks volunteer to go in defense of our country, and then have to be deprived of what would mean more to you than anything in this world, but suppose things are meant to be that way, and just cannot be helped.

When Gretchen was six months old her mother lay at the point of death: that was the one thing that was hard, and I still remember my mother trying to console me. I know she told me the Lord chasteneth those whom he loveth, and I've always carried this in my mind when things seem to go wrong, and I feel I am taking abuse in some form or another, something that seems should not be.

Spring is a little late in this part of the country but sincerely hope we can produce our quota and the war will be brought to a successful conclusion in the near future.

Regards to you, and may you be successful in all you undertake, is my wish to all young people who are starting in life's journey.

Best wishes,
R.H. Boody

Ida and Reuben Boody with children, from left:
Dorothy, Gretchen, Donald

My Darling,

I just this minute got back from N.Y. darling, and found your two letters waiting for me. I never thought I could love you more than I did but they were so wonderful darling, and understanding that tears came to my eyes not of unhappiness but of the deep honor and respect with which I hold you and the honor of having and still loving you.

Before we go any further darling, let me say one thing and that is that we shall see each other again. We shall see each other after I get assigned to my new job and we both have had a chance to get our legs again and walk straight. I know how much you need me darling—do I need you any less? We both need each other and if it can't be as husband and wife it will be as, well darling, it's more than friends. In my heart you shall always be mine and I know that in your heart I know I shall be yours. We are probably the two most wonderful people in the whole world darling, so the hell with everything! I know that we can both go on being happy for each other, no matter what happens to each of us and when we do meet within the next few months it shall be with laughter, fun and joy—not with tears—we shall probably cry but they will be tears of joy at seeing each well and getting on.

I'm not trying to kid you darling, and there would be no percentage in doing that. The past few weeks have been a nightmare but humans that we are we can stand so much then just have to sit up and take it. Darling, we each have a tough job to do and we must help each other. Your letters helped me in knowing that I have a brave Bopsy who loves me and who is going to carry on. Knowing that, I can go on to trying to get a hold of myself.

Bopsy, I'm not going to say anymore right now. I still have so much to tell you about my trip, from Panama and my trip to N.Y. But, that will wait until the next time. Darling, please send your mail to me here at the office and not c/o Dad. He gets the mail and I don't want him bothered with seeing how much we write each other. You and I will write and one fine day we'll see each other. In the meantime darling, be good to yourself. I still want to see my Bopsy of old one of these days and I'll try and be good to myself so you'll recognize me.

Bye for now darling, and God bless the most wonderful girl in the world and I pray and thank him each day for knowing you.

Your Baby—
Smiling?

My dear darling

Your wire & long letter were awaiting me on my arrival home to-night. Can you possibly know dear heart what comfort they brought? I will cherish the letter especially forever, because it was so beautifully written & the expressions were from the bottom of your soul. Darling I thank God that you are so strong, think so straight & reason everything for both of us. I know baby dear that I have really not been responsible & did well to even keep going-but my Edward being the fine & real man that he is has carried most of the load. Bless your heart Bopsy dear for never failing anyone for a moment.

My darling especially to-day something has begun to happen to me-as I rode through the country looking at our America, I suddenly became ashamed at my weakness—& then Bopsy's voice kept saying in rhythm with the tracks, "Be strong, be strong, our love, our love," and to-night baby dear I am strong & thankful & humble.

How wonderful it was to be able to go home & to find love & a mother & father who are faithful & helpful & deeply concerned. My darling, thank you for writing them. You are on a pedestal in their eyes, & they said over & over, "Gretchen dear, be thankful that Edward is the kind of boy you said he was. He is a man & a gentleman & one we are proud to know as the person you love."

Baby dear you asked me not to write. I know that is the best too, but please darling just for a little while. Can't we until all this is just a little more past. Can I be just a wee bit selfish for awhile. My life will be torture month after month if I don't know how or where you are. If I promise darling only to write later on just to say hello & how are you. Please Bopsy dear.

Bopsy how terriable I feel about your mother. I've been unconvinced until now about their attitude toward me-but after seeing & talking to my own mother, I know that they feel deeply about our hurt. Please forgive me dear baby, but I know now that all parents who really love their children share their heartaches. Give your mother my love baby. Tell her for me that she must be brave & strong with us & get well soon. Is there anything I can do darling. Could I write them? Tell your father too dear that he should hold his head high in pride for having his Edward as a son.

Now my dear love. You have a much braver soldier back here who is fighting & winning. So please sweetheart get your own spirits well & in *knowing that—I too will be happy & content again. Keep on being your Bopsy's brave good darling & lets be so proud that we are strong. The world has much for you dear heart & I'm with you always wherever you are & whatever you do.*

Your own
Baby

April 17, 1944

Good Morning, my darling,

Well, baby, here's that old Bops again. I'm starting to emerge from the fog I've been in for the past few weeks darling and starting to see a little bit of my surroundings.

Sweet, sweet baby, I hope that you also are beginning to get a hold of yourself and we shall both soon be the people we are supposed to be.

As for my trip coming up—I got on board a Navy transport on the 29th and we sat on the damn boat until the 31st. Jeepers what misery, wanting to get home and having to sit around in the harbor for 2 days. Well, we finally set sail and we went to Trinidad of all places. Holy Cow, what a dump! Well, finally after 13 days of kicking around we finally landed in N.Y. We sailed past the Statue of Liberty and the feeling I got was a hell of a lot different from what I thought it would be. I got to Times Square and it seemed as if I had never left the place. It was crowded, noisy, service men and women running around. Well, I guess there is no place like N.Y. Well I finally got home on Monday and my brother and Dad met me at the station. I won't go into the details of my reunion with the family. We know all about that. At any rate. Mother has picked up 100% since I've been back and she is looking much better and feeling better. Darling, believe me when I say Dad and Mother feel so terribly for us both and they are going to write you next week when we all get straightened out and tell you that there is and never has been any animosity between you and them. They are proud that such a lovely and fine girl should love me and they expect us to be friends. They are really swell, baby, and as you expressed it someday we shall all meet and be friends. Don't ever, ever, ever, feel that you have come between my parents and me. You haven't. O.K.?

Of course, you and I aren't kidding each other. You are my friend of course, but primarily we are *Mr. Bops and Miss Boo* and I love you and even though the cards are stacked against us, no one in the world can keep me from going on loving you and you loving me, you old sweet thing! Sounds more like Bops, doesn't it, baby. It's funny, baby, I get feeling so lonesome and then I think of you and I know we are really to-gether even though we are miles apart. Time is our best friend darling, as you say we don't know what is in store for us, do we? Just stay sweet and lovely and keep your weight, baby, please?

Please, dear heart, don't be a stay at home. Get out and have a little fun, if you can. I shall try but there's no use kidding anyone, it will be a long time before I'll be able to look at any gal without thinking of you.

I just unpacked my stuff and Jeepers what junk. There's no place to sleep in my room there's so much junk, but who cares. I don't sleep much anyway. Everyone admires my ring, darling, and Mother asked where I got it and I told her you gave it to me. It's on my finger and will always be there so I can rub it for good luck and comfort when things are a little tough.

You old thing you, be happy again darling, one of these days we shall have a reunion when I get settled again and we will talk about all the things about you and us. Our letters must be happy, darling, because we must help each other.

I'm going to have quite a session in N.Y. this week. Thursday I'm going to Tony Pizani's bachelor party in N.Y., Friday to the opener at the Yankee Stadium Baseball game and Saturday is Tony and Angi's wedding at St. Pat's in N.Y. So you see, I hope to have a good time. When you got home you had all those parties and people and stuff and I want some of them too. I haven't done a thing yet Bops.

Be brave darling and remember, you need never ask me again if I love you, now or 50 years from now. A love such as ours lives forever in our hearts no matter where our individual futures lie. Let's get tough, darling, and take this goddam world in our stride. O.K.?

Mr. Bops

My darling,

Hello sweet baby, how are you this evening?

I just got back from a medical meeting at which I addressed the local medical society group and I seemed to have made a hit. They all think I'm sort of a hero or something and I agree, but for different reasons. Bopsey, Bopsey, how are you darling? Gee whiz, in spite of the hell that we have been through for the past few months for some reason or another I don't know just what it is but I'm starting to feel a little better. I just close my eyes and heart to the rest of the world and I just sit and think of my old Bops and how she is and what she's doing and I actually feel as if I am enjoying a little visit with you. Gosh Bops, everything I do I just picture you with me and I feel warm all over. I just feel your love with me all the time and although we aren't together physically, I feel so good inside when I know I love a person such as you. Your letter of the 14th was so wonderful that I keep reading it and reading it over and over again and thank God that I was lucky enough to have known a person such as you. Bopsy, the days are getting a little more tolerable and I can get up in the morning without that hungry gaping hole that existed for so long. I just can't describe it but I think of you now with such love and devotion and such a feeling of warmth that I can't describe it. Do you know what I mean?

In a few days you will be getting a package from me. I walked past this shop today and saw something in the window that I fell in love with and I just had to buy it for you. It's a real Mr Bops and I hope you like him. He's nice and big and you can hug him.

I'm going to N.Y. Thursday and stay until Saturday. Tony's wedding should be fun and baby, I just have to go and try to smile again. Father Laws will be there and we should have a good time.

I'm trying to get assigned at England General Hospital at Atlantic City with Col. Bergamini. I talked to him over the phone yesterday and he asked for you. He's fine.

Bopsy, I shall write you every few days but I know that we are both living for the day when we see each other for our reunion and I promise you it won't be too long. My leave is up on May 10th and I go to Upton in L.I. From there I don't know but when I get settled we can start thinking of seeing each other. We have to be all well, happy and fat when we see each other because there's so much we have to talk about.

Bye for now, darling, I dreamt of you last night darling, I kissed you and held you in my arms and you're sweeter than ever. They can't stop us from loving can they?

Smile darling, please—thank you!

Your Baby

My dear darling

Well Bopsy—here's your brave soldier to say hello & how are you. How wonderful it was to receive a happy letter from my sweet thing. Our correspondence of late has been something for the books hasn't it but baby dear we couldn't help it could we? It was the only way we could do. I promise too from now on to keep my heartaches out of writing—& any way all that interests me now is how you are feeling, & darling if you are happy & being brave.

How wonderful to know that at last my Bopsy is able to look around & go out & have some joy from this furlough. This all to date has been such a wretched homecoming & so tragic. Dear heart you deserve so much & not the past few weeks experience at all—but only my old Scruntchy could come out of it without bitterness & discouragement. We will just keep helping each other & believe me my dear Edward—only your wonderful letters have given me courage to go on & be brave. It's love & honor & respect like ours that make this old world worthwhile. Our love shall never, never die baby—it's too deep & fine & beautiful. Yes we are the two best people in the world.

Darling, darling—when I read those lines about our reunion—I cried for joy. That alone will be worth waiting, hoping & praying for. Yes we'll weep—but tears of happiness at being to-gether & baby dear—we'll have such fun & be our old fun loving selves again. We probably will see none of our surroundings or anyone but just each other & then will walk in a dream & pinch each other to see if it's real. Darling I'm living for that day.

Edward, now I want the truth. What do you weigh—do your panties bag at the seat? Gee whiz skinny—how about that—who needs to eat & get fat again. Drink all the milk you can, & baby please for me stop worrying & take care of my soldier. For myself—I haven't started to pick up much—lost all I had gained & more, but now people are concentrating on my weight—such worry warts. And all the time I couldn't say why my loss was so great. Next letter though dear here's a promise of 3 pounds & for you the same.

Know your trip to N.Y. was wonderful. So Angie & Tony are married—had thought they were married long ago. Tell me all about everything. Bet baby was in heaven at the ball park. You old fan. Am thinking of you each day & right there beside my darling sharing all.

Darling I'm going to try & not be a stay at home-but it's going to take months for me to be able to look at a man. Have a couple of nice girl friends

& we keep company. Honey I'm scared to go out-how will I act. What is there to say? Anyway darling there is such a pack of wolves around here—it isn't worth the chance. If anyone touched me I'd probably kill him dead. Darling can you even half way imagine the agony of having a strange man not respect me even because I'm a woman. That's why I'm scared & I'd only cry & be unhappy. Can't even talk about it. Baby dear we were such wonderful & good people to-gether weren't we & you especially dear heart who thought of me constantly in every act, deed & thought. Such an old spoiler.

Am anxious to know where you are being sent & when & how you are—so keep writing dear heart & be brave & sweet & wonderful forever & ever.

Your very own
Miss Boo

My dear darling

Just finished little duties, bath etc & now I'm all sweet & clean for a date with my baby. This is extra special cause its our Saturday night date. Bops has seen the ball game & probably on the way back to Poughkeepsie or maybe not till to-morrow-but anyway old Tag is right there. Well maybe not in person but in your heart & thoughts that's the way it will always be sweet thing won't it?

To-day has reminded me of Panama—it's been cloudy & rainy all day-spring is terriably pokey round these parts dear. Suppose it is lovely & warm in the east. How was the ball game or was it rained out? Darling did you yell & holler & get all thrilled & excited-hope so darling.

Gee baby dear-your old Bops has just been seen by the press, interviewed, photographed, etc. I was called on to model the foreign duty uniform-some of the other girls modeled the other uniforms. It was sort of fun & if they ever put them in the Chicago, Milwaukee or Detroit papers will send one to you. O.K?

Had a lovely letter from Father Laws to-day-was so surprised. My darling when I think of all our friends & how each & every one is with us & hoping for our happiness even though we must be apart it helps so much. Guess we're a couple of swell guys huh?

Bopsy dear how happy I am to think I gave you the ring—& to know you will wear it forever. Just look at it once in awhile & think of that old Blonde gal in Wis. who gave it to you because she loves you so. It's the same with my watch. Somehow I look at its face & see my baby's.

So a Mr. Bops is coming to stay with me. He'll be hugged to pieces cause I'll make believe its my rascal. Honey what is it a bunny-puppy-doll or what—gee I'm excited my darling. You never forget me for a minute do you? My sweet Scruntchy lovable dear heart.

Edward you never mention Martin. How is he feeling? I've felt more strange toward him through all this baby—maybe it's because he had to write the letters. Darling his letters were so cold & blunt & maybe that's why.

Baby dear I'm being brave & keeping the chin up with a crow-bar & smiling for you. But darling do you care if I cry just a wee little bit—well now for instance on your shoulder. Member how I used to get permission?

Thank God for you my dear darling. My fine, noble brave soldier. Must have been a pretty good girl to have had the privilege of loving & holding anyone so good & wonderful.

Believe me my sweet thing my dreams are full of you. We are always to-gether then.

Smile Bopsy dear—tell me what you are doing & if the fanny's getting fat.

Your very own
Baby

Father Laws on the tennis court

My own Mr Bops

Bopsy, maybe I'm silly, but when I find a letter in the mailbox from you, my knees get all limp, my heart goes to my throat and and—well baby dear, do you know what I mean? It's so pronounced just had to tell you the symptoms Doctor, what is it love?

Glad you liked the picture. Personally think it's a bit flattering—how glad I am that I had it taken when my toes were tickling pink clouds—baby don't I look fat—was almost 114. Weighed yesterday & I've gained up to 107 again. Am also beginning to eat a little better. Anyway the lump in my throat is shrinking. How often you have told me about "time." Well darling heart it helps—but it can never blot out the love in our hearts can it?

Just think darling each day that goes by makes our meeting one day closer. I'm living for that reunion. Hollywood better send for us—we'll really show them how it's done.

Work is O.K. I like McCoy Bopsy it's really a paradise & every one raves how they like it. Haven't even heard any griping & it's wonderful. The Drs work hard—4 med officers for 400 patients, but they don't complain & the days go fast. This is an 1800 bed hospital. Since my ward is restricted (U.R.I.) the boys have movies q.o.d.* on the ward—it's like a picnic. Darling I'm so greatly respected here, get all the gravy—hours, no shifting from ward to ward, etc.

Must hike to the chow line—now aren't I being a good girl & do I sound more like your Bopsy?

Forever & with all my love
Your Baby

p.s. No Mr. Bops yet—he must be sightseeing—the scamp.

---

*   Every other day

My Sweet Old Thing—

Good morning, Bops, how are you this miserable, cold, dreary day? It has been raining every day since I've been home with the exception of only one or two days and I'm getting sick and tired of it. I guess your weather and mine have been alike.

I've been running around with my head chopped off the past few days what with seeing people, etc. I had quite a write-up in the paper and I'll send it to you when I go down to the office. I'm writing this from home. Got my good old trusty typewriter again and I sure can bang them out. My New York trip was pretty hectic. Since I've been home I've just been sitting in my office day after day poking around, etc. Getting it in order and straightening up. It sure is a beautiful office.

Darling, I know how you feel and what thoughts you are giving because I have them too. You are with me always and then I go in and sneak a look at your picture and believe me baby, it's so good to just look at your smile that I feel pepped up. I have gained back 6 of my 22 pounds and I'm still going strong just for you.

I know how you feel about going out on dates Baby, and I hate to think of someone even making a pass at you, it makes my blood boil but you are the sort of gal who commands respect and you'll get it from even the worst wolves so don't worry about that. You're so good inside darling, that people know it the minute they speak to you. I think that's the thing I love about you most, your inherent honor and decency.

You may cry anytime you want darling because I know how things are with you way down deep inside because that's the way they are with me. But believe me baby, I'm really starting to feel better. I don't think of us with hurt or despair, it's something beautiful that I feel when I'm thinking of you darling, and I know I'll feel it forever.

We are both reconciled to our fates but we understand each other so well and so deeply that it will never change. If I ever get married, I'll probably call you up on my wedding night and want to talk to you, I can't help it Bops but no matter where I am and what I do, I feel you with me and it makes me happy even though we are apart. 'Nuf said.

By this time you've probably got my picture and Mr. Bops. Love them both, you old droopy, scruntchy thing you!

My panties are starting to fit again because I know you are coming out of the woods darling and are becoming happy again. (Holy smokes—looks funny on paper)

I think twice a week is about right for us writing Bops.

Smack, smack,
Mr. Bops

27 April 1944

Hi Gunboat,

You wonderful old thing, how goes it to-day?

I'm so happy that your letters are beginning to sound like the Bops of old and that mine sound the same way to you. We're both too tough a pair of old horses to let this get us down and I'll be damned if it will. Right?

The weather started to clear yesterday and I went out and played golf for the first time. It sure was wet out but the golf pro who played with me couldn't get over how much better I had become. As a matter of fact, I was pretty good yesterday and he had a tough job beating me. Tomorrow night I got hooked into accepting a dinner invitation with some friends of Mother's who have a very ugly, unmarried daughter and I have to go because I said "no" five times already and Mother says I better go and get it over with or else they won't stop bothering me. Ouch, I shudder at the thought. People just won't leave you alone will they?

I still don't know when and where I'm going but I'm trying to get to Rhodes General at Utica, N.Y. Tony says it's a swell place and I think I'd like it.

I just noticed that the AMA Convention is in Chicago in June. Maybe that's where we shall see each other, but we'll just have to wait until I get settled before we make any plans for our reunion. Yes, darling, I think of it too, all of the time. I know it is going to be fun, happy and wonderful, isn't it? It has to be that way and I know that it will do us both loads of good to have a wonderful long talk, (and stuff)! Won't it, Bops? Jeepers, I'll just look and look and look at you!

Yes, Bops, your picture is swell and don't ever say that any picture flatters you because it doesn't. You're a sweet, beautiful old thing and no picture in the world could ever portray your loveliness and wonder, so there, you old rascal you!

I've started going to movies again—there's nothing else to do in Poughkeepsie—saw the Song of Russia and loved it, as well as Madame Curie and I've started reading again. Keep up with your reading Bops, it's really wonderful and passes the time. Someday I'm going to write a story, too. Think I'll go down to N.Y. next week and get my 2 months back pay. Money, money, money—

Heard that song Love, Love, love and as you said, it sure is swell—

xxxxxxx (code) Your old Bops

4/28/44

My old sweet thing,

Jeepers how I've haunted that mailbox & finally just a minute ago your letter came. You've spoiled me so Bopsy dear how can I reconcile myself completely to occasional letters etc. What a h—of a world. It's all unfair & wrong.

My darling your picture is wonderful. You have completely invaded the private realms of my boudoir & my old sweet thing sits there on my dresser & looks so wonderful. At least now I have something to smile back at. Its such a splendid photo dear. You look so young & happy. To think your Bops put grey hairs along the edges of that hair line—she's a bad girl.

After waiting & waiting Mr Bops Jr. arrived—in a huge box—on his face. Thought sure you were sending the Empire State Bldg. What a rascal he is & darling I have scruntched him to pieces only he's not very responsive. It's wonderful just to get my arms around something. Thank you dear heart—you just knew I'd get a tremendous laugh & a big kick out of him didn't you? He's the envy of the barracks & won't stay home, all the girls love him so.

Oh my baby when you even mention the word marriage, my heart turns over. Are you thinking about that already? I have no right to ask or say anything but darling it hurts so to ever think of some one else in your arms.

Time is going by-yes-but at times I think its harder instead of easier. Don't you see dear—knowing each day is taking you further away from me in your mind. It's so much easier for a man who can call a girl & ask for a date-but honest darling some days I think I'll go mad if I don't see you. Love like we have for each other never dies. We shouldn't be apart & yet we must become reconciled. Is there such a thing?

Honey if I ever hear of you marrying & being unhappy, it would be terriable. Even if you do marry dear-no one can take care of my baby like his Bops. Darling for your sake & other girls please don't go with anyone but a Jewess, it will only cause heartache all over again.

What ever happens dear heart-be sure you love the girl & she loves you, even if it means being single the rest of your life. There will never be a love like yours & mine-but some of it may be present. Can I have a job in your office baby?

How is your mother Edward. Did our break-up cause her to start feeling better. Sent some posies because I want her to know I feel responsible. Will she understand?

Guess I'd better quit—or this will become worse than it is so far. Darling I miss & pray for you constantly. Be happy darling & I'll keep trying, knowing that you are feeling better.

Any word yet of your reassignment? To-day I hate myself—but love you more & more if that's possible.

A million smacks my sweet Bops—your bad girl.

My dear Sweet Bopsy,

Gee Whiz—after thinking it over, guess I didn't write such a nice letter the other day, but darling you know me so well, certainly you understand. How awfully hard it is to keep the old chin up constantly. No use kidding my Bops about anything—it wouldn't work. You would read between the lines anyway—like I do in your letter. Should never write you I suppose when my mood isn't good, but baby dear its just going to take time & even now can't run to anyone but my Edward when I'm unhappy cause he's the only one that does understand. Scold me sweet thing—tell me to mind my own affairs when Gunboat gets uppity.

Yesterday Elaine & I went for a long walk, then bowled three games. It was simply gorgeous out, we had a nice afternoon. She's so much like me, Edward, we like the same things etc. It helps a lot. How good that golf sounds. Am sure getting itchy to go out. There is a club about 8 miles from here & may look into it. If I only had a car. Speaking of cars dear, do you have yours out & how does it seem to be driving again?

Aren't those "have to" dates awful Bops. Know what you went through, I did the same when home—but lots of times it's necessary for the families pride. (How well we know that huh?)

Mr Bops Jr is fine—he's so fat—can't keep him on my bed—he shoves—& then if I put him on the trunk he pushes Katrina & Pete off—(my two Italian dolls). Then every once in a while he goes visiting. Honey I get such a kick out of my toys. My whole room is a constant reminder of you dear—blue blanket, your picture, my dolls & Mr B. It's fun though darling being that close to you. Baby why have you always been so good & wonderful to this old thing?

Work has really been tough this week, awfully busy & all these new girls are a headache—but on duty I stop thinking & that is best for me. Am still not posted for nights—goodie.

Darling I'm so happy you are saving I am too cause you taught me to. Will hit the 700 mark again this month, even after my loan to daddy. Rich thing, huh?

Seems like your furlough is so nice and long dear. How good it is to know the last part of it is happy. Yes I guess we're tough darling, but you are the only one—& I have inherited part from you. These letters & everything & knowing our love continues as something so beautiful has been my pillar.

Am enclosing a 6th Serv. Command badge—have your mommy sew it on your blanket. Is there anything you need dear.

Bought a new beige suit & dress & will take good care of them for our reunion. Darling am I wrong to look forward to that with such joy?—We'll be a couple of happy kids—& Chicago would be fun. We still have a date for N.Y. don't we?

Be a blessed old sweetheart, I adore your picture—only I will have to put it in a glass frame as I'm wearing it out.

Forever your
Own baby.

Smack & I have a billion due me huh?

Mr. Bops

MAY, 1944

May 1, 1944

Good Morning, sweetheart—

You are a bad girl baby, to think that I am going off to get married and all those sort of things. Jeepers Bops, do you think for a moment that I could even stand someone else for even a minute after you? Of course, not, you should know better and I understand perfectly how you feel about everything but baby, you need never worry about what I do in the future and with whom I go out with. I've been through too much, we both have, for me to throw everything out of the window and do something drastic. So please, dear heart, stop your worrying, and let's have those happy letters of the past week again, please darling? You know that I understand what you think and feel because I feel and think the same way, you rascal!

As for Mother, she realizes just what we are both going through and she will continue to be unhappy and worry about the whole thing until she feels that I myself have become happy again so you see I must be brave and strong and convince her that all is well and that I am making a comeback. She knows it will take time too. Of one thing you must be sure and that is that Mother holds no one responsible for this, especially you, people can't help these things and you must realize that you are not to blame baby, please believe that because it is the truth. Don't continue to blame yourself for anything baby, because even now that things have turned out as they have, I'd do it all over again because of knowing you and having been with you for two years. Please baby, let's get out of this self-thinking and worrying and just think about the future. You know I'm right?

I'm so glad you got Mr Bops and my picture and that you like them. I cherish my gray hairs baby, because they belong to you and I wouldn't trade them in for anything in the world, so hush up sweet thing and say no more about them.

Friday night my brother is having a dinner party for me and a bunch of my doctor friends, strictly stag, and I suppose a lot of talking will go on about me being such a big shot, etc. There will be about 20 and it should be pretty much fun having all the old timers together again.

I still haven't heard about my reassignment and probably won't until I report to Upton on the 10th. I'll let you know immediately what I do find out. O.K.?

I've received all the letters from you so far and Bops they sure are wonderful letters and I love every word of them. I eat them up just as you do mine but baby, it isn't right that you and I write every day. The pace is too stiff darling, and we must learn to be apart gradually and thus ease the pain slowly. Please dear heart, let's help each other as I said before and I don't want anymore 'bad girl' letters like the last one—for both our sakes!

If you don't, I'll only kiss you 4 million times instead of 6 million when I see you again. You old sweet thing!

Chin up soldier, and forward march!

My love,
Bops

My dear Gretchen,

I have intended writing before but I thought that it would be better if I waited for a few weeks until the acuteness of this whole situation had subsided somewhat and we all started feeling a little better about the whole thing.

I know how this whole situation is hurting both you children and our hearts go out to you both but you must believe me when I say that it is better to suffer now and to straighten out your respective lives than see something beautiful go by the boards in years to come and hurt a lot more people—especially yourselves. The idea that any given person can go merrily along his way with complete unconcern for what people think and how they react is pure idealism and just doesn't work out in real life. Whether we know it or not, our entire lives are ruled by others and the cause and effect we have on each others lives. In my years, I have seen so much of the heartache and despair come from such unions that, not from the people themselves, but from outside sources that all my experience and soul cry out for each of you to go your separate ways and trust in God and his wisdom. None of us can explain why things are but we must accept them or else there is no basis for thought or belief.

Of one thing I must assure you and that is that we hold no one responsible, especially you, for all this. Neither you or Edward are to blame for falling in love and we hold nothing but compassion and sympathy for you both in our hearts. Don't for one moment ever think you are to blame. No one is. We must just accept this as it happened and hold no bitterness toward each other. But, for your individual sake's, you must both be intelligent people, as I know you both are, and not let this affect your future lives adversely. You may not believe this now but time will mellow your aches and tribulations and bring you a far-reaching wisdom and gentleness from which you will derive great comfort in the years to come. For that matter, you and Edward must have had two beautiful years to-gether and you should be happy for at least that. Some people go through an entire lifetime without feeling what you both have.

No Gretchen, despair not—feel no bitterness because we feel none. Thank God for what you have had as Edward does, and continue your lives without pain and hurt, because no one can take away what you had.

Our best wishes for your future.

Sincerely,

Jack Siegel

3 May 1944

Hi Bops,

Received your latest letter this AM and it was nice to hear a happier frame of mind than your last one but I understand of course how hard it is sometimes. It's better to refrain from writing when we get in those moods. Isn't it?

The weather is beautiful and I sure have been making the most of it because one week from today it is all over and I go to work again. Bops don't write me after Monday the 8th because I won't be here to get the mail. I'll let you know where to write me as soon as I can after I get assigned. O.K.? Perhaps when I get settled I can call you up, that will be swell! This phone call will be better than the last one—Jeepers Bops, that was an awful few minutes wasn't it?

It sure is nice being in the States in the Spring time, isn't it darling? I've been playing a lot of golf in the past few days but not half as well as I used to do in Panama. Guess I miss giving Bops a few lessons, don't I? We sure did dub around and have a lot of fun, first I'd get mad and then you'd get mad, then we'd quit and laugh like hell all the way home.

Bops, I just bought an album of the records from Oklahoma. I haven't seen the show but the songs are so beautiful and funny that I want you to have them. I have them in N.Y. and will send them to you the first chance I get down there. There must be a record player somewhere where you can play them. I just play them over and over. "All or Nothing" is wonderful.

I bet your room is something swell with all the dolls and Mr Bops holding sway all over the room. If he shoves you out of bed, just hold him a little tighter and you'll see how well he behaves himself. You old sweet thing, you!

I understand fully. My baby, reading between the lines but please for our own sakes let's keep the letters happy. You've no idea what a lift I get when your letters are written in a happy frame of mind. After all, the only one I'm concerned with is you Bops, so please stay the wonderful soldier you are. Believe me, you old rascal, things happen for the best. It may not seem so now, but time will tell.

I think Dad wrote you a letter yesterday. I don't know what he said but I guess he wrote you telling you that he feels sorry it had to be this way but wanted you to know there were no hard feelings and that's the way it should be. After all Bops, we're all sensible people and there's no reasons for animosity is there, sweet baby?

So old Bops is saving her money, is she? Good for you darling—I haven't been paid for two months now and when I get to my new post I'll have a great big juicy bunch coming.

Bye for now darling, and consider yourself smacked!

"Bops"

Dear Gretchen:

Please excuse the delay in answering your letter more promptly, as my daughter came in from school over the week-end, and so we were busy shopping, altering, sewing on buttons, etc.

I want to tell you that my husband and I were terribly moved by your letter that was so filled with pain and disappointment. I have been searching for words that could express what I feel, or that would bring you some comfort. It is hardly what should happen after two years of such a rich, meaningful relationship—I do think you are very tolerant of Mrs. Siegel's feeling—in view of the fact that it blocks the fulfillment of your lives together. Gretchen, I think you and Eddie both know how we feel, because you have been able to write to us so freely.

We knew Eddie was due home, and when we got wondering, we telephoned to find that he had been home for several days, was then in New York. He phoned one day to say that he would be seeing us before his leave was up, but so far we haven't heard from him. I guess, it's hard for him, and perhaps he thinks it is easier, when he is trying to please his parents not to be thrown further into conflict, because we have a different point of view. Then too, he doesn't want to be responsible for creating any ill feeling between his mother and my husband.

Gretchen, you are a brave girl, and I hope that you will see how best to handle this problem, and find happiness for you and Eddie.

If you plan at all on coming East, I hope you'll feel that we would like to have you visit with us—and that you would be very welcome in our home—

As ever,
Aunt Sally

My sweet Bops—

Just received your letter & that put an end to my nap-so will answer pronto since your leave will be up so soon.

Darling I know it's going to be tough going back to work after such a long time away—but how much it pleases me to know that the end of your furlough has been some happier. All I care dear is that your pain is becoming a little easier. We're tough old guys aren't we? It shows just what people can take if need be. Anyway sweet thing we still have our great love to bolster us up & as your daddy says, no one can take that away ever ever.

Whatever post you draw it will mean readjustment, new faces, new friends, the first few weeks there will be the hardest. Guess that's why I was so depressed during our turmoil. Absolutely no one to turn to. You didn't tell me whether or not you intended taking your car. Good luck baby dear & remember I'm always at your side.

Had a beautiful letter from your dad dear. It was so nice of him to write. Tell me if your mom got the flowers so I will know whether to pay the bill or not. Hope they brought her cheer & that she now understands that I hold no resentment or animosity.

Aunt Sally wrote me too, she must be a dear. They were expecting to see you darling—did you go? You can imagine how hurt they were. They feel it isn't right at all, but are bearing with us in our heartache & think we are very brave kids. We are, aren't we darling?

Not much out of the ordinary going on here, have been working hard & liking it. This whole set up is just splendid dear, the hospital runs like a clock. The reconditioning program is going fine. You will hear more about it at your next post. Instead of sending the fellows directly to duty after long hospitalization they give them a program to get back in shape. It's really fine.

Had heaps of fun yesterday in Sparta. Another girl & myself went shopping. Spent some of my hard earned money. The first in months. Got Mother a beautiful dress for Mothers Day the 14th (don't forget yours my pet). Also some things for Charles & Margie's birthday the end of May. Then various odds & ends for myself. Was tired last night. Whew.

Darling I'll love the records. How sweet of you dear. Yes we have a record player here in quarters. Thank you dear heart for your constant thoughtfulness.

How much weight have you regained dear. Hope some. I'm up to 109 now. Slow but sure. Did you have to buy lots of new uniforms? Aren't I the question box?

It's been colder than heck here the past week—34-40. One soldier from Texas said if you took a 3 day pass in August in this country you'd miss summer. Spring is just awfully slow. Daddy is troubled because of his farm work of course.

Gee whiz I miss my scruntchy old sweet thing—but I'm being a good soldier really I am. Darling both of us have so much compared to others. Tell me all the news. I eat your letters up. Am still going to tie a blue ribbon around a few. Can I?

Be good baby dear & a million smacks to keep you warm & happy.

All my love
Your Miss Boo

May 8, 1944

Morning, Miss Boo—

You old rascal, you, how goes it, these days? I'm waiting anxiously to see where in the hell they will send me when I report to Upton on the 11th. May sound funny that anyone would want their leave to be up but that's the way I feel. I want to get working again—but I don't have to explain to you why. Just sitting around the house isn't much fun and I sure could use a clinic full of patients again. Never thought that I'd be saying anything like that. This medical profession is sure funny. You work and you gripe about working too hard and then when you get a vacation you want to start in again. Thank God for work, is all I can say.

The dinner my brother gave me was really swell. There were three judges, 8 doctors, three dentists, and a few more assorted people. After the dinner we just sat around telling stories and jokes and we all had a swell time. Dad was as proud as a peacock and was blown up like a balloon. It was really nice and I enjoyed it.

I played golf yesterday with my brother and it started to rain like hell and everyone stopped playing but not me, I thought I was still in Panama and didn't even notice the rain. It's been around 90 in the shade here for the past few days believe it or not, but today it has become cool again. I even wore khaki the other day.

I'm leaving here Wednesday A.M. and have to report to Fort Hamilton to sign in. I then go to Upton and will be there the A.M. of the 11th. Better not write me Baby, until you hear from me to where I am, etc. I'll wire you as soon as I know where I'll be and I'm still going to try and call you up within the next week or two. May I?

Be brave, my darling, I love you so much, and soon we will have a peek at each other. Yum! Yum!

My love,
Bops

May 9, 1944

My Baby,

This will be a quick note answering a few of your questions before I leave in the A.M. I'm busier than a one-arm paper hanger in a harem saying good-byes, etc.

Mother received the flowers and loves them. She is a lot better and believe me again when I say there is no hard feelings anywhere, so be assured, my darling.

I am taking my car with me. It sure is swell having it. Martin had the whole motor overhauled and it runs like a charm. I haven't had a bit of trouble getting gas here at home but I probably will wherever I go.

As for your trunk, Bops, you can't file a claim against the government because they don't insure the stuff and luggage shipped by the army on route is not insurable so I'm afraid that you'll just have to sit around and wait for it. One of these days it will probably turn up. Your best bet is to contact someone in the QMC there who has had some experience along those lines and see what he says. Another thing, why not drop Lucille Tassin a note and have her snoop around LaGarde where you were and see if she can find anything out.

I packed yesterday and I'm taking only a few hand pieces with me. After getting all my junk home, I was surprised to find that I don't have much at all to pack. But after a few months at my new post, wherever it is, I'm sure I'll be loaded down again.

Bye for now darling and I'll write or call as soon as I know where the "Old Man" is going to be.

My love,
Bops

May 12, 1944

My Baby,

Well, Bops, here I am at the Medical Department Replacement Pool here at Tilton General Hospital, Fort Dix, N.J. Johnny O. and Tom Swift are also here and I live right next door to them. It sure is nice having them around because if I didn't have someone to talk to and show me the ropes I'd probably be going crazy or going around punching people in the nose. No kidding Bops, it makes you sick to see where the officers are being sent and kicked around. I thought for awhile I'd be sent near home but the way it looks I'll probably end up in Oshkosh, Somewhere. I'm staying here and have to wait further orders. Some guys have been here for two and three months and they tell me that being an EENT man I should be assigned within a few days because they need them. Jeepers, I sure had a tough day yesterday. I drove from Home to Upton 150 miles and then when I got there I had to wade through about 90 miles of red tape. I just couldn't drive to Dix so I stayed over in Jersey City where I was a resident years ago and visited with a lot of my old friends. The boys who were my interns are now residents on most of the services and they told me all the dirt about my friends. They sure have gone all over the world and done lots of stuff.

Our barracks are really something to behold. Five million guys falling all over each other and sleeping in the hall-ways. The shower and latrine are a half a block from the barracks. Thank God that it's summer or else I'd freeze here I guess.

Good to be able to write you darling. I know that the best thing I could do for us both would be to stop all this writing but I don't know baby, I just want to write and there's no reason why we shouldn't. After all we've been through, that's the least we can do.

Sweet baby, pray that I get a good job and that they don't start kicking me around like they have a lot of the guys here.

Your picture is right in front of me and you were just kissed, so there! Write me c/o the return address on the envelope, but don't get excited if your mail doesn't get to me soon, I may be kicked around in the next few days.

All my love, darling,

Mr. Bops

Hello my sweet thing

Darling, darling I just finished talking to you-how can words express how wonderful it was to hear your voice. Jeepers I was like a little girl with a new doll, so excited. I'm still trembling. Had expected your call most any time, but fortunately this morning came off duty at 9 & go back at 2-so was in qtrs. God is awfully good to us isn't He dear?

Baby it's a wonderful feeling to know that my being happy & sounding that way, it gives you such a boost. We are certainly doing everything to help each other. That's cause we still love each other so very much.

Now darling the next glorious thing to look forward to is our meeting. I feel the time is growing closer & closer. A funny intuition tells me you will be stationed maybe in Chicago—perhaps it's just wishful thinking, but I do know they need Drs. badly in this area. Perhaps though you wouldn't like the idea of leaving the east but in my way of thinking one place is no different from the other in the Army-just as long as there is work to be done.

Yes dear heart, the passing of time is making it some easier in a way—at least the horrible ache is slowly easing, but one thing it can never do is to change my love for you, feel you belong to me & always will. We will always be to-gether in our hearts.

Edward dear my work is a help in my gaining weight & eating better. That is one time when I think less about my own misfortunes & think of those dear sweet kids. The nurses here are really tops & as I said before they are so willing & appreciative & no griping, it's of course because of the Army being a new career & they haven't learned its ways. Darling it would make you proud to know how many want to work with me because I teach (or try to) them as much as possible, and baby I don't care in the least whether my 1ˢᵗ Lt. comes through cause I hate to leave my little ward.

Called Mom yesterday & expect to go home for the week-end. She was having such a nice day. Fourteen of we girls hiked some 8 miles to the cranberry marshes yesterday. It was gorgeous out & the scenery was exquisite. There are lots of little streams in this section of the country all bordered with huge pines, spring flowers & blossoms. Everything was so calm & beautiful that it gave me great peace. Darling there is nothing like nature to help one forget this ugly war torn world. It's such a great privilege to be an American.

Baby dear you must eat & gain some weight—seven pounds is not enough hear? Your panties will still bag really if you don't. Just can't imagine my old Scruntchy being skinny.

Will run over to the mailbox now so scuse for a bit perhaps the address will be there. Smack, smack, a million times Bopsy dear.

Hi Bops, you old thing!

Here's the old man again still waiting orders at the Pool here in Tilton. It'll be a week to-morrow and still nothing.

We have some swell guys waiting here in the pool. 90% of them have been overseas for about the same length of time that we have. They come from all the active fighting fronts and their stories are swell. There are four of us who hang out to-gether here. Johnny, Tommy, myself and a boy who is a dentist and took part in the African and Sicilian landings. The poor kid caught malaria in Africa and yesterday morning he was taken with a chill and we had to admit him to the hospital. No kidding, Bops, the difference between the guys who have been overseas and these jerks who haven't been over is the same as night and day. Over here at this pool they're more concerned with the correct type of uniform than whether or not we ever get a good job or that there are about 10 of us not doing anything. Oh nuts! Think I'll get assigned to Camp McCoy, Wis., no kidding Bops, what would we do? Something to think about isn't it?

I went home last week-end and I suppose I'll go home this week-end. I don't drive because it's too tiring. Johnny usually drives me to Newark and I take the train to N.Y. and then I go home by train. Boy, will I be happy when I get assigned somewhere and I don't have to go running around living out of a suitcase for a while. If I'm still here when the first week in June comes around you may rest assured that I'll be on my way to Chicago and a reunion with my old baby.

You should be getting a package of salt-water taffy I sent you from Atlantic City to-day. Yum! Yum!

Stay as sweet as you are, darling, and carry my love with you always.

My love,

(Mr. Bops)

P.S. I got about 8 insignias for you. I don't know if you have them or not. I almost had a 7th Army (Italy) for you but didn't quite get it. I'll send one or two each time I write until you get them all.

Note: Gretchen collected insignias during her stay in the Army and sewed them onto a navy blue blanket.

5/18/44

My darling

How's that sweet old soldier man of mine to-day? Just a wee note this time to tell you that my thoughts are with you every minute dear.

Don't know who is most anxious to hear what the reassignment will be, but am sure it's both of us. Darling don't be disappointed in where ever they send you. Just be a brave darling & we still must believe that whatever happens, something good will come from it. Of course Bops I'm selfish & want you close by. It still wouldn't matter what our future is. My Bops is my one & only fella so there. Our happiness hasn't ended at this stage of great disappointment dear heart. We will be just two happy kids no matter what happens.

Be sure to get out & have fun baby. After all that's all I'm concerned about. Can't you go to N.Y. once in awhile during the wait?

All is quiet here. My ward was quarantined for measles this A.M. so it will mean less work for five days.

I'm cold baby. Guess Mr Bops and I will have to take a snuggly nap until lunch time.

Happy days are coming sweet darling so keep your chin up. I keep thinking about our telephone talk & how wonderful it was.

Love you dear baby—so be good.

Your
Miss Boo

May 22, 1944

My darling,

Here it is Monday again Bops and still no orders. I was home again over the week-end and spent my usual quiet 2 days with the family. Perhaps I'll be getting orders this week. I sure hope so. This sitting around is getting me down. I just want to get myself settled so I can start working again and studying for my boards. I'm so far behind in my work it isn't even funny.

Your letters are so beautiful Bops as to what you do and what you think. The photo I got must be framed adequately. You sit right in front of my cot so I can look at you when I go to bed and when I get up, you sweetheart! And you are always smiling. Sure happy you took a smiling picture instead of a serious one. That's the way I always want to think of you and that is smiling. I don't know how to describe my feelings these days. It's very hard but it's like a state of suspended animation in which I go through all the motions but just keep wondering what is going to happen to you and me. I've gone out of my way in getting dates and I've had quite a few in the past 10 days it seems but there's no sense kidding myself it just isn't the same. I just don't have the fun I used to have, Bops, so I may as well quit going around. I'm not despondent or depressed but everything I do I feel I should be doing with you and so there's no kick in it. I suppose that someday it will iron itself out but even if it doesn't I'm quite content to go as I have. That great big, gaping chasm I used to have is really filled in Bops, and it has been filled with a great, overwhelming admiration and respect for you—something that grows with each day and hour when I think of how wonderful you have been through all this and have emerged without bitterness and despair. Anyone else would have thrown up their hands in bitter regret at what you have been through, but not my Bops. God Bless You! As for me, I'm quite content. After having been through the wards and spoken and seen our fighting men come back from the wars, I think I should be content that I am still in one piece and so are you. You've given me so much in our two years. I've had the privilege of looking into the finest character I've ever known, I've been very lucky darling in having known a person such as you and I'm happy for that. Yes, baby, I am content and happy about a lot of things. I'm on my way back to normalcy and I know you are—that's what makes it so much easier for me. 'Nuff said!

Johnny and I have been playing a lot of golf and having a good time. He sure misses Alfy and I know just how he feels but when he gets feeling low I start bawling him out. At least he's married and had a few months with his wife. No kidding Bops, this is sure a crazy world. Johnny caught hell from his brother and family when he got home because he didn't marry a Polish girl. Isn't that something? What the hell goes on with people anyway? It just amazes me the things I hear day after day.

I hope you got the records, the candy and the shoulder patches. Be a sweet old thing, stay happy, don't worry and consider yourself smacked thousands of times.

My love,
Edward

My darling,

Baby, baby. You sweet sweet thing. Why are you so very good to this old gal. It makes a great big lump in my throat to know you still care this deeply & show it by your constant thoughtfulness in sending gifts & your perfect letters. Darling it makes me so proud to feel you think I'm worthy of such devotion. She's just a plain little every day girl baby with great love in her heart for just one person.

The candy is so good. Can see my Bops buying it with a gleam in his eyes & thinking I bet Bops would like this. Am thrilled with the records dear. The words are so cute & the tunes catchy. Like "All or Nuthin" especially & then my sentimental one is "People Will Say We're in Love." The girls in the barracks are certainly enjoying them too, then I brag & say my true love sent them. They think that fellow is pretty wonderful & really must be in love. Next, out comes the picture & the ohs & ahs honey. Ooh lah lah. Can't say the right things in Gretchen talk darling—so just thank you over & over. Any little thing even a common pin would make me happy if it were from you.

Closed my ward yesterday. So am a little lost. It will straighten out though, as the Col. in charge of medicine is my friend & he really made my chest puff out in pride this morning.

Bopsy darling I was quite startled to hear the way you are feeling of late, because my feelings have been identical. Something I can't explain & thought it would sound funny on paper, but would you like to know about my premonitions. I swear darling we're psychic, because at the same time I'm either thinking or writing you—here comes a letter with all my thoughts already written. For the past month the most peculiar sensation of "something's going to happen to Bops & me," has been swimming through my head. Like it isn't the end between us darling—that we have a great happiness in store. It seems like people will influence us some how. Can't quite say who, when, or why-but it's there. Our love is so beautiful & fine & strong that it will be recognized. Consequently baby I've been sort of living in a dream. Sounds squirrely doesn't it, but before in my life I've noticed how strongly my dreams (or whatever they are) have become a reality.

Last week I too was real brave & went to the club—darling it was horrible. The only way I could be comfortable was to know how good it was in a formal, but all the time I was dancing with Bops, looking for him in *every corner & in everyone's face thinking any minute he would break in & relieve the awful agony of a stranger, then darling when I came home I wept myself to sleep. You shouldn't hear me say this but that's part of our love baby dear. It's a crazy world sweetheart-yes-yes-yes-yes. Just won't go out anymore, for the sake of going—these officers drink like fish, have no respect for anyone's ideas or morals & believe because you're in the Army anything goes. Well darling I won't change for anyone & until someone understands that I'm not just one of the gang, I'll sit home. Am reading, sewing & enjoying the girls company in the barracks & at night time I sit with my baby's picture & we just look & talk silently.*

Mr. Bops Junior is fine darling-he looks like he has gotten into the candy but sits & says nothing.

What a chatter box you're attached to sweet thing-but she no can help. Gotta jabber to my old darling, just be happy dear heart & remember I'm being a good soldier & loving you.

Always
Your Miss Boo

26 May 1944

My Baby,

There's still no news about me getting a job so I think we better start making tentative plans for getting to-gether in Chicago. Of course, being in the army, things may change at the last minute but I'm putting for 10 days leave to attend the AMA convention from the 10th to the 20th. Can you get leave for those dates?

I just hope that this works out Bops. If it doesn't, then we'll have to wait a little later but it will be so wonderful being together for a few days that we'll be able to sort of make up for all the heartaches we've been having.

If you think of any other arrangements that you'd think would work out better or some other plan just let me know. I'm using the Convention as a reason to get leave but if I never attend one meeting I don't care. Just want to be with Miss Boo.

I'm making this short so I can send it right out.

My love,
Bops

My Baby,

Well, I just got my orders to Camp Blanding, Florida. All things considered I guess it could have been worse. The camp is at Stark, Florida, just below Jacksonville. I'll be about the same distance from Chicago as I am now. I don't know what I'll run into there Bops, whether I'll be there permanently or whether I'll move somewhere in that locality. As for our plans for meeting Bops—I'll still ask for leave to attend the convention but it's impossible to say whether I'll get it or not. Don't get leave or make any plans until I know exactly where I'll be and what the set-up is. You know how these things are. Well, here I go again on another Cook's Tour. I'm leaving Tuesday A.M. & I have 5 days to get there.

I just came down from home & said goodbye to the folks. Mother was being brave but I can see her starting to worry all over again. Bopsy, Bopsy, when will it all end?

If I can't get leave, I know you'll come & see me—if you can. It's about a 22 hour ride from Chicago to Fla and we can have a reunion there. At any rate, let's just sit tight & see what happens.

I'm driving with my car and I dread the trip down but then I'll have my car with me. I'd be lost in Fla. without it.

I'll call some night after I get there and tell you all about it. I expect to be there by Saturday or Sunday.

I love you, my darling,
Edward

My darling,

What a gorgeous morning this is dear, keep thinking-if my Bops were only here we would go golfing & then to the ballgame this afternoon. Wouldn't it be fun sweet thing? Well maybe some day, some place, somehow—do you suppose?

Darling I'm really leading a lazy life these days. In charge of the T.B. ward-with only four patients who are all boarded & waiting to go out. Its delightful to take it easy. This a.m. we all sat out in the sun. Its so lovely here. Green grass rustly pines & flowers. Must try to get a little tan—gee—if I could only go golfing.

Sweet baby whatcha doin? Still sittin around twiddling thumbs. Golly I don't understand it really do you? Are you being a good boy for your Bops. Darling I'm so proud of you & of us. I think we're swell people—just cause, but what are we going to do now? How soon are you coming part way to see me, darling. I'm chewing my nails awaiting that day.

We went into summer uniform yesterday. Like my new beige dress, it fits good baby, it even has some curves.

Await your letters so anxiously dear—keep playing our records & then I know you're close by listening & enjoying them too.

Need some smacks just awful bad dear heart—& want them from my baby cause I love you.

*Always your own
Miss Boo*

My dear darling

Baby, baby how can you keep thinking of such wonderful things to do to keep your Bops happy? To hear you to-night so unexpectedly was almost more than my heart could stand. It was perfect, perfect darling. I fairly bubbled with joy & happiness. The whole world has been pink & beautiful since.

Was too excited to think of all the things I wanted to say but wasn't the connection excellent? Could have reached right out & touched that sweet, old Bops. Anyway we did get our smacks in didn't we? Edward my darling if it's possible I love you more & more each day. Distance has only made it stronger & proven to me that no one or nothing in the world matters except us.

Am writing to Del*& told her to expect you. It is really wonderful dear to know you are so close to them & the first thing I thought of was how wonderful it would be for me to come down. Del & I mean more to each other than sisters & to have a visit with her & to have you at my side seems like too much happiness for one little girl to have doesn't it?

Darling, darling I can hardly wait. We have a million smacks to catch up on & how are we going to have time to talk?

Am really quite perturbed about your mother dear. It is so very puzzling. I may be wrong in thinking this—but her objection to our marriage must be based from a health standpoint as well as other reasons. She will just have to understand darling that she can't have her sons right at her side every minute. They have lives to lead too. Darling baby I'm so afraid you won't be happy at home the rest of your life. The closeness isn't good believe me—or am I out of place voicing an opinion.

Dear baby-nothing else matters any way now. We will talk about all that later. Just want you to get settled, like your post—let our love make you happy & think what heaven we'll be in oh so soon.

Know your trip was long & tiresome but I've prayed that God would get you there safe.

I love you darling & my call was just too perfect.
Your very own Miss Boo

---

*   Del had been Gretchen's roommate in Chicago, and now was stationed with her husband, a Navy officer, in Jacksonville, Florida.

The Deep Crummy South

Hello Miss Boo, you old sweet thing—

It sure was wonderful speaking with you last night Bops. You really did sound so close but you're never far away from me anyway, so there. I wasn't going to call until I got to Blanding, but the desire was just too much especially when I had the phone right there at my side and all I had to do was pick it up and tell the operator I wanted to speak with that old Sweet Thing—funny she knew just where to call and who to ask for. I guess she must have known . . . !

It sure is a lonesome ride driving all alone in this hot part of the country. I left Dix Tuesday morning and reached Washington that afternoon. I spent the night at the new Statler Hotel and Bops it's the finest hotel I've ever been in. No kidding, each room is air conditioned, has a radio, and it's just beautiful. I drove to Raleigh and stayed at the Sir Walter and that's where I called from. That wasn't bad but to-night I'm in Augusta, Ga and Bops don't believe the picture of the hotel at the top. This is the dumpiest, crummiest hotel I've ever been in. I just had to call up the clerk because there were no bulbs in the room and the water was turned off in the shower. I think I'll sleep with the light turned on tonight to keep the bed-bugs away in case there are any. To-morrow I'll be in Macon. I expect to drive the rest of the way into Blanding Saturday or Sunday or I may drive into Jacksonville and spend the week-end because I'm not due until Monday but I don't know just what I will do yet.

Yes, baby, we shall soon see each other and there is so much for us to talk about. I'm going to try and find a place for you to stay that's closer to the Camp than Jacksonville. Jacksonville is about 45 miles and I'll want to see you even during duty hours if I can so I'll make an estimate of the situation when I get to Blanding and find out how we can swing this thing. Leave it to Bops. I think Tobey has his wife at the Camp and they'll be able to give me some pointers.

Bops, my darling, your last letters seem to be building a little day-dream about you and me. Please, dear heart, don't talk yourself into anything that will let you down again. Don't think, don't plan, don't hurt yourself, my beloved. Just sit tight until we meet soon and then we'll talk until the cows come home and then some.

You sounded so wonderful over the phone, baby, I know how you feel, what you think, and every little thing that makes you tick because you never leave me. I know you're a brave little soldier just for me and I'll always love you for it.

Chin-up, sweetheart, pretty soon I'll kiss each care from your heart—

Mr. Bops

JUNE, 1944

My darling,

I just pulled in here about 2 hours ago and I'm so goddam lonesome that I thought I better sit down and write my old baby a letter. I'm so happy you wrote me the other day because your letter was waiting for me when I got here and it was swell reading it, just like a welcome committee.

I intend to drive into Jacksonville to-morrow and try to find Delma. It will be so much fun finally talking to someone about you. I don't see the C.O. until to-morrow Bops. I was speaking to a few of the men around here and it seems they already have about 3 EENT men already. I spoke to Tobey, who is here, and he says that the C.O. makes all the new officers work in the dispensary at first. But, I really don't know and I won't know until to-morrow.

So my baby loves me more and more each day—how is that possible, you old sweet thing you! Oh, bops, you've no idea how terrible it was driving all those miles by myself with nothing to do but think, think, and think some more. Sometimes it all becomes so horribly confused that my thoughts don't work at all, but my sense of humor comes to the rescue and I think of my strong, brave, Bops and I'm all right again. It's both a terrible and beautiful thing to become so attached to anyone isn't it?

As for Mother, it's so hard to talk of her Bops. She's really ill with her menopause and hypertension and she tries so hard to carry on like her old self. But we'll wait until we see each other and I can tell you more. This camp Bops, is miles from everywhere but in the next few days or couple of weeks I'll get working on our plans because we can't postpone them any longer. I can get off each night. They work here every 4th night. I'll speak to Harriet Dawley, or I'll find out what kind of Chief Nurse they have. Perhaps you can stay out here for part of your leave and the other part you can stay with Delma. I'll be saving all the gasoline I can for your leave. Don't worry Bops, I'll fix things up somehow. Oh my darling, I do love you, smack, smack!

Enough for now, darling, and Bops, let me know how long the "Free" letters take will you? I think they are just as fast as the air-mail so you can save yourself 9¢.

My love,
Mr Bops

6/4/44 Sun. p.m.

My dear darling,

Received your letter from Augusta, Ga. today. Bopsy I've watched the map each day trying to figure out just where you were. Have been right on the seat beside my old baby—did you see me there?

Had to go to the movie with the gals so just got home. We saw "The Eve of St Mark" not so good. Seems movies don't interest me much anymore. Miss my old Bops at my side. Consequently I go very seldom.

Edward dear I'm awaiting all details about my trip to see you. Naturally I want to be as close as possible & knew Jacksonville was a bit far. Do the best you can dear, maybe I could sleep in your car. Will have to spend some time with Del. But we can see about that later. Hope you have a chance to see her soon.

Darling you were right about my daydreams, but after all dear heart you can't take my dreams away. No I'm not planning on a thing—even though our future must always be apart I will always dream & think. It's all I have left dear. No one will ever take your place. My whole life revolves around my love for you & when it is so deep one just can't help but show it even though they try. My darling I know what to expect for us—but even that can't dampen my spirits or my attitude. So please don't be frightened thinking there will be another big hurt. Just think, soon we will be together for a little while & that's all I've asked since our plans for our life together were shattered. We need to talk darling for hours & hours & to be close & so dear to each other again, the days are so long & lonesome at times without my old baby.

Baby dear I'm sort of sleepy, so guess I'll go to dreamland. I have met you there so much these past few days. Last night you were dancing with some other girl & I was watching ogle-eyed.

Good night dear Bopsy—hope you find everything to your liking. Don't be lonesome my big old soldier man. Cause Miss Boo loves you.

5 June 1944

My darling,

Good morning, darling!

Thank god that I have you to write to and tell all my troubles to. I'm so goddam mad that I've been counting ten every minute since I've been in this place. If it weren't for you and my family I'd be in Washington to-morrow requesting overseas duty again. I finally met the Colonel yesterday morning and we batted the breeze for about 20 minutes during the course of which I wasn't asked to be seated or anything like that. After that I went to the MAC adjutant who is a major and he told me that they had more than enough EENT men and that I would be assigned to the induction team for examining incoming draftees. From the Chief of a section in a general hospital to examining draftees on a production line, how the Mighty have fallen. They didn't know how long it would last. To top it off I was assigned quarters to-day in the usual barracks type partition quarters and lo and behold there is a double decker and I have to share an 8x8 room with another Captain. That was a little too much to stand so I promptly called up the Lt. in charge and raised hell. It's the first time I've ever griped about anything and I'm thoroughly ashamed of myself for doing it but I just couldn't help it, baby. Anyway, he said he was cramped for room and that he would take care of a single room in a few days. I'll give him his few days and see what happens. Needless to say baby, I'm a little upset and mad about the whole thing. A guy comes back from over 2 years overseas and they start jerking him around. But I guess I'll just have to sit back and take it.

To talk about something more pleasant, I drove into Jacksonville yesterday afternoon and met Delma and Frank. It was so wonderful Baby having someone to talk to who know you that I was almost in tears from thankfulness. Frank was out playing golf and Delma and I had a long talk about us. She told me frankly that she disapproved of our romance and had written you but after we were to-gether 5 minutes she told me that she was wrong and that I really was all you said I was. You didn't tell me that, Bops. I guess you wanted her to see for herself. We had a wonderful day baby, and when I left last night we were the best of friends and Delma was rooting for us. They sure have a swell little girl. They took me out to their Naval Air Station Club for dinner and were wonderful to me. Frank and I are playing golf next Sunday if I can get off.

Now as to your coming down. Personally I think that if you're coming, the quicker you get here the better it'll be because I don't know just how much longer I can wait, darling, to see you. So, see about your leave darling. If you wait too long, it'll be getting hotter and I don't want you uncomfortable. So get the ball rolling, sweetheart, and let me know. I believe the train leaves Chicago midnight and pulls into Jacksonville the morning of the day after. 24-36 hrs.

I saw some pictures Delma had of you years ago and boy were they something. One of you with your hair parted in the middle sitting on some sort of rock was really cute. You rascal.

Chin-up darling, or rather I guess you should be telling me that. You're the tough guy in this family it seems. I love you darling, love you, love you.

6 June 1944

My darling,

I guess to-day is quite a day in all of our lives. The Invasion is finally here and I don't wonder that you and I would have liked to be in it, come what may. In spite of our two years in Panama doing our little part I know that we would have liked to be over there now working side by side and looking after "our boys." Gives you "duck bumps" when you think of that first wave that landed and the thoughts that the boys had when they landed. It makes you think of all the prayers that they were uttering and all to the same Lord. Perhaps something good will come of all of this and people will realize all the more how we are more alike and all want the same thing out of life. A chance to live your life as you like it and with whom you want in dignity and love. Maybe it will and maybe it won't, Bops, I don't know. People are prone to forget things they learn at so expensive a price. Let's hope that they don't forget this lesson for all time.

I started my job this morning and it wasn't too bad. I always said that if I was on an induction team I'd really not let anyone through that didn't belong and I started to-day. Things are rather quiet and that's good because while I'm on this job we rarely work in the afternoons and we don't work Sat. afternoon Sundays or Mondays so when you come down I'll have all that time to spend with my baby. Jeepers Bops, I'm waiting patiently for that telegram or letter saying, "arriving Jacksonville—love, Gretchen." Jeepers I looked at the map to-day and thought if you had been at Ft. Lewis—I hate to think of it. At least that's one break!

I went swimming at our beach yesterday and it's really nice Bops. When you get here we can spend a few afternoons at the beach.

Bye for now baby, and I'm waiting for Bops's invasion of Florida.

My love,
Mr. Bops

6 June 1944

Gretchen Dear,

What a day—The gang from Panama all are in the living room by ourselves & we have our ears screwed to the radio—oh my—We know that thousands of parents tho happy tonite are mindful of the fact that some of them will get that awful letter saying their son was killed in action—That's the part I hate to think of—but ah Gretchen to get this war over with.

As it gets very cool—our laundry goes out each Fri morning & is returned each Fri P.M. from the week before—very satisfactory—30¢ a uniform & we all get along with 3 (a week) nicely. We pay $10 for a meal ticket which takes care of 30 meals—Each meal is punched & therefore you pay only for the meals you eat. $30 a month covers it if you ate 3 squares a day. We pay $5.00 monthly into the House Fund which covers maid service, Johnny paper, paper towels, etc.—

We have a Coke machine & you know how I love them. So you won't have to worry about that Gret—whoopee!

Our Hospital is brick but a sort of cantonment style you know—halls are heated—floors are cement & it all looks pretty durable. Guess it's going to be a Veteran's Hosp after the fracas is over. Our German prisoners are landscaping the grounds & it will be more & more beautiful each day if that is possible.

Our food is good. Our quarters are two story brick, very comfy, rooms small, but nicely furnished—lovely bed with inter spring, big easy chair with ottoman, dresser, small table & a closed closet for a clothespress which is a joy. We have to furnish our own sheets etc. We have issued 2 white blankets & oh they are lovely. Use them every nite.

Well ole sox I just hope & pray you will be happy in whatever you are doing & going to do—I'm so glad Edward is thoughtful & good to you—I trust the plans for your leave will be successful & that you both will have a scrumptious time. I know you will.

Have to cut this short but I'm praying for you—chin up—be a good girl & don't worry. No matter what happens, God knows best always.

Love,
Kay

8 June 1944

My darling,

Just received your letter of June 4th and it was good to hear from you dearheart. Amazing just what a simple letter can do for you isn't it? Sort of makes everything all-right, doesn't it baby? But I guess the big thing right now is your coming down here. I hope it's really soon before it gets too hot. We shall have a wonderful time baby, just the two of us again—laughing, loving, kissing each other, oh Baby, soon, soon, soon!

I won't think of the future or anything, just our reunion soon. I'm gathering my gasoline, hoarding it, just for our days to-gether. I'll have my Bops in my own car and we'll drive around, go swimming. This job I have now only requires my being here in the mornings and Sat afternoon, Sunday and Mondays off. Hurry, baby, hurry!

Yes baby, I understand completely when you say that no one will ever take my place because I can't possibly conceive of my feeling for anyone else the way I feel for you. I enjoyed Kay's letter—yes baby, everyone that knows us is rooting for us and won't take "no" for an answer. But talking like that gets me nowhere. Thank God there are such things as to-morrow, we can always pray that something may happen.

I am being a brave soldier, darling, because you are so wonderful about all of this. If you weren't I think I'd die!

I love you, Gretchen, my dearly beloved—God bless you—

Edward

P.S. Free mail gets here just as fast so save your pennies.

My dear darling

How anxious I've been about your safe arrival dear—now I can breathe a little easier. It was a tough trip Bopsy but we made it.

They can't do that to my baby—what's the big idea, but honey we have lived in our own happy little private world so long things are hard to take now. You just have to be a good soldier & show them you are big enough to take anything they dish out & make a success of it. Remember there is a silver lining to every dark cloud. We have learned that, haven't we? After all darling none of it makes sense—because some people have no idea how to organize or place personnel, try to keep the old sense of humor (I'm a copy cat) & keep the chin up for your Bops. The important thing is that we still have our love to see us through all these trials & tribulations.

Edward, how happy it makes me to know you have met & like Del & Frank. Darling you mustn't feel that I have held anything from you, perhaps some of your friends reacted the same way, but you never told me. It didn't seem necessary to cause hurt feelings when the judgment passed was unfounded. Del was concerned with my happiness, the religious angle worried her & she only wanted me to be cautious. Knew though baby if she ever met you, all her fears would vanish from her mind & until that time (which I didn't expect so soon) knew she would have to trust me, my judgment & my ideas of the most wonderful man in the world. It's oh so wrong darling to judge people until you meet them; if we would only stop to think it's the person's character that counts & what they are today—not who or what their forefathers were.

Mother was here Tues. & Wed. She got a real thrill out of the immensity of the place. Enjoyed having her so much. She said to send her best to you & is glad you would get to see Del.

As yet I haven't been able to find a place to play golf, in fact there isn't any place to do anything. No tennis courts, nor swimming pools. Am a little perturbed about that.

Don't forget to keep the chin up darling & smile for Bops—cause she loves you so very, very much.

Bushels of smacks—pretty soon they'll be real.

Your Miss Boo.

Mother loved "Mr Bops" & my records.

June 9, 1944 Fri. noon

My dear Bopsy

Suppose you will be surprised at all the letters, but can't let my old sweet thing be lonesome. Just know how tough it is dear, but it will be better as the days go by.

Received the free letter today which was written the day you arrived & the air mail letter written Monday came yesterday. There is some difference, but we can send them free unless it's urgent information, o.k.?

This is an ugly dark cold day, in fact this week hasn't been at all pleasant. Am going to LaCrosse at 3 to do a little shopping—think it is a good day to dig around in the stores. Am already planning for my visit dear & want some comfortable play clothes, swim suit etc. just a few things. You know how something new to wear boosts my spirits. It's about 35 miles to L.C. just a good way to spend a lonesome afternoon. Maybe I'll find a sprise for my baby—remember how I always brought you something from town & then old Bops would look through all the packages. Darling I love on all those memories. They are so wonderful. Well dear, how are things going. So hope your job isn't too unpleasant but I have no fear because you will make the best of any situation. Just show them darling that you are the best EENT man in camp.

Perhaps you will find time now to study for boards. Want you to get that done soon dear—it's important. I've been doing quite a bit of reading "under cover." "The Art of being a Person," etc. right now I'm enjoying Lin Yutang's "With Love and Irony." You know what a task it is for me to read—just get so sleepy.

After Tuesday I've got to move to another barracks as they are getting new cadets in. The kids call 1013 (where I'm going) "Menopause Manor," isn't that a riot? Golly I'll really miss that gang of girls—but will find new ones no doubt. Seems the last few groups are really crumby gals.

Darling I am so lonesome for you. Just think it's been 5 months. It seems like 5 years, but my sweet baby I know now how real our love is to hold us so strongly through time & tempest. Yummy—in a few weeks—just think. It's like a dream darling. Last night I could hardly go to sleep—kept thinking & thinking.

All my kisses to keep you happy. Keep smiling & Bopsy loves you billions & bushels.

Your Miss Boo

My darling,

LaCrosse is a failure as far as shopping is concerned & I came home without spending any money. Don't you think it would be wise to wait & get a few little things I need in Jacksonville?

The weather still remains unpleasant, a little too cold for my comfort, can't even get any tan, there isn't any sunshine, but I promise to look healthy for my invasion. Six of we girls are having a card party this p.m. All my pals who are leaving—darling they are still begging me to go & as their chief. What a grand bunch they are.

Yes darling, the invasion is on. What a peculiar feeling we all had at 6 a.m. on the 6th & news was pouring in. Each of us is so concerned & even though you & I are back here, we feel so deeply that maybe we could help in some way. Our chance may come dear, but until it does we mustn't fail at this end to do our jobs well, for all of us is just a little cog in a great wheel to help make it go round.

There is so much dear Bopsy that I want to say to you—however writing them is unsatisfactory so we will just wait and talk. Those of us who are in the Army know what we are fighting for, we know that irregardless of race, creed or religion all our boys are side by side, thinking of no discriminations except that we are all Americans. Darling I've thought so seriously of this whole thing & interwoven in those thoughts are you & me. It's very sobering.

Expect you will see Del & Frank tomorrow. Have fun dear. How is your golf game—guess I will have to give it up for the summer, just no transportation to get to the one course there is close by.

No news of my coming yet dear, can hardly wait to ask, but am trying to be considerate since our Col. is head over heels in details now. Then too we will be a little short of help for a week or so. Am terribly afraid dear I won't be able to come until July—just keep your fingers crossed. It seems ages away when we both are so anxious.

Hope your work is going better dear, that's right don't let anyone in who shouldn't be. We have seen so much of that.

Nothin much more darling old sweet thing 'cept I love you with all my heart. Keep smiling dear & your letters are so wonderful even though you were a little angry. Be my good soldier & soon I'll come to collect all my smacks in person.

Your very own
Miss Boo

My baby,

Received both your letters mailed from Sparta dated the 10th to-day and the Free mail does come a little slowly but as you say we can use air-mail for the urgent stuff.

I know how swell your bunch of girls must be. You wrote of them so frequently and I have been so grateful to them for taking care of my baby. I know how nice it would be for you to go with them as their chief. I too would like to go overseas again darling, but I won't volunteer also because of you. Funny, isn't it, darling, how we think of the same things and don't do them for the same reason. But, we are so close, that is to be expected.

Yes darling, the boys of different races, creeds, etc., are fighting to-gether and it is so hard for us to understand these things. You and I understand however, about these things and perhaps in another generation there will be a great awakening as the true facts of religion and what it really is, I don't know. But, we shall talk of all these things soon. The important thing right now is for your leave to be granted.

My job, if you want to call it that, is still the same. We seem to have less and less to do each day. We have a pretty nice bunch of fellows and corps men though and it's almost like the old clinic days.

I was admitting OD last night and admitted 98 patients from 4 in the P.M. until the following morning so you can see this is really a large place, usually around a daily census of 2,000. I'm sorry that I was a little angry in one of my letters about my job but you set me straight, darling, as you always do, and I know we all have to do our job. Just bark at me, remember? Bark, bark, bark!

Don't worry about the sunshine. It's been so hot and sunshiny and rains every afternoon, just like the tropics that if I had Bops here I'd think it was Panama.

I'm so sorry about your not being able to get transportation, Bops, but I have my car and I barely drive rarely because there ain't no gas . . .

Sweet dreams, baby, and maybe there'll be news soon about my baby's coming down.

I love you,
Mr. Bops

16 June 1944

My darling,

How perfectly wonderful speaking with you last night. It sure was a long wait though. I put in the call at 8 P.M. our time and as you know it was completed at 1:10 a.m. my time. I had the hospital on the phone an hour before I talked with you but they said they couldn't find you or something but I guess that (they) have to go and tell you instead of ringing after 10:00 P.M. I would have called sooner Bops, but I thought you might be still working on the ward and I didn't want to disturb you, but at least we talked. Somehow, those old phone calls just aren't enough are they Bops. You want to crawl through the wires after each other.

As you say when your night duty is over, you shall have your little vacation as we used to. But this one shall be a super one I know. You asked me if I was having fun and you know I'm not. I have so much time on my hands right now Bops, that all I have to do is just think and think all day and you know how bad that is for us. And you said that I sounded unhappy—well Bops, each time I hear your voice over the phone, so many things happen inside of me that I'm sort of speechless. I guess we both need this meeting badly and it shall all be so wonderful being to-gether again. I too am excited and waiting and it won't be too long now, baby.

Take it easy on your night duty, Miss Boo and it will soon be over. Just think what you have to look forward to. Thank God it's only 2 weeks and not a month.

I'm going to see a heavyweight fight to-night in Jaxonville with a friend of mine down here. I've been sort of paling around with this doctor. He just came back from Alaska and we've sort of hit it off. Bet you wish you could see the fight with me don't you, like old times—remember the old Panama Boxing Bouts.—Old Bops would sit down there and get splashed with water.

Easy does it Miss Boo and don't you think it was silly of you to ask if I loved you?

'Cause I do love you,
Mr Bops

Hi Sweet Thing,

Keeping my Saturday night date with you OK? It's sorta by remote control but that's alright, cause we're sort of miracle people any way.

It's so blasted hot & sticky to-night, keep wondering if I'm back in Panama. We have had too much rain & a couple of bad storms yesterday & to-day. Am trying to keep cool by few clothes & a Coke & was reading Omnibook* until now. Spect you went to the Officer's Club to-night. I try to picture you everywhere in your activities. Darling have a good time for me & be happy.

Last night I made complete rounds with the supervisor to learn the ropes. Whee!! My poor feet. Hope to heavens I don't walk off those precious pounds I've been saving to show you. Have 32 wards to cover twice during the night. It ought to keep me awake hadn't it?

Darling my reservations are made. Isn't that good. Now keep your fingers crossed for me to be able to use them.

My little cadets are so cute. They pile in here with lots of questions. They are really pretty. Think they were picked for their looks. Watch the soldiers whistle now, we anticipate a little difficulty. Most of them went to the Club to-night & were so excited.

Hope you play golf tomorrow & go to Del & Frank's. I'm so terriably happy darling that they are so fond of my Edward.

Not much news—but just had to talk to my darling. Good-nite dear heart. I love you.

Miss Boo.

Little Mr Bops says hello—he's such a good reliable pal—never grumbles.

---

*   Magazine

19 June 1944

Dear "Rock of Gibraltar",

That's what you are darling, just an old rock of Gibraltar—steady and true—dependable—you sure put me in line when things start getting out of hand. It was heartless of me to sound so unhappy over the phone darling, but you know how it is once in a while. I've just made a solemn vow to stop thinking and everything until we meet again and then with you beside me it won't be anything but heaven. The part of your letter about my possibly not wanting you to come down was really something. If you don't come down I'll really be fit to be tied. So we'll just count the days until 'Der Tag'.

I'm enclosing the picture again you sent and Bops, it doesn't do you justice at all. You look so thin darling, but maybe it's just the way you have your hair. Bops, bops, you old rascal. I know just what will put weight on you and me both but I think there's some sort of rule against it right now. Hah! Hah! You rascal, what was that dream you had about me? Was it good and yummy? What happened Bops, did I hold you real tight and scruntch yah? That's be nothing to what'll happen to you when I get my hands on you again and it'll be no dream. Spank my hand!

Another thing, you old Gunboat, you—the way to spell terrible is T-E-R-R-I-B-L-E not terriable as you often have. I laugh like hell every time I see you spell it wrong. So remember.

My radio works swell—remember the old Portable. Well, some gal just sang 'For me and my Gal' over the radio and I harmonized it with her—pretty good but not like that old thing used to sing it. Come to think of it—you were some Prima Donna. You sang just when you felt like it and that's all. Remember the night we sang over the Mike at the Club. I didn't and you did but after all I always was a push-over for doing what Bops wanted. Come to think of it Bops, we sure were a happy couple of things, weren't we, baby? I just sit around and think of those happy days, when we were well off and didn't know it. How'd you like to go back again Bops, just like before and then we could forget to come back home. Day dreams!

Bops, I've always wanted to write some stories and perhaps now with a little time on my hands I may sit down and try to write some. Do you think I could? I might try anyway. At least I have a typewriter. Who knows I may be another Best-Seller!

Terrible how things have to be sometimes but who knows what life holds in store for us. Perhaps there is lots of sunshine just around the corner. I don't know. Guess the best way to be is like the obstetrician, 'Watchful waiting'.

I think that I love you a little too, baby, and please don't think me forward or fresh when I say, please have more and more dreams—aren't they wonderful sometimes?

Your Mr Bops

Good morning my sweet thing

The long old night is about over for me and I suppose the all too short one for you. Just finished my reports and stuff and it is 5:30. Have been trying all night to get a note off to you, but things and stuff have kept me busy.

How are you my darling, any busier (can't find a question mark on this machine). Are you going to get some of that fat back before Bops comes to squeeze you. You know something baby, I bet we both will gain after we see each other, on account of happiness makes you fat they say. We are the craziest guys, nothing seems to agree with us. Each night before I come to work I mark another day off of the calendar, it's such fun to have something so wonderful to look forward to. Yes darling those telephone calls are just teasers, but I sure like to be teased, it's so wonderful to hear my old Bopsy's sweet voice. Guess I forgot to tell you dear that I didn't have to move after all, and they kept me in with the cadets. There are two of us there and am so glad, cause those girls are good for me, so young and full of pep that they keep my chin up. So my telephone number is 1215 as before. Darling you ought to save your money, you spend so much on this old thing. Think it was cheaper for you when you had to take me to the movie every night huh. Anyway I liked it so much better, yummy.

One of the Drs. and his wife invited me down to their place Sunday eve, another couple was there too, and guess what Bops they played poker and wanted me to play too, what a laugh they got and what a razing they gave me, cause I said I had never played, only kibitzed, and then to hear me say I kept a kicker and that I tried to draw an inside straight. Honey they wouldn't believe me, anyway I won 30 cents, and it was fun. We had a nice eve, with lunch.

It has been terriably cold up here the past few days last night it was 45 and I nearly froze my fanny off, think I'll have to come south (and not only cause of the weather.)

Darling there isn't much news, but night duty isn't half bad, especially with this job, so much walking and making out reports, and being by the admitting office that I really don't get a bit sleepy. It's also kinda nice to have a typewriter at hand, it goes faster, but it has been so long since I have used one that I have almost forgotten how.

Time for me to go now to get some sleepy time. I love you darling,

Your Miss Boo

My darling,

How's my baby to-day? No letter from Bops in two days but I guess the old night duty is taking up your time. I'll never forget your love for night duty. Remember the days my old baby would come to the quarters and sleep in Bops bed? And I'd come home and wake you up. Yummy—Old Bops would grunt and bury her head in the sheets and then look up and say, "What time is it, Bops?" Sweet memories, aren't they?

I just heard that Aaron landed in New Guinea and I sure feel sorry for the poor kid but that's the way things go these days—we just never know from day to day. When I hear from him and his new address I'll send it to you Bops so you can write him a letter. He's my best friend Bops and after his having written to you I'm sure he'd like to hear from his best friend's Baby. I've made up my mind that he's going to open up his office in Poughkeepsie when the war is over. I know he wants to and I'm selfish enough to want him there with me. I dread thinking of opening up home Bops if things are the way they are now. I'm afraid I'd just die if I have to go back feeling as I do now. I know I'll be quite successful but the idea of practicing medicine without you by my side, picking and barking, at me is just too much. I know I need you darling and perhaps God in his way will show us a way in the months to come. But, that's something else we will have to talk about. I'm trying to just keep myself in a state of suspended thought. I'm trying not to think, plan or anything until I see you again, and you do the same thing. Just let the next 3 weeks go by and soon we'll be together again. Right?

This afternoon this Doctor McCrudden and myself are driving over to St. Augustine and look at a bungalow to rent. Mac's just back from Alaska and we've sort of hit it off together. Just staying around the post here day after day is terrible and we thought that if we had a place for week-ends it would break up the monotony. It's a 6 room bungalow, right on the beach and all they want is $65 a month so perhaps in a day or so I'll have me a house to go to at week-ends with the boys. How does it sound to you?

Bops, do you remember me telling you about the little colored girl I had as a patient in Medical Center—the one who throughout all these years still says I'm her best boy-friend. She's the kid with *fragilium ossium*—brittle bones—. Well, she just sent me a card telling me she graduated grade school in the hospital school and that the only thing missing was me. Wasn't that cute? I went down to the PX and sent her a string of cultured pearls. I hope she likes them. She's so cute!

The way the news is going Bops, this damn war may be over before long but it'll probably be quite a while before we all get home. Oh yes, Bops—did you see Bing Crosby in 'Going My Way'? If you haven't make sure you do because I think it was wonderful. The old priest sure does steal the show and Bing Crosby reminded me so much of Father Laws that it wasn't even funny! Be sure you see it!

I've sure been jabbering haven't I baby? But, it's what I like best to do. I sent you some flowers yesterday and I hope you get them. Let me know, will you sweetheart?

Vincent Lopez just came in over the radio—remember how we used to hear him 12:30 from San Francisco once in a while?

Take it easy darling, soon the nights will be over and then—us again!

I love you,
Mr Bops

23 June, 1944
Thur Eve 9:30

My dear darling

    I'm so patiently waiting for that telephone to ring. Golly I'm afraid you can't get through, & darling I have been looking forward to our talk so much. They can't do this to us. Have been chewing my nails all evening. Could hardly settle down to do anything—but tried to keep busy & not get too excited & not be able to talk. Won't give up yet. The evening is still young.

    Baby dear—you sweetheart—how can we both love each other more than we do & yet I think it grows stronger as the days go by. If anything happens to my leave it will be terriable. Can hardly wait for our days to-gether. Won't it be fun darling—will probably act like kids with a lollypop. Old Jacksonville & Camp Blanding will really learn a lesson about happiness won't they. Bopsy, it all seems like a wonderful dream & we're waiting for it to come true.

    Speaking of dreams Bops—this morning we were having such fun & were so happy that I overslept cause I had to see what happened next. Just turned over & flicked the alarm off so unconcerned. Remind me to tell you what it was about when we are talking in person. Honest darling it was so vivid & real couldn't believe it wasn't true when I finally got up.

    Nothing more on my leave except it is pretty sure to go through—have been assured by several 1st Lts. Made my reservations & will find out about that to-morrow. Monday nite darling I go on nite duty as supervisor. Will be off July 3rd & then just 7 more days if all goes well—I'll be on my way. Am rather glad for the nite duty, it will seem like old times when my baby always had something special planned when I got off—& this time it's extra super special isn't it?

    The Sat. nite Club parties sound beautiful dear—just tell the gals to be careful of my private property. Did you really & truly miss old Miss Boo dear?

    Will have a few hours in Chicago on my way down so will get a new formal just for Bopsy. What color shall it be darling—it's for you—so there.

    One of the girls just stopped in for a chat & it's now 10:30—so I guess my Bops isn't going to call. Have to make rounds in the Hosp to-morrow nite from 7 to 10 with the other supervisor so hope you call Sat or Sun nite dear.

    Be good darling—Bopsy loves you more & more.

Good nite dear heart
Your Miss Boo

Good morning darling,

Well that's another one to mark off my calendar, was quite busy so the night really flew. Am getting a bit sleepy about now, but you should see this old thing sleep during the day, right straight through till 4 p.m. There isn't anything to get up for like there used to be darling, remember when I would run to Bopsy's house and wait for him to come home.

Ha, Ha, so I got scolded or being a poor speller, aren't I a bad girl though, guess you aren't the first person to tell me that, just negligent and don't think. Oh well I'll do better and that's a promise, even iffen I gotta go buy a dictionary. As long as it came from Bops it's alright this time, honest.

What's new down your way baby dear, bet you are just counting the days like I am for July 10th, it seems ages away, but then I'm scared it will go too fast after it does get here. Darling we are going to have such a wonderful time, and you couldn't possibly keep me away even if you had said, yes it will make me more dissatisfied, so there. You still haven't told me what color formal I'm supposed to buy, remember I think my Bops should be a stylist and has wonderful taste and that's why I ask. Didja know Mr Bops what a scrumptious old thing you are. (still can't find that question mark on this machine)

Can't tell you the dream darling, but it was yummy and anyway my dreams are full of you, guess I just think about my Bops so much that my head is full of movie reels, they are awful good though, sometimes get a little mixed up like all dreams.

Bops why don't you try to write a story, I've asked you to before, or rather encouraged you cause I know you could do a million times better than some of these so-called novelists. Do you know that I still read my poem every once in awhile because it is so beautiful, remember how the tears came to my eyes the day you gave it to me. Such a gal, she's a problem huh Bops.

Darling let's go back to some place like we were, just not Panama though, no we didn't realize how we would want those days back, in a way we did, but we needed to come home for a visit. We were so terribly (spelling corrected from terriably) happy though dear heart. Yes I dream too but can't help it, just like you.

Am awful stupid on night duty dear, nothing to tell you of interest except I love you very much and you probably grow weary of my repetition. How are Del and Frank and have you been in lately.

Must give you some good big smacks now dear and get ready for my bedtime, always my greatest love

Your Miss Boo

My darling

Bopsy, Bopsy, you dear thoughtful baby. What a beautiful surprise to be awakened for. Red roses are my very favorite & it made me so happy dear, almost wept. I kissed each bud which I put them in the vase knowing that is what you meant in sending them. Yes, darling I know you're waiting & old Bops is about to bust from anxiety. Thank you dear so awfully much.

Your letter to-day was so good darling. I eat them up anyway & read & re-read each one. My poor darling has such worries because of this old nuisance, doesn't he? Just don't you fret too much dear, everything's going to be alright I just know it is, be patient & keep praying.

Glad you heard from Aaron, I would like to write him dear, after his nice letter to me, so send the address—poor fellow though. Hate it that he had to go to the South Pacific.

About the house dear. You know I want you to do anything that makes you happiest. If it will help you to relax & get you away from the old camp—then please do it. Am so glad you have found some nice friends dear.

Yes I remember the little colored girl—how nice of you to help brighten the one big moment in her poor miserable life. She was probably thrilled to pieces with the gift. That old Bops of mine thinks of everything.

Funny thing Edward. I thought I had written in one of my letters to you to be sure to see "Going My Way." It impressed me the way it did you—even to the similarity of Bing to Father Laws. Enjoyed it immensely. By the way have you heard from Father Laws of late?

It's beginning to get light out. A very quiet night for Sat. The only thing exciting is one of our pts. is AWOL. We only admitted 4 pts to-nite. It seems the Hosp. is being cut way down. I heard 850 beds instead of 1800. That means a lot of changes in the next few months. Wonder what will happen to Bops. Am so darned scared I'll be shipped to an overseas unit—since there are an awful snag of them being formed. Jeepers darling it bothers me. Sure don't want to go, really I don't.

Just think dear baby only 15 more days to wait—golly will time ever pass. Got a special corner in a pair of big strong arms that I want to cuddle in—so there.

Must write my night report & seal this with all my love.

My flowers made my whole day complete darling & I love you.

Your Miss Boo

Monday night

Hi dear Baby—

No letter from my love to-day. Bopsy we are such spoiled old things. Resolutions just don't hold in our family do they? Keep wondering what my old darling is doing from day to day beside chewing his nails. Are you still on the same job with all that free time? How I hope no changes are made in the next few weeks.

Had a letter from Del to-day. She said you hadn't been in for a week. Gas shortage? Darling are you going to be able to have enough when I come or will we have to use bicycles? What did you decide about the house?

We had some excitement last night. One of the patients on psycho cut his wrist at 5 a.m. It's rather wild up in that section to-night. So hope nothing else happens.

What an old sleepyhead I was to-day. Didn't flicker an eyelash till 4:30. It was cool & nice sleeping. Yes darling I used to sleep awful well in Bopsy's bunk. What heaven we had those days dear, & such good kids we were. Just no one like us is there baby?

Honest, there is nothing to write dear. I'm fine. Gained two pounds on nights so far in spite of all my walking. Need a few more, but it seems impossible. Are you gaining my sweet thing?

Yummy, yummy soon darling—each day seems a century. Will let you know immediately when my orders arrive.

I love you dear—Bops

28 June 1944

Dear Miss Boo,

Glad you liked the flowers baby—but I enjoyed sending them just as much as you did getting them, so there!

I didn't write you but Dad was down to see me for the past 5 days and I just put him on the train for home. We had a very nice visit Bops and he's sure a great guy. The real reason he came down was because of me and how I'm getting along. My letters home have been anything but happy ones and they figure I'm still brooding about us and I guess I was so he came down to talk to me. Nothing has changed as far as he is concerned Bops and we talked and he still feels the same way about things, so there's not much to say except I'll tell you all about it when you get here. They know I still write you Bops and feel that as long as I do we shall keep this flame going forever. But, you know what all the arguments are and I'm not even thinking of a single thing until you get here and we have our wonderful time. As you said in your last letter, I'm not going to fret but just sit tight until I see you again. I just can't fret anymore because I'm outfretted. Hah! Hah!

I also hope that they don't send you on foreign service again, baby, but I may go too so there's nothing we can do about it except wait and see. Jeepers, supposed we got sent to the same outfit again. WOW ! WOW!

I know that as soon as your 6 months are up you'll be a 1st Lt. so keep punching. You must be the finest and best nurse there and they can't keep you down.

I'm still on the same job but who cares anyway. It can't last forever and the way the war is going perhaps it won't be too long and shorter than we think.

Be a good girl, be happy, don't fret, I love you—

"El Senor Bops"

Wed p.m.

My dear darling

Just finished my blfdinnersupper, so will spend my free hour with my old sweetmeat. Your letter was waiting for me when I awakened this afternoon, it was so good baby. Get so anxious when the days go by & no letter. Aren't I a bad old thing & so spoiled?

Well darling the days are slipping by, still no definite information but we have our fingers crossed haven't we. Just two more nights & that graveyard shift will be finished. It cooled off a lot to-day & was wonderful sleeping. Had good dreams too dear.

Bopsy I'm so glad you rented the little house, but I betcha that sweet thing wasn't thinking only of his relaxation on week-ends. Just know you were thinking a little of your old Bops & wanted some extra special place for her when she came. Isn't that right? Darling I can read your every thought & more so well, just because we love each other so much. It will be such great fun dear & I'm so anxious.

My poor baby is melting away with the heat huh? Know how hard it is on you dear, so hope it cools off some. How's the forehead dear—sunburned?

We had a German P.W. in last night for possible app. Bops you've never seen such a build on anyone. A regular Hercules—all muscle. One of Hitler's health program subjects. It really made me sort of sick inside to see a fine looking boy who had been raised for gun fodder & to know nothing but killing. Lots of interesting things take place round here.

Tell Mac to take good care of my Bops till the old "barker" comes. Baby do I really bark & fuss awful much. Well it's just cause I love my old sweet baby isn't it?

My calendar is getting more & more black marks on the dates—oh Bopsy I'm so jittery—chills & fever & everything run through me when I stop to think. Awful fraid I won't want to come back here. Then what'll you do with this gal?

Love you trillions of bushels dear heart. Be a good baby.

Your very own
Miss Boo

JULY, 1944

2 July 1944

My dear darling,

 Well sweet thing the old night duty term is over & there are now nine long days till your old nuisance will be on her way to you. Know the time will be endless.

 So your daddy came to visit you dear, how nice. Know you had a pleasant time. Did it help you to talk to him again? It made my heart ache pretty bad to hear his reactions. Had hoped after the test of five months he might change. Oh well darling it's nothing more than we expected, that is we thought it would be hard but would straighten out. We have gone through so much for our love & it makes you wonder which way to turn next.

 Any way darling I still want to come to be with you & in your arms, cause all our worries & cares will disappear for a few days won't they? From then on dear we'll let what's going to happen, happen. We both have promised each other not to fret any more until we talk it all over, so I'll be your good soldier.

 Bopsy do you really think there is a chance of your being sent overseas. Am sure if you went I'd sign up right away. Couldn't think of staying here with you over there besides it's most unbearable even now.

 If you were here tonight darling we would have a Sat. night date. Yummy. Instead I'll have to crawl into my little bed and dream of us.

 Let's try to see Father Laws darling. Am sure he would make an effort too.

 There isn't much news dear—except I'm lonesome & that isn't news. Good night dear baby, I love you.

Your Bops

Tues. 4th July 1944

My darling,

    Well old sweet thing. I have my orders in hand & now we can talk with more confidence. Isn't it super baby. I've really held my breath & now am so excited can hardly write. Even have my bag 2/3 packed & it's only Tues.

    Guess I'd better give you a few of the details now but will wire later & write Friday. Will leave Camp Sun. night—arrive in Chicago at 6:30 a.m. Mon. & can't leave there until 2 p.m. Mon. Will spend some of those hours shopping—may meet Mona for lunch (she is the girl who returned from Africa.) I am coming on the Dixie Line & arrive Tues eve about 10. As I say I will wire exact time from Chicago. Oh darling is it really so or a dream? Am sure you'll have to pinch me when we meet—so I'll know it's true.

    Have to be back to work the 22ⁿᵈ but will make my reservation in Chicago before leaving there. Still am not accustomed to doing so much myself cause I've had my old Bops to depend on for so long. Darling our parting is worse than any divorce could ever be isn't it?

    Today was the 4ᵗʰ but celebrated all by myself—living in the clouds waiting for Sunday. Worked this afternoon—it was like any other day.

    Called Mother last night. They are so happy for us & are certainly unselfish about my taking a leave with the one I love instead of coming home. They wanted me to say hello & wish us both heaps of fun.

    Have so much to tell you darling & five whole months of T.L.C. to catch up on. Will try to be patient until Sun, but I'm like a fly on a hot skillet.

    Be a good baby & remember I love you now, always & forever.

Your Bops.

Thursday

My dear darling

    Well sweet thing your badly disrumpled girl has arrived home again, the most unhappy creature in the world. Darling that trip was awful awful—too much time to ponder & think & besides that the horrible mistakes the agent made & causing me to leave one day early. I was wild when I found out. Wanted to get off & run back. Wanted to cry my eyes out yet what was there to do but go on.

    Arrived in Chi. at 4 yesterday. Tried to eat. Went to a movie & couldn't see it as my heart was aching so with lonesomeness. Got in camp at 4 this a.m. Only one advantage to coming early—it gave me a day of rest. Go to the office in the a.m. Horrors.

    Darling you were so wonderful to me. Nothing seems too good in your eyes for Gretchen—my bond, the flowers, dinner & most of all your love. That is so priceless dear heart. We were happy & unhappy—the latter because we want do to be to-gether, to have our family & be secure & yet the same old problem. Our days to-gether were heaven though dear heart because of our love for each other. It's so wrong that they must be stifled for awhile.

    Edward dear I must urge you to fight for our future. Try not to think of the awful thing that will happen. Please hurry as fast as you can dear—I need you so.

    Baby I can't help but be a little angry at the awful pounding you are taking. It's so wrong. I want you to be kind & considerate & I'll wait that period as I promised, but darling above all don't be wishy washy. Once more put your cards on the table even though it hurts. It seems it must be your family or me at least for awhile—but sweet darling they will have to stand what you have. I can't let them beat you darling—it's like killing me—for you are the only one I'm concerned about. Just keep remembering that because of this I shall not be bitter toward your family. I so want to love & cherish them with you. Please let me write them soon.

    Darling our evenings together were so perfect. We are such good kids—if your family only knew.

    Be brave darling heart. I love you so much & please let me thank you sweetheart for all you have done. Such a priceless darling. Do you wonder why I hang on like grim death?

    Called home this noon. All is fine. Send their love here.

Darling when I left you at that station it was even worse than Panama believe me. All I could do to be brave. You looked so forlorn & lost. Poor baby.

Talked to Chaplain Schwartz. He has a copy of that letter & will mail it direct. His initial is "W." He was perturbed because you had never received it & said it should make you angry because your mail hadn't reached you for no apparent reason. And so it goes darling. How do we stand so much.

It's cold here dear. Wore my winter suit this a.m. Wish I had my baby to snuggle to. How wonderful our dreams are dear.

Am staying right at home—resting—eating & trying to be brave. Darling there is no one in the world but you. So please be brave & keep fighting. Don't forget to say your prayers & have courage.

I love you dear heart
Your lonesome baby

Fri. Eve

My dear darling

Oh sweetheart how wonderful it was to hear your voice. It completely vanished that awful empty lost feeling in the pit of my stomach & took away the awful taste of that dreadful lonesome trip back. It's amazing darling what we do to each other. Just to hear each other or to be to-gether, our letters, wires, and everything. My Bopsy you are what makes my heart keep going from day to day. I love you so.

Baby please forgive that blue letter yesterday. I was so completely bewildered & lost—felt like an animated cartoon, no feelings, no emotions—just moved automatically. That's why I had to call you to-night. Couldn't wait to make plans & wait for an answer. It will be easier now to keep the chin up—for it was so hard to see you stand there forlorn & choking tears back. Old baby me had to bubble over—just couldn't help it darling, it tore my heart out to leave you there.

Darling I'm waiting & please don't worry about my becoming impatient, for I promise not to. Knowing how deep & wonderful our love is, how we talked & planned about our home & family. It was heaven baby even though we had to be a little sad, it proves our devotion doesn't it.

The office is so strange dear, like a new world. Am a good secretary but my typing needs brushing up & plenty. Will not have much contact with the girls dear, but have lots of friends & I won't deceive them. Now another group that is alerted are begging me to go with them. Isn't it odd dear. Girls have never made a fuss over me before. Maybe our love is making me more tolerant & understanding.

I told you about Tollefson one of my friends here. Last week she married her Dr. He is Jewish & his family had a fit but he said they would get over it. He couldn't go on without Tolley. She is so happy, relaxed & says she feels like a new person. So see baby we aren't the only ones with problems.

Imagine Bops it was 48 here this morning. I shivered my head off. Yesterday it was cold all day. How has the heat been down there? My poor baby almost melted & ran away Monday night didn't he? What two old happy things we were building our castle & getting all our smacks. Yummy.

Must write to Del. They were awfully nice to us dear, but guess you know that I felt uncomfortable. It's odd, because Del has always meant so much to me. She really seems different now. Perhaps her home & family & contentment has changed her.

Darling my first Coronet* came today. Know I will enjoy them. Bopsy you think of this old thing every minute don't you? Every time I pick something up it reminds me of you—seems you've given me all I own. Darling I'm so proud to wear your bracelet. Have had lots of questions asked but no answers—ha.

Keep up your courage darling & remember we have a whole lifetime of happiness ahead. I have such faith. Pray darling—pray—pray.

Good-night darling heart.
Your baby.

---

*   *Magazine*

My dear darling

One long long week ago to-night darling, we were in heaven, dancing under the stars holding each other so tightly for fear those moments would pass too quickly. Baby dear I was so proud & happy. Wearing my dress especially for my Bopsy & like a little peacock with my gorgeous orchid. To-night nothing but contentment fills my heart. Staying home when all the gals are out carousing. I'm really so much happier just dreaming & being true blue to my darling.

Your letter to-day was so beautiful dear, it was filled with real courage & hope. Darling we both grasp at the tiniest spark of relentment in any part of your family's letters. I do feel it's becoming a tiny bit easier & now that Martin is experiencing real true love he can't help but be a different person. Let's just hope awfully hard that his plans materialize this time.

Worked quite hard today. Typed my head off, but Edward I'm learning a lot about what makes the Army Nurse Corps tick. Am off in the morning again. Ann Dorsey & I pitched horseshoes on my hours today. Got some sunshine & exercise & felt good after being out. Really must try to get out sometime during the day. You should have seen me eat today baby. It would have done your heart good. That telephone call really straightened me out in a quick hurry. Wasn't it wonderful dear heart?

Such a busy bee as I was to-night. Went through all my possessions, sorting, packing & darling I re-read some of your letters. They are worth their weight in gold. So beautiful dear—full of joy, sorrow, despair & courage. You know sweetheart if we ever accomplish our happy end, it will really be written in sweat & tears. Bopsy Bopsy what courage & faith you have had—more & more it amazes me. Sometimes I wonder if I'm worth of such wonderful love. No girl in the world is as lucky or blessed with such a dear baby's love friendship & true devotion.

Darling to-day I wrote for my course in Interior Decoration. Must do as my baby says & study & progress.

Edward I am so anxious for you to join the Masons—it will be a great spiritual as well as moral help; and darling I know you will gain so much from the fellowship. We will have a nice insignia put on your ring after you've joined. It should be lovely.

Old scruntchy. Bops would adore some of those big luscious kisses. They always come from the bottom of your heart & go right to the bottom of my toes. We are awfully wonderful people aren't we dear?

Yes dear darling I'm praying too. God will listen if we really show Him that we have faith. There really is an answer for us & that silver lining is bound to show up. I'm being your good soldier because I trust in you so much dear.

Just cause I write often Bopsy, don't feel you must do the same, I know it's a strain & you have so much to do. Darling it completes my day just to say hello & send my smacks.

I love you my darling
Your baby

My darling,

Thanks so much darling for your calling me to-night. I know how lonesome you have been baby because I've been lonesome too—but you must believe me I really don't have those bitter moments like I used to have anymore, sweetheart. Since you've gone you have been so much closer to me sweetheart. I'm really getting back on the ball, eating better and feeling much better about a lot of things, and I want you to start getting back into the shape I once knew. Please Bopsy, don't worry darling, as you tell me not to worry. O.K?

Funny my letter wasn't there to meet you because I especially wrote it to be there when you got back but I suppose it was held up. I'm so happy that people were glad to see you back—as if anyone could help from wanting you back—I want you back too darling!

Nothing much new with the folks Bops. As I told you I'm going to wait awhile before I spring us again on Dad. He will continue to keep Mother in the dark of course as long as he can and I dread the day he has to tell her all over again but it has to come again, I know, perhaps they will see a little clearer this time. All I know Bops is that I love you darling, love you so much that I know I shall never be able to feel this way about anyone else. It isn't possible to love as strongly as we do again—I know that. But, as Father Laws says, time will tell so chin up, sweet-thing, and we'll see what our guardian angel has in store for us.

Darling, for my sake, you mustn't be unhappy or sad anymore. I know that we just can't take it as we have any longer and we must now just be grimly determined to get a hold of ourselves and start getting back to what we were. The next time I see you I want round, soft, shoulders or else I won't scrunch you, so there!

I've been asked to go down to the County Hospital to do some bronchoscopic work for them so you see they are beginning to see some good for the Old Man to do and maybe before long I'll get some recognition, I hope. I played golf to-day, Bops and had a 45. Not bad, after a 2 week lay-off.

Everyone asks for you especially Wally and Mac. I'm grateful for the two of them. They really look after me, good.

Be happy, don't fret, and you must know by this time that

I love you
Mr Bops

My dear darling

Your awfully sweet letter of the 20th came this morning. They are all great big tonics to me dear. It makes me ashamed to be such a baby Bops—but please rest your mind at ease, I really have a strong hold on determination to be a big girl from now on. Darling for you nothing is too hard to accomplish.

Don't like that threat about "no scrunching" darling—& I'm eating like a Trojan, sleeping oh so much better & my heart has stopped that awfully pounding lately especially on awakening. Darling to tell you the truth, a great calm has come over me; it seems our love for each other is a great foundation & we are even more sure now than ever before. I no longer have that panicky feeling that maybe Edward is sorry or discouraged, for I feel so strongly darling that just a little more time will find us together forever. Oh baby when I even think about that part it makes me all duck bumps—you too?

Am off this p.m. Going into Tomah with one of the girls. We are giving a little party for Tolley. Darling do you know her husband's mother is having hysterics too, won't eat & all that—can't believe that Mothers feel they get anyplace by being that way, when darling, it would be so much easier if they would try hard to be reconciled. Poor Tolly is going through what we did, but they are married. Bopsy I'm really so glad we waited & we are trying to make our peace first. It will be much easier, & baby dear I'm sure your mother will take it easier this time. Remember that they have told us that, "Time would erase many feelings," & certainly they can't expect to teach a lesson that they haven't learned themselves. So sweetheart don't dread this coming news to them too much. Am sure God will give you strength & wisdom & your mom & dad will too. Wish I could go home with you to meet them so they could see how much in love we really are.

Bopsy I am so proud of you. Remember how I told you they would soon find out what a wonderful Doctor my Bops was if you just were patient & did your work well.

Everything is turning our way, so slowly, but it definitely is. You see dear, God is showing us that we must have faith & determination & not be sissies & quit when the going is tough. It really shows what we are made of baby—& we are the tops. We old conceited things.

Went to the movie with one of the girls last night dear. Saw "Sensations of 1945"—entertaining—also saw one of those army shorts, #32. Very good—on the invasion.

Sweetheart how's the manicure I gave you while you dozed? How good it was to take care of my old sweet thing again. To see you relax & rest was such a comfort to me dear. If we have our own little home some day dear, the rooms will be filled with the sunshine of our contentment, won't they?

Mr Bops is fine dear. Ruth got such a kick out of keeping him. She said she loved him so hard he got his tummy dirty. Ruth is on night duty now—is sending for her car next week, so we probably will get around a little. She is a large very motherly person dear & really watches your Bops for you.

Darling I sent my bond home the other day. Am so very proud of it—& it was a wonderful birthday gift dear. Fear the 28th won't be anything this year. Just another day. Remember our glorious party in Panama last year—baby you are so good to me.

Will rest a little while & then go for a ride to Tomah. It's beautiful & cool out.

I love you darling,
Your own Miss Boo

Wednesday a.m.

My dear darling

 Your old Bops is all curled up under the little blue blanket on her bed, it's cool & rainy out, and ideal for writing her sweet thing while all is quiet.

 Having morning hours, then back to the steno's job at 2. I'll have that sitter's spread darling if this keeps up—but it is getting some easier—you know how uncomfortable new jobs are at first.

 Oh darling—a call on my birthday? How wonderful. Shall be sitting right by the telephone waiting. That will make my day complete and say there guy, if I want to spend my money to call—gee whiz can't I? Anyway what's mine is yours & what's yours is mine too—so there.

 Bops I've been trying to figure out all sorts of things to get some fat on my shoulders. Ha-ha—you have a ditty for developing to "The Farmer in the Dell,"—now professor put on the thinking cap (bad girl huh?) Anyway get weighed today & promise to report & as for you old skinny better grow out of those new trousers.

 Wasn't it hot bowling Bops? Your score sounds wonderful—suppose I could keep up? Expect to go bowling myself one of these eves, but have to find a girl that would enjoy it.

 Last eve I wrote & wrote letters, had too many to answer. To-night Tolley & I will see "Mr. Skeffington." Wish I could hold my Bopsys hand.

 Have you done that bronchoscopic work yet dear, & where is it being done? Don't be nervous & do a fine job darling.

 Think I promised you in my last letter that I wouldn't worry anymore. Baby dear, it's strange how confident I'm beginning to feel. Just don't hurry the barrage on the folks dear, give them plenty of time only don't sound too content in your letters—you rascal. It all has to turn out perfect dear & keep counting on me to be a good brave patient little gal.

 All my hugs & smacks are for my baby. God is taking good care of him for me cause I'm praying so hard for all of us.

 Don't forget to get your laughter back darling & remember I love you.

Your own
Miss Boo

My sweet old thing—

Received both of your letters to-day and you're not such a bad letter writer yourself. Old thing! I must admit that your spelling is improving all the time and I haven't found a mistake in any of your last three letters. Keep up the good work Bops.

Sorry to hear that Tolley is having her ups and downs right now but she should have expected it all along. It is a shame that people appear to lose their sense of balance and intelligence, especially when it's their children that suffer when they are that way. It accomplishes nothing but heartache and misery. The Deed is done, no matter how cruel it may appear to them so they should make the most of it. Parents fail to realize that they can make or break a marriage if they so desire. If they fear for their children's happiness why they don't go out of their way to make it a happy one and keep everyone content I don't know. They say you must be a parent to know how they feel but after all is said and done. Why, oh why, do they forget their youth and their desires. Beats me!

I received another letter from Martin today in which he states that he has definitely decided to let his gal know just how he feels about her and that he expects to propose something or other within the month. His letter is quite nice although he seems to have forgotten all about me and how I feel in his moment of having found love. I hope that now that he has a girl he will change his tune a little about things. His letters are really something to behold, Bops. He continues to tell me what a great guy I am and how much he loves me and then he goes right around and does nothing to help me. But, I'm not worried too much about it all. I will of course do nothing to spoil his plans, etc. I don't intend to let him get worried about me at all at the present time but will wait for the right moment. Wally and I finished writing a joint letter to Dad yesterday and it's really a pip. We are saving it until we think the moment ripe and then Wally will send it in his name. If there is no response to that letter then I will have been convinced that my family is made of steel. However, we must be patient darling, we've waited so long and I think God wants it this way for the time being. I pray each night and all I know is that God can't possibly let a love such as this go by the boards. If he does, I won't know just what to think!

I'm so happy that a serene calm has taken over in your heart. After all Bops, it took our reunion to bring it about and I feel the same way. Gone is that terrifying feeling and it has been replaced by a resignation to take whatever comes for us. It's the only sensible way to be and thank God we both have found it out. Perhaps Dad and Mother will recognize the inevitable one fine day and see the light.

I enjoyed the poem you sent. Bops it was really nice and hit the spot. I don't think there is a Mother in the world who doesn't resent a daughter-in-law at first. Why they suspect them all of ulterior motives I don't know but I can understand how they feel all-right. I'd probably be very wary of anyone who wanted to marry a child of mine and would want to make sure that they are the best.

I bowled again last night and knocked off a 225 so I'm getting plenty good. In spite of my starting to do some work at the hospital in Jax, the Old Man (Col. Callard) decided I was setting a bad precedent in doing civilian work and made me stop. However, I don't give a damn anymore. I'll just sit on my big, obese Tochas, and let them do what they want. Mac and I had a real gripe session last night that Tom Swift could have taken lessons from us but it made us feel good, so what the hell!

When I get started there is just no stopping me is there Bops? I just sort of go on and on. But it's fun to be able to sit down and write just what you damn please. Isn't it? To-night Mac, Wally and I are going to drive down to Lee Field (Naval Air Base) and get us a couple of bottles of booze. We know a bunch of fellows down there and they are a hell of a swell bunch. We can't have any fun around here. We go down there and play the piano, sing, jump around, I can sing all my dirty songs, no women around and all have a good time.

Yes Bops, you sure were a pretty little thing Saturday night with your pretty flower. All dressed up like an old sweet thing, weren't you?

By the time you get this letter we will have talked with each other so all I can say is that it was swell talking with you Baby and I love every dollar of it. Hah! Hah! With all your bonds, you're getting to be a regular old money bags. I'll probably have to borrow some money from you one of these days, but I'm not spending a damn cent. I realize now what an expensive old thing you were down there in Panama. Not really expensive though considering that moments of delight, happiness and wonder cannot be bought. But you know how I feel about money, don't you? I wish I had all the money in the world so I could just give it away to people who need things and appreciate what money is really for.

I'm just jabbering along a mile a minute, aren't I?

Work hard at your interior decorating course Bops because it may come in handy some day. May God in his wisdom let us have that home so you may plan it all yourself—with suggestions from me of course!

'Nuff said. Keep eating and when you get to 115 pounds I'll let you talk to me again over the phone.

There's something I seem to have overlooked for the moment but whatever it is I know there's nothing you'd rather hear than

I love you,
Mr Bops

My dear darling

What a gorgeous day it is, cool, yet sunny & bright—more like spring than mid-summer. One of the girls & I just returned from a long walk. My face feels a wee bit stiff. Must have gotten a little sun. Have found a new friend dear. She is attached to the Hosp so will stay awhile perhaps.

Last night a couple of the cadets came in & spent the eve. Got all my pictures out and it was fun to see their enthusiasm. We gabbed for hours. Did write a few letters too. One to Wally, do you mind?

Darling your 1½ page letter was super. Yes dear, it is fun just to sit down & write. That's why my letters are so long-winded. Have to tell you all the little things that aren't important to anyone but us.

Oh Bops you're way out of my bowling class now. I'd surely get skunked, but good. How happy it makes me dear to know at last you are laughing and happy again. Glad there is a good bunch of fellows for you to go with. After all darling, feeling the way you & I do about dating, we are so much better off keeping company with our own sex. The only thing I don't want is for my Bops to become depressed & lonesome.

Darling I don't know whether you will approve of my serious thoughts of the past week, but this is it and I want you to answer me frankly. Have been wondering dear if I went ahead & took my instructions in Judaism now, if when the time comes for you to approach the family again, it would make it easier. Now would be an ideal time, while I'm here & know the Chaplain and all. The only thing that makes me hesitate is the fact that I wouldn't want them to think it's a scheme, believe me darling, all in my heart is the thought that perhaps it would be easier for you. Have laid awake nights wondering & looking at it from all angles, & now baby dear I need your help. You see dear, it's definitely my Bops or no one & what ever I can do dear is no sacrifice, but a wonderful happiness to do for the person I love so deeply. One time they say, faith mountain & now I say, faith will bring us together. So see darling I'm bound that neither of us shall go down in defeat.

Don't think dear that I'm brooding cause I'm not, things are much more clear since we saw each other & now it's our future to think about. Something keeps telling me that all will be well.

Bops my 1st lesson came of my course, it looks very interesting—imagine planning our home—that's food for thought. This sort of a course has always been my ambition, rather a hobby & in taking it, felt that it would take up long hours of idleness & give me much pleasure. Of course darling there would always be your suggestions, that's why our life together would be so perfect, neither of us has a selfish hair & always thinks of the other. I get duck bumps, do you?

Guess I'll go to the 6 o'clock movie. Will have to hunt someone to go. How I miss my old sweet thing who was always ready to do anything. Those happy days will be recaptured though dear—just keep praying.

(Bubble, bubble) I love you, dear heart. Be happy & get fat.

Your own
Miss Boo

One and thirty years ago you saw the light of day,
I didn't know what color eyes or how much you did weigh,
Don't know if you cried a lot or whether you were mean,
Cause I was only one year old and not yet on the scene.

I've known you now about three years and that's what makes me mad,
Because I miss the twenty-eight I know we should have had.
For all those years that we have missed, I know it's not to late
To find in love and happiness those missing twenty-eight.

Right now, my dear, the going's tough-the end is not in sight,
But for our love I shall go on and fight for what is right.
My daily prayer to God above is that soon you will be
Esconced in my dear Mother's arms to love as she does me.

And when God brings that day about, my family will know
Why I love you and you love me and why their hearts should glow-
For love like ours is endless and they will then realize
That with their own son's happiness there is no compromise.

Some day the folks will know you and will lift their arms in prayer
That God would deem it right some day for them to have an heir.
I pray that when you're thirty-two, I'll find you at my side
With Dad and Mom and Martin too, with happiness our guide.

AUGUST, 1944

August 1, 1944

Dear Gretchen,

Words cannot express how honored I felt on receiving your wonderful letter. It is I who is very proud to know a person as fine as yourself and to have your friendship and trust as well as Edward's.

Let me again assure you that you and Edward are not alone in this battle. Whatever I can do, no matter how infinite, to aid in your ultimate reunion, will be done. Ed is far from discouraged for he knows the path he is trodding, and though many miles separate you, you are always very close to him. Yes, he is very unselfish and grand, yet never underestimate your own wonderful unselfishness. For as true as there is a Lord above, so are your lives so entwined that never for a minute doubt what the ultimate end will be. It is simple to know that a love like yours and Edward's was meant for a lifetime, and not as a casual thing to be broken at anyone's desire.

I have never met so fine a man as Ed and I certainly do not blame you for fighting for that love. But I also have never met so wonderful a person as yourself, and Ed too is fighting for the most precious thing in his life—you.

Walk around with a light heart. Don't let that awful little word "if" torment you. Even before I met you, I felt that only one outcome could be the result and having had the wonderful pleasure of meeting you, no doubt or fear remains.

You can rest assured that little Wally will never let you down. We are inseparable and I promise that I will take the utmost care of him. Perhaps Ed told you that I went through a tough two year session before I could convince my mother-in-law that I was the man for her daughter. Naturally, circumstances were different, but the battle was rugged. I fought tooth and nail for the one I loved and can honestly say that today everyone is happy.

It is needless to tell you to have patience, because yours has been wonderful. Believe, and believe strongly, that God is watching over you. His heavenly hands are placed on yours and Ed's shoulders, ever drawing you closer to your richly deserved happiness.

I, too, am sorry that we could not have spent more time together, but when this war is over, I am confidently looking forward to visiting you and Edward in your home. I know that my wife will be crazy about you and we will have many happy times.

Gretchen, I can speak so much easier than I can write, so try to imagine how many more words I would say if I could only talk to you and reassure you of your wonderful future with Ed. Never have I seen two people so meant for each other.

Believe me when I tell you that these words are not written to qualm your fears temporarily. I write with all sincerity and feel certain that in a very short time your dream of happiness will be a glorious reality.

All goes well at camp, although we are still in the throes of organizing the program. With all the wonderful news about the war, perhaps it will not be in the distant future, that this war will be over.

The only thing that you can do to help, is to retain your patience and confidence. You must keep your health and not worry, because you will want to be the very lovely bride you will make.

Thank you again for honoring me with your lovely letter. I will be very grateful should I be honored again and if at any time you feel as though you must get something off your mind, remember that my shoulders are broad and my heart big and understanding.

Grateful for knowing so grand a person, your most ardent admirer closes with wishes for a speedy end to the war and the culmination of your dreams.

Ever sincerely,
Wally

My dear darling

So you have me cause I'm a *"gunboat"*—well all right Bops. To love me feet is a pretty big part of Gretch—so that's good. Thank you dear for the shoes & the sweet note. They must have come by dog sled though—just arrived yesterday.

Rather pokey about getting my letters off to my sweet thing. Yesterday was my half day & my intentions were good, but it was so beastly hot out here that I went in to see the Johnsons. Took a little cool dress along & just loafed all afternoon & eve. It was most enjoyable. Dorothy is a perfect hostess & makes one feel so at home. Got home rather late & transportation is a big problem.

Am working split hours to-day. The new nurses will be in about five & then my work begins. The dumb bunnies should know better than to take this career at this stage-but maybe they'll replace some of us who have had enuf—huh?

Just had a long talk with the chaplain. He was so pleased with your letter. Am sure his understanding of everything is better, although I had told him most everything. I discussed starting my instructions & according to some new rule among Army chaplains they aren't to do any converting—but he said if we said nothing he would instruct me anyway. Darling I so want to go ahead, but told you the final word is yours. Certainly dear it would not make any difference cause even if they still say no, we would be that much closer in our hearts. Then too dear if it takes 3 months it would be less time for us to wait in the end if God sees our love. There is also that chance that it might make a difference when time comes to tell your mother. Baby dear we have to venture some things & this is the only way I know. Darling the blood that runs through my veins can't change I suppose, but to change ideas & views is our privilege—that's why we are Americans, isn't it?

Did a little bowling the other night myself—only averaged 130 but it was fun. Can feel it in my pins a bit—old & stiff—gee whiz.

Wish I had my trip to look forward to again all over—now I can think of so many things to do for my baby.

Know it's time for another shampoo & manicure but golly you're so far away. Then too Bopsy needs a big scrunch & things doesn't he?

Was it fun doing some surgery again dear? I hate it so that your eye surgery is being neglected. Wish you felt like studying for Boards but know *it's too hot to concentrate. Bops would soak the old books & papers & be sittin in a puddle. Have you done anything more about becoming a Mason dear? Don't be slouchy now just cause I'm not there to hen peck-ha-*

Nothing much more except I'm terribly in love with that one Blanding Doctor. Isn't it wonderful to know dear that each of us has one special person to love & adore.

Be my good baby
Your own Miss Boo

4 August 1944

My dear sweet baby,

I also have been thinking of your conversion Bops, and I have given it serious thought. I also have looked at it from all the angles and the only one I have in mind is you and you alone. Your love for me, Bopsy, is something that I like to look at objectively. There are times when I just sit back and look at your love for me as I would at some sort of "wonder of the world." It's so hard to try and tell someone how you feel about someone unless you have felt the same way yourself. You've done so much for me Bops, your spirit and faith is splendid and should be shouted from all the housetops. I want you to be the same as me in spirit as well as in thought. But, we already have been as close as any two people can be in spirit and thought. We think alike Bops, react the same, in other words even without being married we have already learned to live for each other and to be as one. Some people never learn that in a lifetime of living to-gether. To be perfectly truthful Baby, there would be nothing I would like better than for you to start in your lessons. What greater token of love could anyone ask than for you to be as I am. My heart says, "Yes, darling, go ahead." My mind however, tells me that I haven't the right to tell you to go ahead until there isn't the slightest doubt in the world that we shall be married. In my heart, I feel that we must be married someday or else if it isn't marriage I know that I shall never give you up. I need you to talk to Bops and to love. I could no more stop loving you than I could stop breathing, Bopsy, and I know you need me too so with our faith and our love there must be only one answer. Before you go ahead I wish you would contact Rabbi Schwartz and ask him how long it takes and a few of the details if you can and let me know. I haven't said, "no," Bopsy to your question. The thought of my baby being just like me in the eyes of God and all Judaism is wonderful—not that we aren't already but it sort of makes it legal or something like that. For the time being, my darling, hold off a little longer, I think. We are gradually getting closer to the day when we launch our offensive and perhaps your already being started would help our plans.

You see Baby, the only thing I'm frightened of is that if you had started and something happened I don't know just what I'd do—although I can't conceive of anything happening that hasn't already happened.

I wrote a poem the other day Bops and I sent it into the Sat. Evening Post if they want to publish it—what do you think of it. The simple slab of stone is supposed to be the 10 Commandments in case you wonder about it.

I'm so happy you have found a friend Bops and that you are starting on your interior decorating. You'll be a regular Whiz Bang when you get through.

I love you darling, with all my heart and soul. I pray each night that we shall be to-gether—we are right and they are wrong—I pray for your health and well-being—I pray for the quick end of the war—I pray for my brother's early marriage—I pray for everyone Baby and I pray that God will grant me the power to make you and my parents happy because I know that I can and that all we need is a chance to prove it.

Don't fret darling about your age darling, because you're young and beautiful and you'll always be as long as

I love you,
Mr Bops

My darling,

Hi, Bops, you sweet, old, baby, you! How's it going this fine day?

I'm right up to snuff and feeling right chipper these days. I love you, you love me and what else really matters?

Before I go any further Bops, let me say that you have my complete permission to go ahead with your lessons from Rabbi Schwartz. I've been thinking of nothing else since writing you yesterday and I think you are right in that it will help us no end when the time comes. How you love me darling, and I thank God day after day for having been given your love and devotion. May God in his Wisdom show us the way and show my family that we are right. The Jewish religion is quite beautiful in its simplicity darling, and I'm sure you will have no trouble following it. You will learn of the heartaches and tribulations our people have gone through and it is no mean step to undertake upon yourself. Part of the conversion is to try and talk the person out of doing it and therefore show them that you want the religion and that the religion is not looking for you—do you follow me? Yes darling, go ahead, and when it is all over you shall be in the eyes of God just as me and my family. God Bless you, my darling, for everything you are doing to ease our burden and help us attain our final goal.

I heard from Martin to-day that he definitely made up his mind that he wants to marry this girl and he'd let me know the end of the week how he makes out. I pray that he too gets what he wants. In all the letters I have been getting from Dad and Martin lately they ask more and more how I am and that I've gotten over you. I omit the question completely and I've got them buffaloed about the whole thing. We'll bide our time darling until Martin is taken care of and then we'll see for ourselves.

I had a long letter from Aaron the other day and we went on at length to discuss you and me again and he's still on our side if we are both convinced that's what we want. I wrote him that I knew I wanted you, etc.

You didn't mention your weight Bops, in your letter. So I shall have to call you up Thursday about the same time as last time and find out so you be there, hear?

It's been raining here every day, worse than in Panama. Oh yes, I had a date with Lt. Col. Maley, our chief nurse, last night and we went to the

Club Saturday night dance. She's a little older than I am Bops and I felt a little funny, but she's a nice person and has a lot of drag with the powers to be here and there's no harm in knowing her well in case we may want a favor from her. I may want you down here one of these days, who knows, in case my St. Louis job falls through.

So until Thursday darling, take it easy, keep eating and getting those shoulders fixed up because there will come a day soon when I'll just have to throw my arms around you, kiss you, and then look in your eyes and say

I love you,
Mr Bops

60th Gen. Hospital
APO 211-c/o Pres.
San Francisco, Calif
27 July 1944

Dear Gretchen,

Thank you for your sweet letter which came in this morning's mail. By the time you receive this, I expect that your visit with Eddie will be over and that you will have returned with good spirit to McCoy.

I can only hope that your visit together has been good for both of you. Throughout these many months, I have been with both of you through the thick of your differences. War is strange—because all of us, so indiscriminately involved in something of such great magnitude, are impeded by long distances. The distance, however, does not—or should not—color the problem.

There is little I can tell either you or Eddie that both of you don't already know. I don't even know whether you or Eddie would want me to say any more than I have already said.

I couldn't feel closer to Eddie were he my own brother. Because of what you mean to him you share that closeness. There is nothing more that I could hope for but your own great happiness. But this is one problem that no one has the right to advise his fellow man about regardless of how close they are. You both know, as I know, how fundamentally important it is to both your lives that you resolve the situation. Both of you must have happiness and free yourselves of the torment that is now going on within you. You must, therefore, in justice to yourselves and to each other decide your course—whether it be in pleasant reflections of the happiness of the past or in a future positive course. Thank the Lord that both of you are mature and sensible enough not to let your emotions interfere with your good reason in realizing that the future happiness is based, not only upon your mutual love, but also upon those things that make Eddie, Eddie, and Gretchen, Gretchen.

I am now waiting for transportation from the Depot to my assignment at the 60th General—also "somewhere in New Guinea." I am looking forward to it—because of all the assignments this gives promise of the greatest professional opportunities.

My sincere regret, Gretchen, is that I haven't had the good fortune of knowing you personally, for I know how wonderful you are. I join you in prayer that this war will soon be over so that I can meet you.

Remember, only, Gretchen, whatever you or Eddie decide, don't lose sight of those things that created this mess for both of you. Chances are you will have to face it for a very long time.

Cordially,
Aaron

Monday Eve

My dear darling

Gee whiz what a gorgeous evening, cool & beautiful. Do you know what? If Mr Bops were here, he'd have to go for a walk. We would head for this big hill in back of my house & watch the moon come up. Yummy. Instead we'll have our little chat & then a little studying is waiting.

Darling your letter today was so perfect. How that Bops thinks of so many lovely things to say about & to his old gunboat is amazing. Only people in love can write letters of that kind & I betcha that's it dear, huh?

Well! At last someone wants my Edward for his ability. That's good dear, however, don't you feel it is his place to make the request? I do. Feel it would be a fine opportunity & hate your giving it up because of me. On the other hand time in the Army may as well be spent in one place as in another. Darling while you're at Blanding I feel so much better with Wally & Mac at your side & certainly feel it much to our advantage when the offensive is once more launched. You must have someone to help this next time & they are the ones to do it dear. Couldn't bear your struggling alone again among total strangers. Have him request me. Wouldn't that be a super spot for old Gretch?

Edward the poem is splendid, there is much food for thought & lots of sincerity & truth in those lines. I'm terribly proud that you sent it in.

Went into Sparta today & bought a few little gifts for my six pet cadets. They are all finishing training within the next two weeks. Will certainly miss those dear kids. Had to get my Baby a little something too. Saw & ordered it last week. Tomorrow I'll send it just cause I love you so.

Had a lovely letter from Aaron today most sincere & wishing us the best. He realizes we are not letting our emotions rule our hearts, but says even as close as he is to you dear, he would hesitate to advise anyone how to run their lives. Am most happy that he answered my letter, & he certainly must be a fine person.

Dear baby I realize how difficult it is for you to give a definite answer about my conversion. Never would I want you to feel it was your responsibility. The only thing I wanted to be sure of was that you wouldn't feel—& your family too—that Gretchen was a scheming vicious rascal. That is all that matters. Somehow dear heart to be that much closer to you regardless of end results would be the one final step I could do to show you how sincere & deep my love is. In my heart darling & even in my mind there is only one answer

& from that you must not feel you are indebted or responsible. It's only our love that counts, don't you see darling no one or nothing else matters except your happiness. This life of ours will never be spent apart in spirit & as the chaplain says a few miles between you & Edward is a small matter when neither of you are jealous & probably couldn't be together right now anyway. Edward dear I love you so it's only that knowledge of it being mutual that keeps my little world bright.

Work is going much better—getting smart maybe—typing is improving & all those dangling ropes are being spliced gradually. Wanted so to go home this month, but it looks a bit unlikely because of restrictions. You'll be so tired of my scribble—better quit for now & smack & smack & smack my sweet Bopsy goodnight.

Oh yes I saw Mr Skeffington. It was wonderful & so true.

Your own Miss Boo
Who loves you.
—It rhymes.

My darling—

That was an awfully lonesome sounding sugar report found in my mailbox this morning. Know your idleness is the cause of it. So wish they would give you some work. Don't be lonesome & blue dear heart please.

Had to be up at 5 this AM to do a little inspecting of the wac's ishy.* Whata life for those gals. Sure happy I'm not in that field. They are treated almost like enlisted men really, all the beauties of womanhood seem so far removed for them—poor kids. Have a little extra time today plus my half day consequently I'm off duty now at 11:00 AM. Nothing to do either. Have my lesson with the Chaplain to-nite at 7:00 really looking forward to it.

Yes, dear, I will fight any overseas assignment—it would be awful—another two years. Know if transfers of any type come through it won't be until Nov. 1st. Of course anything can happen anytime. Darling I too want to be out of the Army like so many others. Guess it's impossible under the present circumstances.

Bopsy dear will you do me an errand? I am enclosing a piece of notebook paper and need a notebook to fit it—a nice soft one. Can't find anything here. Will you look in Jax for me sometime? Don't make a special trip—also get some paper to go with it as I had to borrow this from one of the gals. Thank you, sweet thing.

Sorry about the poem, anyway we think it's good & that's what counts. Shall I send it & the other one (first one) you wrote to Good Housekeeping?

My sis said she wrote you. She has put it off for a long time but has wanted to write before. Darling they all want us to be to-gether so badly.

Anxiously waiting word about Martin. How I've prayed that all goes well. Wonder what their reaction will be about my conversion. Darling you aren't sorry I'm changing are you? Don't you really feel it will make it easier?

How is your mom these days—hope her health is improving. Would you like to go home to see them, would it help your fidgets?

Your arm filly is still 112. Another week or two & maybe it will be 113. The awfully hot weather reduced my appetite some.

We'll think up a good hobby some time baby dear-have lots of them in mind-ha-one is washing dishes for me.

I love you sweetheart.

Keep happy—
Your Miss Boo

---

*   *This* was a check to observe symptoms of syphilis and gonorrhea.

My dear darling—

The way this thermometer chases up & down-whee-ee roast one day, freeze the next. It's 62 this a.m. & I'm all curled up under my blue blanket, awfully lonesome cause my Bopsy isn't here.

Your Sat nite letter with Dick's arrived to-day, a day after Monday. That's the reason I hadn't received it. How I would love to have you get in on the ground floor of this project. Dick is a peach to keep your interest at heart. It sounds most encouraging, but we shall just keep the fingers crossed.

Last night was lesson night again. It is most interesting darling & I am terribly enthused. Chaplain was pleased about the amt. I had memorized. To be so happy inside dear is wonderful & know it is derived from the fact that soon we will be alike in the eyes of God. This is the last thing I can do sweetheart & it pleases me so to know that it came from my own heart not because you said, "Do this if you love me or because I love you." Keep faith my dear darling remember we are practicing one of the fundamentals of Judaism in living our lives here on earth as we want it & not being discouraged & saying, "Oh well, there will be something better for us in the next."

Darling I wish you weren't so far away cause I want to see my sweet thing so very much. How I wish you could be here the day my final lesson is finished. It should be finished about on your birthday. To have you at my side the day I'm confirmed would be the most glorious present imaginable. There I go again-day dreaming.

The old days are so long. I just know how restless you get, but whittle away & don't forget to be happy. Your moods & mine are like this Wisconsin weather up & down, aren't they? As long as I know you are not worrying too much. Am not sorry for anything, stay at a pretty even keel—but the minute you feel upset down mine go-just because all I care about is you & your happiness.

My sweet old angel face I adore you—to be in love with my wonderful Bops is my whole life.

Our new piece on the radio is "Day After Forever." It's beautiful dear, listen to it.

How's Bopsy's little room & how is that sweet darling who lives in it? I love you

Your Miss Boo

1 August 1944

Hi Fatty,

In this corner weighing in at 112 pounds we have that stream-lined, lassie with the chassis, the one, the only, the inimitable Gun-boat Groody, the Gretch. Take a bow, Champ! Bops, you old sweet thing, I'm so happy that you are gaining and I love every little ounce that you put on. Keep it up, sweetheart.

Needless to say, our phone call was super and it was so good talking with you. When I called the second time, they told me that you had left the hospital but I said try the Chief Nurses office and there you were. Leave it to persistent me.

So Bopsy has started her lessons. Oh darling, what a wonderful person you are. Bopsy, you've done everything that any person could possibly do and it all—it adds to our mutual love, something more we have in common. I promise that you'll never regret it and that someday all this will pass as a bad dream only to emerge as a splendid, ever-widening panorama of love, happiness and devotion. I too share your faith that everything will someday be all-right—it just has to be or everything I hold sacred, my very code of life and religion will no longer mean anything. Please write me about your progress and if there is anything you don't understand, please ask me, but you'll probably end up knowing more than I do if I know you correctly.

Dad wrote me yesterday that my cold letters are hurting him. He wrote he understands why I do write that way but asked me to make an effort to write better letters. Jeepers, what does he expect me to do. I'm writing him to-night what can he expect when there has been so little understanding on his part. I'll keep you posted.

Still good reports from Martin's front. I include him in our prayers and you do too that he'll get married because I'm sure when he gets engaged things will be a little easier for me to spring on the folks again.

So Bops is sending me a present. I bet I could guess what it is but I'll wait until it gets here and let you know if it is what I thought it would be.

I love your long letters Bops and I want you to write me everything you feel and anything you have on your mind no matter what it is. There can never be any secrets between the two of us, don't forget.

Your poem was cute but I want you to sit down and write one of your own to me one of these days. I know you can do it, so sit your lovely Tochas down and do it. Do it! Do it!

I've been doing some model airplane work in my spare time lately and it sure is fun. I sure have plenty of time on my hands but I like it because I have more time to think of you.

For the time being Bops, I think it best that you stay in the 6th SC if possible, don't you?

In expressing my fond adieu

May I say that I love you,

Mr Bops

Fri. Eve.

My dear darling,

It's late & your Bops is sleepy, but have to have a little chat with my dear baby to make my day complete.

Darling, thank you again for your call, they are always are so perfect. Must confess I get a little lonesome after we hang up—cause it seems you are so close it's hard to realize that soon you won't be over to give me my smacks. We do pretty well for two old things & really get a lot said. Afterwards though dear I can think of so many things that we forgot.

Bopsy, all afternoon & eve I've wanted you so to be with me to enjoy the pleasures experienced. Just got away from everything today & had the best time since being at McCoy. Tommy (Lt. Tompkins, the girl I told you about) took me out to the cottage of some friends & we really had a perfect time. They live on a lake 4 miles out of camp, privately owned by 10 families. We went for a swim & what a joy to get away from camp. Then we dug worms & went fishing off the end of the pier & Bops I caught 25 sunfish. You should have seen me dragging them in. I was so excited. Together we caught about 40. Tommy & I cleaned them (pewey) & we had fresh fish & corn on the cob for supper. Jeepers it came out my ears. After dishes we went for a walk & how beautiful dear. This little lake is nestled among the pines & the sunset on the water was scrumptious. Just ran around all pm & eve in my swimsuit & did exactly as we pleased. This couple has a daughter who is an Army nurse & they seem like your own mom & pop. We came back at ten & so tired but a good tired. Darling those are the kind of things I dream about for us. Please God make it come true.

Some cooler today. Hope to be able to sleep tonite, it was wicked yesterday & I was exhausted this a.m. Really need some of that rain from Florida.

Felt so relieved to hear about Martin, it just has to be the real thing for him dear, my fingers are cramped from keeping them crossed. Only hope it helps make things easier for us. Funny how he has forgotten about my Edward's happiness now. Makes a person sort of wonder. Darling please don't ever feel that I hold his unreasonableness against him, there really is only love in my heart for all of your family. You see it's cause I love my Edward & they are part of my Bops. My sweet, sweet baby.

Guess we better say good night & have our dreams. Need a big bear hug awful bad, really.

God bless you dear & keep you well for your Miss Boo.

My darling—

You fooled me—I thought it was to be something else.

It's beautiful darling, thank you! I really needed some too, because I went into Jax to buy some the other day. May I use up the old stuff first, darling? I want to save this for extra-special letters to you.

It sure is fun getting presents, isn't it Bops?

Hey Bops—what am I getting for my birthday? Remember how you used to tease me and how I just couldn't wait to give you your presents? Is it big? Small? Round? Flat? Square? Do you wear it? Eat it? Wood? Cloth? Animal? Vegetable? Mineral? Holes in it? Handles on it? Glass? Leather? Heavy? Light? How are you? How's the folks? Are you happy? What're you doing? How's tricks? Am I crazy?

Enough of this tom foolery—I'm just a man & I love thee

Mr Bops

My darling Mr. Bops—

What a scamp you are. Besides you're only allowed three guesses on your birthday present-not a whole page full.

Glad you liked the paper, it's so much fun sending you things dear-but those bugs up here don't have things worth buying. Please now, tell me what you thought it was. It won't effect your birthday present, that was decided long ago.

I'm sleepy this a.m. read & studied for a couple of hours after my lesson last night. Think the body will curl up & take a nap with Mr Bops-it's cool & cloudy-feel human again.

Darling the lessons are wonderful. Am thoroughly convinced no one should voice opinions or study religion until they are adults. Have learned more in two hours than I have in ten years & it's simple & so beautiful. Chaplain is just a prince, being privately tutored is a real privilege. He thinks it will take about 6 weeks & then says I will be better versed than most Jewish girls. Isn't that wonderful dear? Naturally the work is very concentrated because we both want it finished before transfers go into effect.

Darling I'm so happy-a feeling of complete euphoria & optimism & the knowledge of being right has taken over the realm. Baby dear I love you for it all.

Have written the poem. Will send it next letter. It's extra special really—if gunboat has to say so—so there.

Be a good baby—keep your nose clean & be happy for us. All my love for that dear, yummy, Mr Bops—

Your tag-a-long
Miss Boo

16 August 1944

My darling Miss Boo,

I've been a bad boy in not writing lately (I missed two days) but I've been as mad as a hornet. I got a letter from Martin yesterday that he is afraid to get married and that he isn't sure. Well that's all I had to hear. You told me that I would get mad one day Bops and I really did. I just finished writing him and when he gets through reading it he'll either never speak to me again or else it will wake him up. I told him that of all the goddam things I'd ever heard was that he was afraid and didn't know his own mind. I promptly reminded him of the day he stood in my office and told me what to do, what was wrong and right, how he tried to lead my life, etc. Bops, it was the opening I was waiting for and I really told him off. I told him that I didn't care if he married a Chinawoman, a Negro, or a Fifi Islander, because I would love anyone because she would be my brother's wife and I'd break my neck to do everything to keep them happy. I wonder just what his reaction is going to be. I spoke home Monday night and I asked Mother when Mort was going to get married and she told me he would when his heart told him to. I told Martin that too and asked him if there was a different set of rules as far as I went. My heart told me to marry you but I guess I'm supposed to be different.

Wally and Dad have started a letter writing friendship and they say that when Martin is straightened out we shall start our own offensive. No kidding Bops, I've been mad now for two days and I love it. Martin's letter started it all and I hope he sizzles. I told him that he was getting older and that he wasn't too much of a prize after all and the simple fact that he may want to marry Ruth wasn't enough because she might not want him. I told him to "sh—or get off the pot." Yeh man.

Your letters have been beautiful darling and thank you so much for writing so often. You see I love hearing from you too. Your description of your fishing and trip into the country was wonderful and I could just picture you squealing with delight when you pulled in your first fish. I love fishing and used to be pretty good at it so one fine day we'll do this together. This goddam war won't go on forever, will it Bops?

I received a lovely letter from your sister, Bops. It was really cute. She said that if and when we get married she hopes it will be in or around Hudson. It sure made me laugh. I haven't even asked you yet! Hah! Hah!

Oh yes, the cartoon of you and me meeting was really cute and I laughed like hell all the way from the post-office to the mess hall.

You really sound busy these days and I'm glad. Keep up your lessons baby, and study hard and keep gaining that weight. I dream about you once in a while and Bopsy we really had a wonderful time last night but I can't go into details.Yummmmmmmmmmmmmmmmmmmmmmmmy! Whoopee!

Take it easy Miss Boo with the Bumps, mine baby, aren't you?

I love you
Mr Bops

18 August 1944

My darling,

I shall be speaking with you over the phone to-night, I hope. It's only a fitting reward for that beautiful poem you wrote darling. No kidding, Bops. When I first got it I didn't know if you had written it or not because your "Free" letter mailed on the 15th got here the day after your air-mail of the 16th. So I didn't know. Bops, it's really beautiful and you should be congratulated. It's better than anything I've ever done so I guess I have to get on the ball to keep you from showing me up!

The reason my mail has been sporadic lately is because I busted my typewriter and I never realized how much I depended on it before. Now I have to wait a chance to get to one not in use. You know how tough it is for me to write in longhand. I just get tired and my letters are therefore much shorter.

I shall try and get into Jax one day this week and get that paper and binder for you. I think I have a soft leather one just like you want home to fit the paper, so I think I'll write for it before I go buying one for you because this is extra-special and if it fits you'll like it. It's a book I used for 8 years in college and medical school and has a lot of memories attached to it. I'll write for it soon.

As for the lessons from Chaplain Schwartz, don't ever for one minute think darling, that I am not in complete accord with your doing it and loving you more and more each day for it. It is the most magnificent gesture of love that I have ever known. Who could ask for any more sign of your love and devotion as that. Keep going darling and the Chaplain is right because the majority of girls to-day don't know a damn thing about their religion. To them it is just a birthmark and they haven't the slightest conception of what it is all about.

Wally is fine and we have really become good friends. He thought your poem was terrific and I still can't get over it. What we'll do Bops is just keep all our poems to-gether and keep writing them and maybe someday, God willing, we'll print them and bind them and have them published under the name of Mr and Mrs Bops. How's that? You old sweet thing!

Oh yes. I have only 4 tires on my car now and it's tough as hell getting another one and I won't leave the post with only 4 and without a spare so I'm tied down right now. However, I don't mind. I've been bowling but I just can't get any callous on my thumb. I bowl swell for two games and then the damn blister comes out and I'm through. I haven't played golf in over a month but I don't care because it's too damn hot.

Jeepers, when I get going on a typewriter there's just no stopping me is there? I just go on and on. Now you can see why I hate to write longhand, I'd have quit long ago if I had to sit down and scrawl out all of this stuff.

Have I forgotten anything. I'm waiting patiently for an answer from Martin. I wonder how he'll take the bawling out I gave him in the last letter but he had it coming to him.

There's just been a lapse of 15 minutes while we were out just discussing the war, etc. Lot of the officers here think it will all be over shortly and I hope they're right.

I hope the call goes through darling, to-night. I know it will be wonderful. Take it easy, keep that weight—

I love you,
Mr Bops

Hi there my sweet thing—

This is your lazy gal calling. It's dead as a morgue around these barracks to-night. Did want to see "Dragon Seed" but decided to wait & go with Tolly to-morrow night. Will be through with my lesson at 8:00 & the movie starts at 8:00.

Worked this p.m. what a long day just tired from doing nothing & didn't feel like getting dressed. Kinda lonesome baby, need my Bops so much.

Just called home—dad said for me to bring him a wig the wind had blown all his hair out. He's such a card. They are glad I'm coming home. Such dears as they are.

Four of my little cadets left to-night, how I'll miss them, they have been my closest friends while here. We took some pictures the other day, will send some if I ever get them developed.

The music is beautiful on the radio—just beginning "the hour of charm." Will curl up in my little bed in a few minutes with my book & dream of my sweet baby.

Hey Bops you are evading the subject, what did you think I was sending you. Now tell me pretty please.

Be a good darling & your Bops loves you-every inch-need some big smacks, will have to dream about them, that's all.

Don't forget to wash your hair & don't forget the comb. I love you sweet old scruntchy bigely, wigely

Your Tag

My dear darling—

Ooh how I like those long talky letters Bops. No you just couldn't write in long hand all those good things—better get the old typewriter fixed. What's the matter with it dear?

It's cold & cloudy to-day-certainly the craziest summer ever. The bed & my little blue blanket are my best pals. Nice & cozy baby. But I do believe I'm beginning not to feel the cold quite so much. 112 ¼ now-a little more padding huh?

Another disappointment-weekends canceled again. Too much going on. Such moving & jumble. I've never seen the like. Poor mom will hate it, dread to call her, but that's Army life isn't it? Another nurse & myself are covering the ramps, it's a real job with so many new girls on the wards.

Would love to have your notebook dear. I would really treasure it, hope it isn't too much trouble sweet thing.

Chaplain Schwartz couldn't see me last night, his wife left for the east this morning, So will go Wed. Instead I went to see "Dragon Seed." Didn't like it as well as the "Good Earth." It was long & drawn out & not as good as the book. Maybe I wasn't in the mood for a movie.

Have meant to ask you something for several weeks darling. The funniest thing happens in the morning just as I awaken. It seems that if I turn over you are there beside me. Your face is so vivid & right then I feel so awfully lonesome. Does it happen to you darling or it is just cause I think of you so much? Hope it's an omen that some day when we awaken it will be true. Darling sweet Bopsy it's just got to be. Miss you so dreadfully & neither of us would have it any other way but to wait for our day would we? Got the old skitchers this morning. Do you know what that is? My own new invention of a word—ha.

Darling I'm afraid to have you bowl & tear that thumb open all the time. It's not good—hear? Two games then stop-now mind me. Your hands are too valuable to have anything wrong with them.

Hope there is news from Dick soon-but again it takes patience, that's our middle name isn't it?

I love you sweetheart-keep well til to-morrow.

Your own
Miss Boo

23 August 1944

My darling,

You're sure a good old thing when it comes to writing each day and I'll get better too when my old machine is fixed. The gadget is busted inside—now do you know what's wrong? You weasel!

You have asked me twice now what I thought you were going to send me for a present but I'm not going to tell you because if I do you'll go out and get it for me and I won't tell you, so there! I know you!

I heard from Irving Firstman, my cousin, who's been in Normandy since D-day. He's the boy who is now a Captain in the Anti-aircraft and lived in the Castle. He met some gal by the name of Parks (Army Nurse Corps) and she told him about what a swell gal you were and how we went to-gether. I wrote him that I still go with you. He sure is a swell kid and once you know him, you'll love him. It's sure tough going over there he writes and I sure feel worried about him—we never know do we?

So you like the way I jabber along, do you? It's so easy to sit down and just talk to you Bops because there's always so much to say and even when I get through I usually think of something I've forgotten.

I'm sorry to hear about your week-end, but we have no control over those things. I'm sure that things will straighten themselves out one day and we'll all have to quit worrying about weekends. I was just thinking what fun it would be if I was stationed at Grant doing the same job I have here. Jeepers, I'd be off Sat. noon until Tuesday morning and I'd be able to go up and see Scruntchy all the time. We'd sure be spoiled babes, then wouldn't we Bops?

So you feel lonesome in the mornings when you get up? Don't you remember me telling you I felt the same way when you were down here? That's the worst part of the day for me baby. Getting up in the morning, I know I should just roll over and find you there beside me. It's something I've thought of for so long I actually make believe some mornings and I sort of mumble to you as if you were there. Oh darling, it will be some day—it just has to be. We were made to be to-gether and I know we shall have our reward someday. I get blue sometimes, just as you do, and worry about the wasted days and weeks but darling, there are so many thousand just like us waiting for something.

We have to wait like the rest, dear heart, and if we want something enough we'll get it. My thoughts are no different from yours darling and I think of being to-gether too, close in each others arms and consummating our deep love. It's good to think of those things darling and you know I need you just as much as you need me. Yummy to talk about it, isn't it darling?

I've been trying to figure out just what that new word of yours is and it sure has me mixed-up. Come on, Bops, tell me what it means. If you do, I'll tell you what "Schpilkies" are. That's a good one, Bops!

I'm waiting on pins and needles to see what Martin has to say. Even he should be convinced by now that I'm serious and mean business. I should hear by next Monday or Tuesday. Here we go again!

I promise not to bowl too much, Boss, and I'll do as you say. You old, picky, thing you! Pick, pick, pick, pick, but I love it.

I'm happy that Tolly and her husband are doing O.K. now with their family.

So you've got my birthday present picked out, have you? Gosh it's almost time and I don't even have a clue. I wonder, I wonder, I wonder—Let me see, is it—? It isn't? Is it—? It isn't? Well, what in the hell do you know about that. I could have sworn it would be—. Jeepers I just can't guess anymore.

I remember what you always said you wanted for Christmas, darling, but now between you and I it will be a Chanukah present. Do you still want me for that time, darling? I pray that this time you can have what you want darling. Wheeeeeeeeeeeee!

You know Bops, sometimes I think of how much you and I have in common to-gether. How much we have been through, how closely our lives have been for the past 2 ½ years. I don't think that any two people could ever get to know each other as well as you and I do, could they? But in spite of it all darling, I still don't know you well enough. Sounds funny, doesn't it? I just want to look at you 24 hours a day and then be able to wake up in the night and look at you again and again, don't I Bops?

Enough jabber for now or else I'll be spoiling you, you rascal. Just take the rest of the day off while you use up these four hundred trillion, eight million, nine hundred and sixty thousand and four hundred thirty-two smacks. Wow, what a work out!

I love you,
Mr Bops

My dear darling

At last the old mail-man came through. Two big fat letters from my Bopsy to-day. Darling I practically devoured them. All your letters are read over & over & over they are such companions & so beautiful.

Sure was an old mopey pants yesterday. Know you will give me a mental spanking on receipt of my letter written in that mood. Know you understand though, get so awfully lonesome for my baby.

At last the letter from Martin—glad he agrees with you on many of the facts.

Certainly he will reflect your Mom and Dad's opinion, be it changed or otherwise. Can't help but feel dear that they have thought this over seriously & are not too happy. Your mother would never have cried over such a thing if it weren't true. I've been pondering just how are we going to reveal the facts to them about our feelings after "not writing" & what manner we will let them know that I've been converted. Should it be a single letter to you saying my love will never die & because of that I went ahead of my own accord—or just what? We have to begin to think about that dear. Perhaps they will hold hope & state it to you that because you say you will not marry as long as I'm single—that time will find me married & then you will be free. Darling that will never be, believe me & they may as well know it even if they have great doubts (Do I make myself clear—kind of jumbled as I reread it). Martin will probably be very perturbed about the contents of your last letter, but certainly darling he has no right to do anything but help you. Not if he really loves you as a brother. Firmly believe too dear that if your mother knew the contents of many of your letters to the family, she would be deeply hurt because they have withheld so much. Darling mothers are wonderful understanding people, deceiving her is no help & they will find out that she is capable of intelligent thinking of her own kind if they give her a chance. Perhaps I'm wrong but which is worse to suddenly shock her into reality or let her gradually get accustomed to it? As for you baby dear—try to keep from worrying about me & what I'll do or say should it mean waiting again. Bopsy I'll always be at your side, patient, understanding, loving & willing to take the bumps as well as the glories of our love.

So my old sweet thing is having fun too. I'm so glad dear-just make the gals understand that they can enjoy my Edward but they better not get ideas—so there now too. Do you know I haven't had a drink or a date for *five weeks-just can't make myself go out. Am concentrating on my lessons, getting fat, my sleep, keeping the chin up & trying to keep my darling happy with frequent letters. That's a big job my pet for one little gal—but I love it. Oh yes. Guess what. The scale now says 113#-super huh?*

Called Mom last night-she was so disappointed—their plans are shattered but that's the way it goes. Will see what next week has in store, but it won't be as nice everyone going back to school, my Auntie gone etc. Mom & Dad are all that counts as far as I'm concerned though.

About the chaplain dear. I've already thought of the gift idea. Am afraid you will have to do the purchasing in Jax just nothing here. Am sure you can think of something—what about a port-folio, book, pen & pencil set or something useful. He would never accept a fee. I'll be almost half through this coming week just think.

Oh Bops look at the length of this scribble-just forget you might grow weary of reading—it's so wonderful to talk to you darling.

Be a good Mr Bops—keep the chin high & a smile always. Remember you're my darling & I love you.

Miss Boo.

26 August 1944

My darling,

You've been spoiling me so, lately, darling, that when I didn't get a letter from you to-day, it sure felt funny. I've been getting those yummy old things each day and I sure love them.

Nothing much going on these days. That induction station job is slowly driving me bats but there's not much I can do about it. I stare at those damn eyes and ears all day and I dream of them at night. I still haven't heard from Dick yet Bops but we old, patient things will just have to sit and wait.

A few of the nurses and the doctors have been coming around to see me about various things wrong with them and the regular assigned men in the clinic don't like it a bit. There are three Majors there now so you can see what sort of chance I have, but I'd rather be where I am than in that clinic. Funny, them coming to see me for treatment. Women are sure funny, Bops, aren't they? You try to kiss them good-night and they get mad and if you don't try, they get mad too. Jeepers, what gives! Don't think I tried to kiss her good-night you rascal, because I didn't. Besides, there's no one with soft lips like you darling, even though you do make me do all the work!! Hah! Hah!

Wally is OD to-night and he just came by the information desk where I'm typing this letter. He's been getting blue letters from his wife. She's lonesome as hell. Funny Bops, isn't it? There's Wally and his wife, there's no reason why she can't be here but there is because they can't afford it. Oh, nuts, what a world!

Martin must have got my letter to-day and I'm just waiting to see what he has to say. Gosh, Bops, if he writes me all that old stuff again I think I'll call him up over the phone and punch him in the nose. There! I started to write Mother the other day but tore the letter up. Bops, I pray that one fine day soon they will all get some sense in their domes and realize that you and I are more important than anyone else in this world as far as we are concerned. Aren't we, Bops?

I went to a double feature to-night and sat there for 2 ½ hours just grunting and groaning. I just don't enjoy movies without you darling. No pick to pick at, no one to hold my hand, and no soft, pretty knees to play with, is there Bops? Bops, I sure wish I had you here right now. It's raining, and we'd sit out in the car and listen to the radio and I'd give you a little smack. Good, isn't it?

I've finished my two warships and they look pretty good for an amateur Bops. They are right pretty, if I say so myself, and I say so myself. I'm working on a Stuka Dive-bomber now and my room is just a mess of wood, glue and junk. I wish you'd keep my quarters a little cleaner, Miss Boo. You just don't take care of my house anymore and I don't like it.

Think I'll write a note to Dee and Murph. In case I didn't tell you, Tom Swift is finally back at West Point. Now he probably wants to go on foreign service again. By the way, darling, do you hear from Annie?

I love you,
Mr Bops

My dear darling

How do I know just what you're going to do? Such two old rascals as we are, even distance makes no difference. Baby you're such a sweetheart to keep Miss Boo the happiest lonesome little gal in the world. Each call is more perfect dear, but you ought to save the pennies for our house or something ha.

Have fun to-night dear, be good & miss me just a little. I'd love to be dancing in your arms, but anyhow I'll be there no matter who you dance with.

Can't imagine it's being hot down there, it's terrific up here, we all are uncomfortable. Now I enjoy my pretty little blue sweater-the one you gave me-remember?

Right after your call dear, one came from home. Dot & Auntie are coming down Monday-isn't that nice? No one wants me to be lonesome baby. Auntie is heaps of fun & I'll really enjoy them. Will have to skip my lesson Mon. eve but will go Wed.

You're a naughty bad boy sweetheart. Please tell me what you thought I was sending & besides that what do you really want for your birthday—well I know but won't tell ha ha so there.

Darling I'm so happy about your application to the Masons. Let me know all about it. Do you know any of the members there in Jax.A committee will probably interview you.

Out of one ear I'm listening to the Colgate program-it's so funny. The little tune they sing is "If it's kissin that you're missin & it's huggin that you need, buy Colgate." Golly if buying toothpaste would bring you here to fulfill my wishing—gee-ee-ee.

No darling-no one is to have the poem except you—it's just for you—my public. It's time we wrote more for our book to be.

Watcha going to do with all the planes darling. Why not make one big enough to hop in & come up to see the old lady? What else are you doing?

About us dear heart—you asked how I feel about it. No change-just feel very good & most optimistic. It's got to be all right. Time—time darling. How's our twinkley star these days. Bops is she getting brighter? We just will never forget that will we dear?

Be careful at the beach to-morrow my pet. Who all is going? Wish we had gone again while I was there, the sun & sand were so nice. You know baby

I knew you were in a mood that day—but just being with my Bops-nothing else mattered.

Darling I want to snuggle—oh so badly, when will it be true again? Good-night dear baby-I love you with all my heart & soul

I'll pray for us as every night. Your calls are so wonderful-your baby.

Aug. 27? Sun. P.M.

My dear darling,

It's really a good thing my week-end had to be spent here. What a miserable cold day it is. Rainy, cloudy & typical fall weather. The heat is on all over the hospital & my little room is cozy & comfortable. Had to run home quick & take Mr Bops off the radiator, his little seat was hot as anything—poor guy.

There really isn't any news to-day dear, so we'll have to chat about us. Thought it best to get a letter off in the a.m. as I won't be able to write to-morrow.

Darling, Friday's letter which arrived this morning was the sweetest one ever. Such a cute old thing as my Bops is just my dear baby. Thinking & saying all the things that constantly fill both our minds & hearts. Two people could never think & act more in accord than we do dear, it's such a glorious thing, honest it seems like a dream, that one day almost three years ago

I should pick the right one for my life. Can always hear you saying—"you really tied & roped me Bops out of all those people." It's another miracle sweet baby in this life of ours.

Bopsy what is "schpilkes?" My word meant goosebumpy inside, the gadgets were playing hopscotch with the thingamabobs-you know-ha.

Shame on you naughty boy-you spelled Chanukah like this—that's wrong—it should be Hanuccah on the 25th of Kislev—so there—aren't I smart? Any way darling remember I've always said that to have you for a present on that day was all I wanted. It still is all I want, ever, ever-for my birthday, Hanuccah, & every day of the year the rest of our lives. It will be so baby just cause God wants it that way. The struggle we're having now is to make us know for sure & because all the good things in the world have to be fought for.

Edward dear you have completely spoiled this gal—my telephone calls, presents, letters & everything, but it's so wonderful. Darling my day to really spoil you is coming—have millions of things that have to be done, but have to have my snuggle-bug right beside me. Oh darling do you know what I mean. All those little things to do to make my Bopsy happy inside & for him to know that Gretchen's whole life is spent to make him thankful & glad.

Just think scruntchy if you were here to-day. We'd read all the funnies, cuddle under our blanket & take a nap—raid the icebox, then go to the movie—home to our little house &-oh darling my day dreaming seems so *real & so easy to be true. Bopsy would your mom & daddy like me if they knew me—please God make them.*

Guess I'd better stop dear, the first thing you know I'll be on the next train speeding toward Florida.

All my love & those kisses we both cherish so much—

Your Pick-Pick

28 August 1944

My darling,

Hello darling, how is my baby, this morning? It sure was wonderful talking to you Saturday night darling and we should do it at least once a week. It's so good for both of us, so you let me know the best time to call and we'll do it each week.

Wally and I went down to Jacksonville Beach yesterday and we had a pretty good time. We went swimming and I got my bald-head good and burned. We went back into Jax and had a good meal and then a movie and then back home. It was a lot of fun except that you weren't there darling.

I'm still waiting for those tires from home to get here. I had to borrow a spare to get to Jax yesterday because I won't drive without one.

I got an answer from Martin, Bops, and it was just as I expected. He still feels the same way about things even though he admits the logic about all of what I wrote him and the various arguments, he still feels that he's right and we are wrong, but that doesn't bother me much Bops because I'm just biding my time until you are through with your lessons and then I'll write the folks that if it isn't Bops, it won't ever be anyone else, that they can take it or leave it. They need a real jolt and I know why Martin is still fighting on because as long as he sees a chance of his winning he'll never give up. Don't feel badly about it baby, because I don't. It's what I expected from him. He just doesn't realize that if I'm not happy the folks will never be happy and one of these days he will see it. I feel no way to blame because I've been honest about us all along. I know that God wants you and I to be to-gether and that one day he will give us our wish. I know there is only one girl in this world for me darling, and that girl is you. I love you more and more with each passing day. I'm proud for you to love me and I thank the Lord each day that I was given the privilege of knowing you. God bless you, my darling.

Martin wrote that Grandmother (Bubby) is pretty ill these days with hypertension and the folks are worried over her, but she's getting so old that we have to expect it sooner or later. Martin is still seeing Ruth and I hope that one of these days he'll get a move on and pop the question.

I'm so happy darling that you are putting on more and more weight. I bet you're a pretty little thing right now. I'd sure like to scruntch you for about two or three hours, sweetheart.

I'll drop in to see Del one of these days Bops as soon as I get a chance. I thought that they had gone away for their vacation or else I would have gone in sooner, I just hate driving all those miles back alone. When I had scruntchy to see, of course, it was a different story.

"Bye for now darling, and please don't work too hard, you race-horse you!

I love you,
Mr. Bops

My Darling,

I've been thinking of you extra-special to-day darling because of the extra-special long letter you wrote me to-day. It was real scruntchy baby, and I enjoyed every line of it.

I enjoyed it and read it very carefully darling, because you are thinking of the day that I tell the family again. I think you are so right about it being better for Mother to know a little gradually then all at once, but I think way down deep she must know darling how I feel. I had felt that Martin would have changed a little after the letter I wrote him but he still feels that I must subjugate all my feelings because of the family and I guess he'll go on thinking like that unless a ton of bricks falls on him. I feel sorry for him Bops because a man that thinks as he does can't be happy. But his reaction has left me madder than ever. I feel so badly that he should continue to take such an attitude but as I said this morning he'll probably go on fighting until he knows he's licked. As long as he sees there is a chance of his winning he'll keep it up but I know that I will win in the long run darling and that someday, God willing, you shall be my wife to have and to hold until death do us part! Your love and devotion, your patience, your all-seeing vision, are constant companions to me in this trying hour and for all of that darling, I am deeply grateful. I feel so sorry for all the people in the world who don't have anyone to love them and I do for Martin as well. With all the heartaches we have been through darling, I find you still that rare combination of all the things I have ever looked for in a woman, I know that you will always be the same, my dear, no matter what anyone may throw at us. Thanks for loving me darling!

I haven't figured out the details of how I'm going to tell them about your conversion darling, but don't worry about it because I will know when the time comes. One fine day, they will have it on the line and don't worry your pretty little head about a thing. Just stay fat, eat a lot, don't worry because God will not deny us this baby, I know. I can't conceive of my Mother denying me the right to live with the woman of my choice and when the time comes we shall have it.

Bops, there's a serial running in Collier's that started the last week in August and baby, someone must have written our story because it is all there. It's about a Jewish lawyer and a Christian girl who fall in love and the objections come from her family. Bops, it's really terrific and the most prominent people in the country have written much about it. Get the back issues and start reading it. I have read the first two chapters and I can just tell what's coming before it happened. It's called "Earth and High Heaven." If I can get hold of the whole book, I'll try.

Bops, I have written home for my leather book but they can't seem to find it so I guess it has been misplaced somewhere. I'm sorry darling.

We played ball to-night darling, and we won 3-2. It was a pretty good game and the old man got a hit and scored the winning run. Proud of me? Bops, remember our code as to when I would get home? Hitting a home run? Golly, baby, I'm sure glad those days are behind us. They were sure bitter and black for awhile but all this has left me and you strong and eager to go ahead with our lives, hasn't it? It has made us better people darling.

My Bops sure has an awful lot of work to do these days. Study, interior decorating, letters, how do you find time for it all, baby? But, you are an amazing person and can do anything once your mind and heart is set on it, can't you darling?

I shall be on the lookout for a suitable gift for the Chaplain, darling. Do you trust my taste? Hah!

Guess it's time for me to sign off for now baby.

To-night I shall tuck you in bed beside me and hold you close in my arms and just kiss you and kiss you baby. And if someone asked me why I'd just have to tell them that

I love you,
Mr Bops

Blanket on which Gretchen sewed military insignias she acquired. Center is her copy of the book, "Earth and High Heaven" by Gwethalyn Graham.

My dear darling

   Just have to talk to you to-night darling so while I'm waiting for the call to go through will have a good old jabber-gab. My baby has been so neglected the past two days & that will never do.

   Your sweet letter came this morning, darling they are just like your arms around me, so comforting & confident. Need your big old arms awfully though.

   So Martin still isn't convinced that we won't give up. What a struggle dear, sometimes I wonder why you don't tell me to go away—poor dear, you are going through so much for our love. Expect after my confirmation the fireworks will really begin, but it doesn't frighten me dear heart except for the awful beating you have to take. Darling sometimes I believe Martin isn't reflecting your family's true feelings because his letter to me was so different from your daddy's. Maybe he's just afraid Bops will beat him to the draw huh? Baby sometimes I feel we should take a furlough & both go up & face the music to-gether. Gee Bops, what would happen-golly. Let's just sit tight until after the Holidays dear, they probably will accept things a little better then.

   So sorry to hear about Bubby isn't she over 80 dear? Your poor mom has had a hard time & lots of work even while she was well.

   Had such a nice time with Dotty & Aunt Lela. They really enjoyed their first visit to an Army camp. Auntie has always been my favorite & she's such a good scout. She even insisted on sleeping in a top bunk just for the experience. She's a little thing about 3 pounds more than me & has a son 21 who is a gunner on a B29. That sweet Mom sent down a box, fried chicken & all the trimmings, so we had a little party.

   Last night the nurses had a huge party (hens) in the recreation hall sort of a farewell to those leaving & by eleven old lazy bones was a weary chicken & had to go to sleep without writing.

   This place is like a morgue dear, so sorry Tolley & Chris are gone, really miss them. Bopsy, still lots of rumors around but never know which ones to believe. Darling I so wish they would put you someplace sorta permanent like so I could be transferred. All this constant moving gets under my skin a bit & it makes the work so much harder.

   Chaplain couldn't see me to-night, we've had a delay this week, but shall see him to-morrow noon. Darling I love my lessons & am learning &

believing so much. Our faith dear will bring us to-gether someday darling & please never believe anything but what I'm sincere in my new faith.

Will finish writing after we talk dear. Smack smack for now.

Oh my sweet gumdrop—how good it was to her your voice. Aren't I an old sissy sometimes for getting so lonesome. We're bad rascals dear-look at us calling back & forth twice this week-but isn't it good & aren't we spoiled? Somehow darling just hearing your voice gives me new life for days. Golly I'm being as expensive as in Panama Bops & that's not saving our money like good kids, but I love it so there.

How was the ball game, did your side win, how many runs did you make Bops?

Bet the beach was lovely Sunday. How's the sunburn baby—be careful of my Bops & don't let him get sick cause he's a precious old thing & he's mine.

Feel so happy now after our little talk—surprise wasn't it? I love you darling with every beat of my heart.

Your own
Miss Boo

30 August 1944

My darling scruntchy baby,

Talk about people being good to one another, you're every bit as good to me darling. Your call to-night was wonderful. Thanks so much darling, for making my day complete. I get such a bang out of your dropping those coins in the machine. Sure sounds like a lot of money doesn't it Bops when it goes in. I can just picture you sitting there with a whole snag of quarters waiting for the operator to tell you to put in the money. Good thing there aren't any quarter machines around. Remember that old baby of mine saying, "Just one more quarter, Bops."

Martin's reaction doesn't worry me at all darling. I'm still mad and I get madder each and every day. Just take it easy darling. I'm just as impatient as you are, Bops, more so because I haven't been scrunched or moused in so long, have I baby? You old sweet rascal!

I'm writing Dick a note to-night after I finish writing to you darling to see how things are going. No news is good news for the time being. If there wasn't a chance he would probably know and have written me. Everything happens for the best, at least for us darling, and I'm sure this will turn out for the best one way or the other. I want to get settled so we can start pulling some strings to get us to-gether. I bet your friend in Washington will help you when the time comes. We'll just get her in a corner and say we have to be to-gether if they want this war won so they better get going and do something about it.

We have an Officer's Club ball team Bops and we are pretty good if I do say so. Of course, we are all getting a little old, but we have won two games in a row and if we win tomorrow we play for the championship of the league. Pretty good, eh?

Darling, you're a rascal. You know so much about Judaism already it's wonderful. But, after all, I know you so well darling. You'll probably want me to teach you to speak Jewish when you're through. God bless you, darling for being such a wonderful person.

Dad called me up yesterday morning in case I didn't tell you and he was upset about Martin apparently getting cold feet about Ruth. Bops, he asked me what I could do about it and I saw red and really told him what I thought of Martin being afraid, etc. I told him that I am sick and tired of everyone home acting as if the world was coming to an end and I said it was about time they woke up and realized how lucky we all were to still be in the States and alive and well. I really poured it on Bops and I had him on the ropes. Bubby is pretty sick these days darling, she has a blood pressure over 225 and is in and out of bed most of the time. She's an old lady now and I guess her time is about up. Dad wants me to come home for a few days but I told him it was impossible. Perhaps I may be able to wrangle one of the patient trips and get home for a day or two. I really don't want to go home, I'd want to get a trip up to Chicago so I can see you darling and I'm in the market for one.

It seems that my application for the Masons must go through my home town lodge and that means letting Dad know so for the meantime I'm letting it ride darling because in the first place the meetings aren't until Oct. 15 and by that time I don't know where I'll be so I'll keep it in abeyance for the time being. I'm still going to be one, though.

Just because you called to-night I'll have an extra-special dream about you darling and I'll kiss all the cares away from your lovely face. If I keep on loving you any more than I do I'll set some sort of record.

I love you,
Mr Bops

My dear darling—

Just came from an unusual party. Rosalie's boyfriend in France had a birthday today & his sister sent her the cake. It was good & so was the coffee.

How is my sweet thing today? Darling your letters become better & better, maybe it's cause each day I love you more & more. Bubble Bubble— that's me.

Darling I hope you listened hard last night cause we had an extra special talk—about Hanuccah gift & together we prayed for our hopes to be fulfilled. You seemed so close—right beside me in fact, then we cuddled & went off to dream land. Your voice was so clear & close because of our telephone call. Such spoiled old things we are. To hear you talk about us in your letters makes me all goose-bumpy. Together darling neither of us should be afraid of anything. Our love is like some great shining light that leads us over all the rough roads on to brighter & smoother paths.

Had a most interesting hour with the chaplain today. He is so anxious to meet you dear & he feels his stay will be extended longer than he thought. Am so glad because I'll be able to finish now for sure.

Scuse me dear—I beg your pardon & forgive the "naughty boy" phrase. Hanuccah can be spelled both ways. Not so smart after all serves me right.

It's so cold dear—still need my snuggle bunny—that's you—darling we have so many good things to look forward to cause we've been good kids—haven't we? You may as well know I have cold feet literally.

Yes dear—never fear about your judgment in gifts or anything. Remember how I've told you about the hours you will have to spend in a dress shop someday. Ha.

Lots of work the next few days. Have all three ramps now & I sure get my mileage. The girls are most cooperative & everyone realizes the extra work with sixty just having left.

Must go to bed, say my prayers. Talk to my baby & tell him

"I love you"
Your baby

Goody, goody Saturday soon

SEPTEMBER, 1944

(Sept. 1?) Fri Eve

My dear darling

 Have all my little chores finished, washed my hair so it would be sweet & clean for our date tomorrow night. Will be waiting so anxiously to hear my baby's voice. Bopsy you're an old sweet thing did you know that? What a glorious privilege to love the dearest Bopsy in the world.

 Whatcha doing darling—how are all the planes & boats? Golly that room—it's full of chips & glue & I'm a lazy negligent gal but as long as making a mess makes you happy, who cares. I'll clean it up some day & can't you hear me fussing anyway.

 Would like to have gone to the movie tonight "The Impatient Years," but have too much to do. Must study my Mon. lesson—it's history and takes concentration. Next I have to complete my 3rd examination paper in Decoration. Suppose it will be bed time by then. Darling my first two exams were a "B" and next an "A." They really are quite difficult—but it's good to be doing something worthwhile. In between times I finished a little knitted sweater for the Johnson's new baby who is coming. They are the people in Sparta who have had me to dinner so many times (where I played poker).

 Darling why don't you save the serial in Colliers & send the story when it's completed. Can't seem to find any of the copies here. Gee dear I wanted you to write our story before anyone else got the idea. Undoubtedly it will cause lots of comments.

 Heard another rumor today & that is we are getting Negro nurses here at McCoy—what next.

 I'm glad Wally liked my letter dear—it's an awfully good feeling to have Bopsy's friends pleased to hear from his nuisance. You see I have to keep Wally on his toes to take good care of my baby.

 Hope by tomorrow night there will be news from Dick. Hope he has some idea at least about the possibilities of it's materializing soon.

 Darling you know your comments about Martin fighting as long as he thinks he can win, sounds a little like his young brother. Ha. Remember how definite you were about us & then it took my coming home to change all that. Some people are from Missouri sweet thing, they have to be shown. Am sure, though dear, Martin isn't happy, how can he be & I feel so sorry for him cause we have so much happiness. Yes dear heart it's wonderful to be loved by some special one—how will I know. Yours is the most priceless possession I have.

Just must get my studying done dear. So old jabber box will accept all those trillion million smacks & return each one in thought until the day they become real again.

You're my sweetheart & I love that dear baby just awfully much so there.

Miss Boo.

Isn't the war news splendid?

Hello Bops, you sweet, rascally, scruntchy, lovable, beautiful, gunboaty, old thing . . .

After that lengthy introduction, all I can say is that I'm exhausted. We just finished playing our softball game Bops and we won. We beat the M.P.'s and boy were we happy to do it. We mowed them down and to-morrow we play for the championship of the Post. Think of it Bops, if we win I'm liable to get a medal or a traveling bag. It sure is fun to have a ball game and play. My wind has improved and I actually stole second to-night. Hey Bops, remember the day I slid in home and bruised my legs and couldn't walk for a week? Wow, that sure was something, wasn't it.

Hey, Bops, you sure are an old rascal calling me up like that last night. Save your money Baby, because we're going to need it someday. Save, save, save. Not me, as long as we can eat and have some left in the bank, we're going to have a good time, aren't we?

Nothing much exciting to talk about Bops. Martin is going away for three days this week-end with Ruth and maybe someone will hit him over the head and he'll ask her to get married. I think we'll have to anesthetize him some fine day. What a guy. He's a wonderful guy too, but where he gets some of his ideas from I don't know. But, he'll wake up one of these days.

The girls around here are sure getting orders. It's purely on a volunteer basis here Bops and they are going fast. Col. Maley is a pretty swell head nurse. She really bawled the gals out though the other day. They've been yelling for foreign service and when she asked for volunteers all she got was one. So she really let them have it. I guess that's natural though. Lots want to go but don't want to volunteer.

Don't be lonesome baby with all your friends leaving. Wally is going to school at Washington and Lee next week and I'll be alone for a month too. He sure has been a swell friend to me and if he weren't here I don't know what I'd do.

I got a letter from Bea, Aaron's wife, and she was happy that I've gotten out of the emotional jag I was on and have made up my mind what I'm going to do. She writes that she and Aaron are behind us 100%.

Yessir Bops, they're all on our side except three, but we'll get them too, so there!

Go to bed and dream of me baby and hug and kiss me and hold me tight all night, will you Bops?

I love you.

I love you.
Mr Bops

My dear Baby,

Darling, our Sat. night date was so perfect. To hear you say it will be every Saturday night until we are together was like a beautiful gift. Having that to look forward to each week dear gives me such courage & happiness. Bopsy darling how could I be so fortunate in having your love? Never for a moment have you ever failed me & please God make me worthy of Edward's devotion.

Had to kid you a little bit punkins about a date tonight. Yes darling I know neither of us want any other person to enter our little realm the rest of our lives. We are so spoiled dates with others only seem dull, drab & a waste of time. Someday darling we hope & pray we will again be with each other days & weeks, months & years. It will be our heaven. Until then we keep on as we are, giving strength & courage to each other by other ways. Certainly in all these months we haven't faltered.

It's such a gorgeous evening, a big full moon & just the kind of an evening we would love together. Couldn't find our twinkly star the sky is so bright, so maybe she has gone on an errand for us or is shining in your window. Dear baby I know you are lonesome, Bopsy has wanted so to be there in your arms to snuggle & scrunch, but I was there in my heart.

Know you are going to miss Wally dreadfully. Hate to have him go for that reason, but glad to hear of his promotion. Hope he goes to see your dad & mother, he will almost have to tell them that he has met me. Bopsy we sure wait for lots of things & people to help us don't we.

Am really weary tonight. Should have stayed home, but hadn't been out all week. I'm covering all three ramps now—hope that doesn't last too long. Gee.

Baby I have to go to sleep now to be with my darling in my dreams. Think about you so much dear that when I go to sleep you are still with me. Darling some day soon we hope, we can both go to sleep, free of all the cares & worries of all we have been through & reach out to find each other side by side. Darling, God will make it so. Keep saying your prayers & good nite my blessed sweetheart. I love you my Edward.

Miss Boo

Hello my darling,

Gosh Bops I know just how you feel when your pals leave you. I just put Wally on the train for school and I'm as lost as a pea without a pod, or something just like that. Never know how much you get to depend on someone until they go. Wally's scared to death he won't make good. You see he never went to High School and the idea of going to a college for work scares him but I'm sure he'll make out well.

It was so good speaking with you darling. You do sound so close when we call. Makes you feel as if you want to crawl through the wire and get some smacks. Yum, yum!

I don't know what I'm going to do these days. Martin is sending me two brand new tires for the car and I've run out of gasoline so you can't have everything, it seems.

I guess I'll be running in to see Mack more often now. I'm such a popular guy I have to divide my time with my friends. Hah!

As to the story Bops, I guess you have this week's so I'll send you the first two copies of the ones you missed. I can't wait until Friday when the final issue comes out. You can get the final issue yourself at the PX but don't read it until you get the first two. It's funny Bops, because in this story it's the gal's family that object, etc. I haven't gotten to the part where he approaches his folks so I don't know if they enter into it, but the story has followed us so closely that the author must have gone through it herself. I fully intend to write her a letter when I get through the story provided it ends as I want it to.

I accept your apology for telling me how to spell that Holiday! I knew you would find out it can be spelt both ways and I was waiting to see what you had to say. I'm so happy darling that Chaplain Schwartz is staying and that you will finish. Won't be long before the fireworks start again, will it Bops? I can see only one ending Bops, so we'll be right in there punching.

Yes darling, we have been good kids and there is so much for us to look forward to. The victory and its rewards will be so much the sweeter for the bitterness of the fight. (Golly, that's pretty good.) There is so much we have to look forward to and God grant us the ability and the health and strength for our future.

I'm just about through with my model airplane Bops and no kidding, it's a beauty. I've put in about 2 solid weeks of work on it and I'm quite proud of it. If you're a good girl I might send it to you when it's through along with two little ships I made. Would you like to have them in your room?

I wrote Dick again yesterday and I hope he may have some news for me. This job is getting me down Bops. The complete lack of knowledge anyone needs to do what I'm doing is pitiful. But, I'm used to things like that.

Your letters are good too baby and I also eat them up. It's so easy to write what you want to hear because I feel all those things as you do, so there, you rascal.

With you being in charge of three ramps they'll probably make you a General or something. Take it easy Bops and don't walk too fast. I know you though, you old bundle of stuff and stuff. Be a happy darling and sleep tight to-night darling. My arms will be around you.

I love you,
Mr Bops

5 Sept 1944

My darling,

Bops, it has been so hot here for the past few days that I don't use matches to light my cigarettes anymore. I just hold them up and the hot air lights them. I had to turn my fan off because it was blowing too much hot-air at me. Heh! Heh!

I'm so glad that you are an old smart thing darling, and that you got an A and a B in your courses. I'll bet you really are busy what with that and your lessons. I bet you know more about Jewish history than I'll ever know and I really used to know it. I also bet that you are the best student that Chaplain Schwartz ever had and that he is getting as much a kick out of all this as you are. Lucky guy, sitting down and talking to my Bops all the time.

I sent you the first three installments of the story by mail yesterday. Friday the magazine comes out on all the newsstands so you can buy the last copy yourself. Saturday night or whenever I call we can talk about it. I can hardly wait until I see what happens. Save the copies I sent you Bops. I may want to send the story home to Dad if I can't get the book.

One of the medical officers here who I ranked by almost a year was promoted to Major yesterday and I went up and raised a fuss about on what basis they used. It seems rank doesn't mean anything here. It's who you know and how long you've been at Blanding. I don't care about a promotion anyway. The way the news is going, I just want out, but for a doctor that's impossible.

The Navy doctors just came in and want a bridge game. We never start work here until about 10 and we knock off a fast bridge game before we get to work. I play with an enlisted refugee from Poland and he's really good. By the way, Bops, have you played any bridge. I'm sending away for a bridge book which is pretty simple and good and I think I'll send it to you. You'll like it. Maybe I better not. You have so much to do now, you'll be toppling over with knowledge, you smart thing, you!

I'm going into Jax this afternoon. Now that Wally is gone I'm like a needle in a haystack or something. Sure do miss him but I'll make me another airplane to kill the time. Think I'll look around for the Chaplain's gift and get some idea of what there is to be had.

Stay sweet and fat darling. I could just eat you up right now because I haven't had anything sweet since you left.

I love you,
Mr Bops

My darling,

Nowhere near a typewriter this a.m. darling and I must say, "Hello" to my baby.

I just got back from Jax this morning. I went in yesterday p.m. I stayed over with Mac last night. Looked around for a present for Chaplain Schwartz but couldn't see anything I like as yet. But, I'll find something soon.

Bops I'm sending you a play called "Cyrano de Bergerac." I first read it in college and it is my favorite piece of literature. I think I told you about it and it is quite famous, the lines are beautiful and fun. Have to read it 2-3-4 times before you get it all. It's a beautiful love story. Someday we'll read it to-gether and talk about it. It should be fun.

The news in Europe is sure good and here's hoping it ends a lot sooner than I've dared to believe. Things should be popping in the Philippines soon. It's been too quiet lately.

I love you, darling, with a deep indescribable devotion. God Bless You for loving me!

I love you,
Mr Bops

6 Sept 1944

My darling,

Now that I have my good old machine fixed I can write my Baby as often as I should. I've been a little lax Bops but have had to wait until I could get to a machine.

I spent a day to-day darling in which there were so many things to remind me of you. I went to the show and who did they have but the purple-lidded woodpecker. After the show another medical officer and myself went to the fights here on the post and one of the infantry officers asked me if I cared to be the doctor for the night. There I sat at the ring-side just like old times but I looked all over Bops and you weren't there, you rascal. The fighters even spit down over me, just like the old times.

I'm enclosing a set of the new overseas stripes for you to sew on your uniform darling. Each one stands for six months overseas. You had 25 so you are entitled to wear the extra one because of a partial 6 month period. Now sew them on your left sleeve down at the bottom above the cuff and you're all set.

Just listening to the news and I sure hope we break that damn Nazi West wall. I think it will be over soon darling in Europe and then we'll get to work on those Japs. Talking about Japs we have a regiment of American Japs here and they sure are good soldiers. They had 5 fighters in the fights to-night and they all won.

What do you think of the new demobilization plan, Bops? The only hitch is that I don't think it applies to officers so maybe it lets us out. Jeepers, imagine getting out of the army. I don't think I'd know what to do, would you Bops? I know what we'd do. We'd just run to-gether so fast we'd meet halfway to heaven. Yummy!

I just took a shower Bops and I'm sweet and clean only there's a part of my back I just can't get to, would you mind running down here Baby and taking care of it for me? Only hurry up Bops, I just can't wait, you sweetheart!

It sure has been hot the past week. No kidding Bops, I'll just never get used to hot weather. I'll take cold weather and your cold feet any day of the week.

I'll bet you're getting to be a smart old thing, aren't you Bops. Gosh, I'm going to have to watch my Ps and Qs pretty soon. You're getting to about the end aren't you darling. Soon, you'll be just as me darling, not that we haven't been before but sort of more so. Oh Gretchen, my beloved, I love you darling, love you, love you. Scruntch, scruntch, scruntch!

Sleep tight darling, and get those feet warmed up a little, they're cold—Hah!

I love you,
Mr Bops

7 Sept 1944

My darling,

How's my baby to-night? Sure would love to have you beside me right now darling curled up in our little blue blanket. It will be soon darling, soon, it must or else one of these days I'll just bust wide open if I don't hold you close to me soon and be able to scruntch and slide, and a little mouse, darling, please? Enough of that or I'll explode. I'm a rascal, aren't I darling?

Got sort of a sad letter from Daddy to-day darling. He approached Mort about Ruth and Mort gave him some sort of cockeyed answer about not knowing, etc. Bops, I hate to admit it, but I think there's something wrong with Martin. I just can't figure out what's wrong with him. It's reaching a point where I don't think he is capable of falling in love. I feel so damn sorry for him Bops that he has never felt the thrills of love and happiness as we have. I never realized how lucky we both are darling in spite of the troubles we have had. Holy smoke, I'd do it all over again a million times to know the thrill of your love, the tenderness of your kisses, the complete devotion that you have for me. I've never completely realized it until to-day darling, how lucky we really are. I feel so sorry for all the people who aren't in love and who don't have someone to love them and worry over them. I'm not talking of parental love, but of the deep, all consuming fire that burns in my heart for you and yours in your heart. Thank you again and again darling for loving me. I'm truly grateful and I promise you that I shall make it all up to you one fine day. I'm proud of you darling for what you're doing, for what you stand for, your beliefs, your Godlike ways. I'll never give you up darling, come hell, high water or anything they throw at me. I get so goddam mad at times that it's all I can do to keep from going home and really telling them all off. I've been waiting for two things, first Martin and Ruth which seems to be hopeless, and your conversion. I've given up on Martin and his chance for happiness. The day you are finished darling, we'll go at it again only this time there can be only one answer. If they only could see beyond their noses that they will never be happy until the day you and I are man and wife. Only by me being happy will they be happy. Please the Lord that they finally see it that way. I'm stronger each day darling in the knowledge that I am totally right and that they are totally wrong.

If anyone gets any ideas about you going overseas again you're going to do the following—you're going to put in a letter that your Mother's health and your father's business requires your presence near your home and that as long as you are near home things are all-right. However, if they insist on trying to send you overseas again you will have to put in your resignation from the army. I just won't have you go overseas again darling. You've done a good job and you've done your share. We'll fight them to the end because you're too thin, etc. to go over again. Don't think for a minute that you're shirking your job because you're not. There are thousands of girls who haven't seen the least little bit of foreign service who can go. You've got me to worry about so there and besides I'm thinking of the best way to get you out of the army anyway. Whoopeeeeeee! Bops, I'm blushing! Well, I love you and if I can't think of you and me doing stuff and stuff like that. Oh, Bops, you know what I mean, don't you baby! Bops, tell me, do you think of it all the time like I do? Can't help asking baby, cause I want to talk about it a little, can I? Heh! Heh! I'm a wolf.

I'm really not too lonesome anymore darling. Every time I get lonesome I get mad that we should be apart this way and that's good for me. I'd rather be mad than lonesome.

Golly, when I started this letter I didn't think I had much to say but here I go again a mile a minute. Be a sweet old fat thing for me darling cause that will give me so much more to eat up when I see you again.

I guess I'll be speaking with you by the time you get this. Yummy old baby, you!

I love you,
Mr Bops

(?Sept 11) Monday p.m.

My dear darling,

This is just the kind of a day when Bopsy & I would be curled up taking a nap if we were back in our little house. It's chilly & dark & gunboat is so sleepy.

Darling I have so much to do can't take time out for my nap today so will have to go to bed early tonight. Have my lesson at 7 & need to do some studying, besides that my art exam is due & I've only completed half of it. Baby it's just like going to school. My book arrived today & there it sits with me anxiously waiting to read it.

Thank you darling for Mr Cyrano—it looks most interesting & I like the manner in which it is translated. Think it will be easy to read. When you were in school dear did you read it in French? Another piece of literature I've been meaning to get to some fine day is Pope's translation of Homer's Odyssey.

My baby, don't burst please, wait a little longer cause I want you all in one piece, then if you're a real good boy all those things we both think about will come true. Darling do you ever wonder how it will be for neither of us to have a worry, just to be able to relax & have that big old burden of trouble taken from our shoulders? Bet we wouldn't leave our little nest for months, its perfectness would overwhelm us so.

Yes darling I know how you feel & what you think because we both think & feel alike & certainly because of that we should be able to talk about those things & be understood by each other.

Bopsy at night after I say my prayers, my mind wonders off to us—just automatically I build all sorts of air castles, build dream houses, make plans & then wonder how we will go about everything. Even think about a wee Miss Boo or a wee Mr Bops & how wonderful it would be to take it home to make your Mom & Daddy proud & happy. Aren't we rascals sweetheart, but after all it's what we both want isn't it? That would be the day Bopsy would burst—just from pride. Darling when I close my eyes I can see you with a big broad grin from ear to ear. Yes darling I think of it all the time. Very few hours go by without my Edward running around up there in my mind.

My darling you mustn't keep thanking me for loving you—because it isn't like a gift dear, it's a great privilege & honor. Darling do you really know what is in my heart & how I'm at a loss for words to tell you what being loved by you means to me? Never for a moment have you let me out of your *thoughts, it's always Miss Boo first, sometimes dear I can hardly believe it's true & that God has sent someone at last into my life who is so wonderful & good. Baby you are good clear way through & I'm so very proud of my Edward.*

To hear you talk with such confidence, pride & determination darling is the greatest thing ever written in your letters. It is the one thing I had always hoped for, to hear you say, "this is what I want & no obstacle is too great." For you to meet the blows which will undoubtedly come in another few weeks, that determination must be seared in your very soul for darling it would just about kill me to hear you say, "they are stronger than me." To say this darling is not mere chatter, for that is what had to happen to me before starting my conversion. "It's what I wanted because of my love for Edward," & now it's what is happening baby.

Don't want to talk about anything else but us in this letter. We come first & sweetheart whenever you feel anxious & jittery just tell Miss Boo about it & know that she feels the same. Let's hope it won't be long baby dear until we can talk these things over instead of writing them. I pray for it darling & for God to keep our love pure & beautiful.

Be my sweet sweet thing & have courage darling, cause I love you

Miss Boo

My dear darling

    How's my lonesome Bopsy—but it seems worse with Wally gone—just don't fret though Darling. We are both lonesome but have our love to keep us happy. Blue Mondays is right. How badly I need my baby for some smacks, cuddles, scrunching & all those funny words for good things.

    Have about 20 minutes before time to leave for the chapel. My lesson is on the Holidays tonight. I'm glad you are pleased with my progress dear, but it is all so simple & beautiful it isn't difficult to assimilate a little knowledge. Darling just think so very soon we will both be alike—we have often said we couldn't before but this is the climax & someday dear when we are together, we will be able to talk together & understand each other even more than we ever dreamed. It will make our lives complete.

    There is so little news, just a lot of confusion. Chicago wants all the names of those eligible for overseas again. My feathers will sure ruffle if they try to get me again. Darling I guess you'll just have to come up & take care of that situation. It would be beyond me—oh dear.

    Only 5 more days till Saturday—yummy. Our date, darling you are such a dear for being so wonderful. What other words are there besides I love you.

    Must get dressed—will add a line when I get home before sealing you up in the envelope.

    Your scrunchy—fatty.

    Oh Bops the scale says 114 now—you'll have to stretch your arms next time. Home again dear—enjoyed my lesson much . . . feel happier now dear, cause I'm that much closer aren't I?

    The pictures weren't very good were they Bops—maybe the film had too much Florida heat.

    Wonder if Martin got brave this week-end. Hope so. Does your family like her dear?

    So Daddy had to be told—well darling it doesn't hurt for them to know the truth. You know dear I think if Martin had been able to get in the Army, he would see a lot of things differently. All he has had are the breaks & good business & hasn't had to give up a thing—isn't that right?

    Better do a little studying on my next Decorating exam.

    Dream about me at night baby, & just remember I have my arms around you every night loving you for hours & hours.

    I love you sweet baby

Your Miss Boo

My darling,

Here's that old thing, darling, dashing off a sweet missile to that scruntchy, sweetheart of mine.

I appreciated your description of the way you felt on reading the ending of the story. I could just picture you reading it and thinking ahead, please make it a good ending, etc. Am I right? I don't know what the title means—just one of those things, I guess. Funny isn't it Bops, the way I used to tell you all those things the same way about what it meant to be a Jew, why we couldn't be to-gether, this and that. I still can't get over it darling, but yet there are so many just like us. Even though we love each other so much, there must have been and there will continue to be similar cases along the same lines and it's so unfair, so cruel. It's just a case of people being their own worst enemies and continuing to make things worse for themselves. The answer to the problem is not intermarriage entirely. I still don't believe in promiscuous intermarriage, because it takes two exceptional people to make a real go of it. But, for anyone to come out and say that all cases of intermarriage is wrong is the same as saying that all Japs are bad, that all Germans are bad, that people do this or are that. Mass generalizations are wrong. The majority of the times people would be right but the simple fact that there are always exceptions which prove the rule. Times change and so do people. Religion by itself must change—not the fact of the belief in God, that doesn't change, but the fact that a religion to be a success must be fluid—it must change to meet the demands of the times. Much of all religion had certain rules which must be obeyed. For example, the Jewish people were not supposed to work on Saturday but their lives in a Christian community made it impossible for them to obey that rule, so they worked on Saturday. There are so many things which change with time and use.

You remember how I used to tell you how impossible you and I getting to-gether would be darling. The thought of my ever mentioning a thing like that to my family would turn me inside out and I've never told you the miserable nights I used to spend in Panama thinking of how much you loved me and I loved you but I couldn't do anything about it. The nights you would cry and look in my eyes and I'd explain all the angles to you and you'd sit there just listening to me and saying yes, yes, yes, but all the time asking yourself why, why, why? You see baby, I knew all those things and I wasn't even honest with myself because I couldn't even answer why to myself. Even the folks don't know the answer, they just accept it as impossible to themselves. Why people put up such impenetrable barriers to their own happiness, I don't know. But they do. The old argument of oil and water not mixing always gives me a laugh. You eat and live with a person, do business with him, go to the movies with him, wear the same type of clothes but yet we are different. But, if they knew how alike you and I are darling. We think alike, we do the same things, etc. Oh well, I better save it for someone who doesn't know. We know, don't we Bops? Golly, How'd I get started in all that?

I got my new tires to-day and they sure are pretty. Everyone had their tongues hanging out when I put them on.

Some days the war looks so good and then it looks bad. I get to thinking of that Pacific business and it's enough to make anyone sick.

You've been so good writing, Bops. Is there anything you've asked me in the past week I've forgotten to answer. There is always so much to talk about that I guess I forget every once in awhile.

I sure miss Wally these days but I manage to get through the day. There's one thing I'm getting plenty of and that is rest. Oh yes, they want me to run the bingo parties here starting next week. How they find these things out I don't know, but they do.

The Holidays are next week and I'll be taking them in and on the 25th I think it is. I think I'll fast for good luck. I'm so happy about your weight darling, please keep it up.

Thank you for the scruntches and kisses and don't ever forget that

I love you
Mr Bops

My dear darling,

The only pleasant thing about having to work this afternoon is that I can have a nice talk with my old sweet thing. It's so beautiful out Bops, balmy and like a summer day. Wish you were here to take me for a nice ride and then we'd go to the movie this eve. Guess I will have to do the latter by myself as it sounds good. "Since You Went Away."

Am the only one working this afternoon so have had to stay in this stuffy old office, didn't even have a chance to make ward rounds, but it's such a long hike to cover them all. Anyway, things seem to be pretty quiet.

Well darling more news. I am getting my transfer this week sometime, as yet I don't know where it will be as the Col said Col. Clemonts in Chicago told me to be ready as my orders were on the way. She probably feels that since I wasn't a yes man I would find things made a little difficult for me here. The atmosphere has been very cool darling and I am on pins and needles to know where it will be. Will wire you the instant my orders arrive. Never a dull moment darling. Oh if you were only in a General Hospital so we could pull some strings. If it weren't for the fact that undoubtedly Dick will be letting you know soon and then a transfer for you I would like so much to come there, but it seems a little unwise when things are so uncertain don't you think dear?

My Saturday was incomplete darling, no Bopsy's sweet scruntchy telephone call. Guess I'm just the spoiled baby. My plans are to call you on your birthday dear, but in case I should get my orders to be out of here or should be traveling on that day I may call the fore part of the week. So this week dear it's my treat on account its your 32nd birthday. Hope your gift arrives in time. I have sent it. Darling I hope you won't be disappointed, but honest trying to shop here is impossible. You never even made one guess did you baby? No it isn't something to wear. Have to take good care of my sweet thing and make him happy don't I?

Did a little celebrating last night Bops, I was invited to a party at the club to help give a farewell for Tommy and some of the other girls that were leaving, and I really had a nice time. Even had a date what do you think of that, aren't I a bad girl? It was our last chance to all be together and I have stayed in so close and been studying and stuff, thought it would be a nice chance to brush the moss off my feathers. Feel a little sleepy today, and there area lotta spirits floating around, even feel a little shakey from that because

I hadn't had a drink since July with you. How I hate to see Tommy go, she is a peach. She still hasn't been able to get her husband, and is so upset over it. They leave tonight for Ellis.

My being transferred will change my plans again for finishing my lessons, but Chaplain says he will give me the name of someone to finish with wherever I may go. Anyway dear we are through the most important part of the lessons. Just don't worry about it though because I will finish come hell or high water, so there. Darling I think you ought to get the Chaplain's present for me because even though we aren't going any further I want to do something for him as he has been so perfectly wonderful to me. Think the pen or pencil would be lovely, just do the best you can and I know your judgment is good.

Darling my things are all packed, even got Mr. Bops stuffed in a big box, cause he will go with me. Am getting so sick of packing and moving, it seems that's all either of us has done all our lives. Won't it be a treat to get all our things in one spot some day dear?

The tires sound beautiful baby, I feel easier now too, because it is so easy to have an accident when the tires are bad. You were awfully lucky to have gotten them dear. Have you been down to the beach lately, or is the gas situation still a little bad?

Guess I have jabbered long enough, we sure have lots to say it seems, but darling I enjoy writing to you just cause we talk along about anything and everything.

Be my sweetheart and don't work too hard. How are the planes coming?

I love you darling
Miss Boo

My dear darling,

Guess I'm finding out how awful it is not to get a letter for two days. Honest darling the days are incomplete without your letters. We are so spoiled. The only thing that I think of when those letters don't come is that you are ill—but that's silly isn't it? Baby dear your letters become sweeter day by day & the thrill of getting them & all the wonderful things you see is greater with each passing day. Honest darling my heart goes a mile a minute when I find that air mail from Florida. Do you get excited too?

Had a nice talk with Chaplain last night. We discussed the completion of my lessons & he will write you. He feels dear when the time comes for the final step that it would be best for me to have it from a civilian Rabbi. Oh darling how I want you here for that day. Suppose it's only wishful thinking, but it will be such an important step for me to take & I hate to be alone. Really don't expect to be finished until October which isn't too far off.

We had fun Sunday. Some of we girls played Royal rummy with pennies. We ate, gabbed, laughed & were silly. It's a good game Bops & the final pot I won which had $2.25 in so you know how many games we played to get that many pennies. Just an old gambler at heart—that's me.

Hope to go to services Friday & then will go Sun. nite if I don't go home. Don't know for sure yet, will wire you if they give me my weekend.

Darling, right now before it slips my mind—a Happy New Year dear heart & as we say from now on, "May you be inscribed in the Book of Life for a Happy New Year."

Bopsy let's hope it's our happiest one & fulfills all our dreams.

Be a good baby & here are all my hugs & kisses for my darling whom I love.

Miss Boo

Are you having some days off for the Holiday's dear?

Wednesday noon (20 September)

My dear darling,

It just takes one good letter from my Bopsy to make me ashamed & angry at myself. Thank you dear heart for ever giving me the courage & strength that seems to be lacking without you.

Darling I want you to know that all in your big fat letter is true, it was beautifully written & now sweetheart I've got to make you a promise. This past year or 6 months has been tough. Perhaps my recovery from your trials & tribulations has not been complete, undoubtedly that is the reason for my instability—but it isn't getting either of us any place & it's high time I became a normal sensible human being again & stopped all this nonsense—else my Bopsy won't love me anymore for sure. First of all dear you must love me because you can depend on me & it is so unfair to make your already heavy load heavier. Certainly by this time I should fully realize that whatever happens, my Edward will always be there to set things right. My faith has to be strong enough to put asunder all doubts. Darling I'm ashamed. Will you forgive me just this once again? Dear baby from now on & since it's the new year, I will have started a new clean book of braveness understanding the true value of things & faith in our future. You see darling all my life it's been a fight by myself & now that my Edward has come into my life I've grown so dependent on him. Baby dear my promise to you from now on is to have utter faith in your wisdom & not to be a spoiled baby any more.

Yes dear I realize there is a possibility of your going out again, but we will face that as we have faced everything else. Let's hope that God sees fit to keep you here but if not darling you will always have me to come home to & I shall be waiting with open arms.

Do you know something darling—you wrote two letters in one day. Golly that's good. Our letters to each other would make a wonderful book & would certainly show people what real love is.

My things are all ready to go. Have cleared the post. So now I can go away with two more E's on my efficiency record & a good feeling inside. Have an appointment with Chaplain Schwartz at 2:00 & he will give me all the necessary information about completing my lessons. Will feel so relieved darling when at last I am that much closer to you. So sorry my transfer couldn't have been postponed for another week or so but, thank heavens I started when I did & have the most of it.

I'm happy again dear, & from now on I'm going to be a big grown up lady with lots of good sense & no more panics-ha-so there. Please don't fret anymore sweetheart, let's just be happy. Mother & Daddy Siegel are going to be on our side soon darling. We know that & then we will show them how we love them for it & how our happiness will be theirs.

> *I love you sweetheart.*
> *Take care of my Bopsy, Your Miss Boo*

My darling,

Thank you darling for your wire, I didn't expect you to call tonight in as much as we have kept the wires from here to Florida busy. Betcha you have a big date for Sat. night-ha-well have fun baby dear & think of me. Also thought perhaps all of this may have precipitated a rush call for an understanding talk with Martin. Darling I hope & pray I haven't caused trouble again.

Darling I've read & re-read your letter commenting on the story. Please don't deny this Edward—you are dreading another talk with the family, aren't you? You feel they will still say no don't you dear & then the decision will be at your feet again. Bopsy my dear heart whatever happens, you've got to be sure & satisfied within yourself. Couldn't face the consequences if you were ever sorry for anything. Darling I've changed my religion because I love you & because it will make me more understanding of the barrier we have to face, because if God sees it our way, we have got to be bound as one in thought & action. Baby I would never fail you, believe that, with all your heart & soul, your faith in me has got to be supreme. It would be foolish not to admit my emotions are a bit mixed up, just because I fear your dread of the coming months. There isn't any other factor darling because I know you love me with unbounding devotion.

Baby I went to services last night, enjoy them more each time. Wanted so to go. Sun. eve may have to work. Please go Edward & may you find strength & refuge in God to give my darling courage & the will to keep thinking straight & being strong. Want you here so badly darling. We should be together on these Holy Days. There will come a day though won't there sweetheart.

Am more positive a transfer will come through soon Edward. Wouldn't mind going to Blanding if you were sure of staying there, but have a feeling Dick will have news for you soon. There have been several meetings in Chicago of late on this reconditioning so it is probably going on in every command.

Isn't it symbolic dear that the lights in London are to go on again the eve of Rosh Hashanah. What a glorious new year for those people.

Need lots of scruntches & things baby & the only person who can take care of it all is my Bopsy—because I love him so.

Be good dear darling
Your Miss Boo.

Thank you sweet baby for all the courage & promises you have made while I was facing this problem. It always seems so unfair of me to burden you with all my problems. May I make it up to you some day?

Monday Sept. 25, 1944

My dear darling—

Look for your letters more than ever now dear. They are such a necessity. We sure have heaps of fun kidding & writing all sorts of things don't we darling?

Work is going fair, it's really quite discouraging, but everyone is so nice & very friendly. One happy family with only eleven of us to do all the work. I'll do my best though darling & hope it won't last over six months.

Capt Butler our Chief Nurse took me to the movie last night, believe I'm on the inside track in that respect. She is really a sweet little person & has her hands full. We know lots of people in common.

Wonder if the girls there are in seersuckers. We are & it seems good. No messy starched uniforms to bother with.

Yesterday I received a New Year's box from Chaplain Schwartz. Thought it very sweet of him, & you can see Bops what great confidence he has in my conversion. It's so wonderful dear & I'm so enthused.

Darling I'll just have to tell you what your gift is—can't understand the delay. Was really disappointed in the necessity of sending a years subscription to "Fortune"—but my hands were tied because of shopping facilities. Anyway each month when it comes you can think of your old thing huh?

Received my election ballot to-day but Edward I'm in a quandary. Guess it will be Roosevelt again, certainly have lost my respect for Dewey's nasty speeches. What a mess. One hardly knows what to do.

Bopsy I do believe in spite of everything my weight is picking up again. Am eating well & don't feel nearly as cold & miserable as of late. You'll see an old fat scrunchy thing yet—so there.

Guess the news & jabber is exhausted. Wish my darling could be here to talk to in person, but I never lose faith in our dreams coming true. No! Sweet baby you're not a bad boy-just a normal human being with hopes & desires & you just go ahead & dream & be my sweetheart for I love you.

Miss Boo

Sorry you had to be OD on your birthday but know you enjoyed the week-end.

My dear darling—

Your letter this morning was like manna from heaven darling. It vanished all that nostalgia in the pit of my tummy & made me realize more than ever how wonderful it is being in love with my sweet scruntchy Bops.

Left McCoy Wed. eve at 9:30 by bus to LaCrosse. What with civilians grumbling about my luggage & saying, "It's probably full of jars & bottles," it was rather an ugly start. Waited for two hrs. at LaCrosse for the train but took a sleeper until they detached it at Rock Island. The coach the rest of the way was a cattle car darling—1492 vintage & my face looked like I'd spent the day in the coal mines. Transportation came for me at Ipana & my wild trip ended at 3:00 p.m.

The camp & especially the Hosp. area isn't nearly as bad as people paint it. My quarters are much nicer than at McCoy. Have a bright sunny room on the main highway. A group of the girls who were at McCoy greeted me at the door, so it was like old home week. Got quite settled by bedtime. The unit I was to be with is here & their chief is Kay Harris, a wonderful girl, whom I knew at Ft. Bragg. Golly it was sure a surprise & I was thrilled to see her as we were very best of friends at Bragg. She is most capable & the girls will adore her.

Our C.O. of the Hosp. is Col. Jacobson. He was the Capt. who gave me my physical at Grant when I entered the service in '41—funny huh? He said my face looked familiar. Our chief nurse is Capt Butler—young & pleasant.

The nursing situation is acute here, 9 nurses assigned to the Hosp with 500 patients. The girls from the units are helping out now. You see dear this is a training camp for engineers, quartermaster & medical corp. All the units being formed to go to Point Of Embarkation are here, & when that project is completed it will undoubtedly be curtains for Ellis. I go on duty tomorrow on the wards—hurrah—in charge of contagion it seems. Will let you know more about that later.

Darling the worst part of all is the transportation. It's going to be a real problem getting anyplace. Oh for a car. It's 160 miles to St. Louis. We do get 2 days off a month so it can be arranged. The very first chance I have to go in I shall & will get all the details in the meantime. It is 225 miles to Chicago & most difficult—so that would not be an easy trip to make.

Chaplain Schwartz gave me the name of the Rabbi in St. Louis that he wants me to go to. He feels I am ready for my final step but would like to *have me go into St. Louis to make the plans. Now darling there will be a little time entailed & since everything seems to be going to happen Oct., believe it is alright for you to approach your family in the manner you planned. In the meantime we will know what they have to say & I can go ahead with my conversion. Think we shouldn't stall once Wally and Father Laws see them. Just don't lose your courage, sweetheart & keep praying every day. Naturally I'm expecting the worst but darling I keep thinking they won't continue to be cruel to my baby. So hope your mother doesn't go to pieces again darling. That part worries me terribly. It could all be so sensible & simple if they'd only let it be.*

When you find the gift for the Chaplain send it direct to him dear from both of us. He has indeed been marvelous in helping me with all my troubles.

Gee darling what will I do if I don't gain weight. My Bops will scold. If I do they may send me overseas again. People & stuff better hurry up & decide. We can't be separated or else off this gal might go. Anyway darling I've always done everything for my baby, so fat it will be regardless.

> *I love you my darling.*
> *Your Miss Boo.*

By the way our calls can be made direct to quarters so-o-o if you get ideas, it's Camp Ellis 5143.

My dear darling

Goodness but this doesn't seem like Sat. at all. No call from my baby which seemed so strange, but of course I didn't expect it. Darling it seems eons since you've written or I've talked with you. This strange land, strange people & a hard days work has all been so foreign.

Its no wonder they say you need the Distinguished Service Cross after serving at Ellis. Bops the hospital is a filthy dirty place. No nurses and all 4F help which is as good as nothing. Had five wards to-day and seven to-morrow so imagine how utterly futile it seems. I'll promise you though darling to go along with my eyes closed & not see the dirt—but it bothers me. Anything is better than facing overseas again though & perhaps none of this will last too long.

What is the news from home dear. Oh how well I realize your dread of reopening a wound. Wonder if they think you have forgotten me or just what. Darling you never have said just how you planned to tell them that we are writing, etc. Baby dear I pray for you almost every hour of the day. Pray for your strength & courage & thank God for all you are facing because of me. Bops I will be so anxious for Wally to return to Blanding. Just wonder how your family will accept his suggestions.

How dreadfully I miss my lessons dear-it doesn't seem right at all. Am trying to do some studying with what little material is at hand and am anxious to make the trip to St. Louis. Do you think Dick will mind terribly helping me. Rabbi Isserman is the one I'm to go see and Chaplain Schwartz doesn't want me to postpone it because he wants my memory fresh. Sweetheart please never consider the fairness of my conversion. It's what I want to do & believe in my heart & it's not a mere gesture believe me darling with all your soul.

Miss you so baby. Miss Boo needs so much scruntching very badly & for my Bopsy to hold her close & brush the cares away. What heaven it will be dear heart.

Better get sweet & clean & crawl in this lonesome little bed. My Mr Bops is sitting on the end of my bed waiting to be hugged, but it will be my Edward in my thoughts.

Tell me all the news dear & I do hope the Holidays have given you great strength & consolation.

I love you darling forever & ever

Your baby

OCTOBER, 1944

My dear darling,

Bopsy Bopsy, your voice never fools me, can always tell by the tone just how things are going. Am afraid it sounded like the going is a little tough again—but you wouldn't tell me—either way it seems Miss Boo must sweat it out. Darling to hear you say, "You shall be Mrs Bops" tells me one thing though & that is you haven't lost your courage. How wonderful those words sounded dear, it almost seems like I dreamed them. Don't be too down-hearted baby, it's going to be tough, we both know that, but the struggle doesn't seem near as hard & your hurt at their remarks not nearly as deep. Bopsy we can win them over, even though they still think you're making a mistake.

Golly I feel like I've been beaten tonight. That horse sure hit all the bumps. Do you know Bops Capt. Butler has as much pep as I do & maybe more. We make a good race horse team. She & I went riding from 5:30-6:30 & it was lots of fun. When we came home we had sandwiches & coffee & then played two rubbers of bridge. What a wonderful group of girls & so friendly. The best women I've met since Bragg. My riding is not that of an expert dear, it's been four years, but can post fairly well & this pony could really gallop like silk.

Bet I know what you did today—listened to the World Series* Didn't hear the final on St. Louis & the Yanks, it was 4-2 last report—imagine St. Louis won. Those two home runs were very exciting.

Well darling, I must take my turn at the old night duty shift starting Tues. with only nine of us we must share & share alike. Have 15 wards—all ward men in charge—really dread the responsibility. Only two nurses for the whole hospital at night. It really seems wicked with our census at 480. So why don't you call me next Friday afternoon about three. Will have two days off at the end of my two week term & that is when I will take off for St. Louis. That will be about Oct. 17-18. OK?

Have just got to crawl in that little bunk sweetheart. Oh if only my Bopsy were there to pat the bruises. Would you, huh?

Good night sweet baby—chin up & now that Wally has returned he will be your moral support & I promise not to worry.

All my smacks & bear hugs I'm saving for Bops cause I love you.

Miss Boo.

---

*   This was not the World Series which did not begin until Wed., Oct 4. She seems to be anticipating that by the time he receives this letter, he will be listening to the World Series.

My dear darling,

Another day has rolled by & soon I will have been here a week. It all becomes a little easier as I become familiar with routine. One thing Bops it certainly is not at G. I. as McCoy.

How are you my darling. You haven't told me for a long time whether or not you are again gaining weight & how's the appetite & are you sleeping better? Baby are those old sleepy hours still full of worry & thinking or are you now calm? Honest Bops since I've gotten here, my mind feels so much more at ease, just like nothing drastic is pending like before & that soon we will be two happy old things. In spite of all the strangeness dear you seem so much closer. Above all I hope everything gets straightened out with the family, then distance or time for us won't seem so hard.

Darling, at last I've started reading Cyrano de Bergerac & it's really wonderful—have chuckled to myself—especially over the description of his nose. It's very fast reading too, the translation is so simply written.

Tonight I'm going to try to do some studying on my Decorating, have neglected it somewhat.

Bopsy what does Martin have to say these days. Why don't you have him come to see you after Wally comes back? Is he still going with Ruth or is it definitely all off?

Darling, can I go to bed tonight & dream good about all those wonderful smacks & scruntches that only Bops knows how to do. Golly it's so hard to wait to see my baby, but with all of it sweetheart, our coming happiness will be all the more perfect.

No news tonight, punkins but just had to have a wee little chat. No letter today but betcha there will be one tomorrow.

Good night baby dear & I love you with all my heart.

Your baby

Tues. Eve (3 Oct.?)

My dear darling

Have an hour before taking off for the first night of my wild night duty term. Gee Bops how I dread it. Under normal circumstances it's bad enough but have a feeling this will be a nightmare.

Baby you're a sweetheart for taking care of all the shopping. Think your choice of gifts was excellent. Am sure the receivers will be well pleased, but honest dear I feel like a heel for not sharing the expenses. My money is good too you know. A thousand smacks isn't very many, but they sound awful good.

What a fairy story we gals lived yesterday. Went to bed exhausted, one of the girls got her boyfriend's 1934 Chevy to drive to Peoria—four of us went & I was the only one with a driver's license so it was my job. Never again. I'll take a horse. It poured like nothing I've seen since Panama. We went through water up to the fenders & you can imagine what happened to mechanical brakes—there weren't any. It took all my skill & nerve to get the gang safely there driving through city traffic. After our shopping the darn thing wouldn't start, so the gals had to push. Bops it was a scream. We all laughed so hard. No one had any strength. Next we parked on a hill to go get a bite to eat, locked the car & when we came out, couldn't get the damn thing open. Finally rounded up two M.P.'s and they helped us. From then on all went well but missed a junction along the way & drove 10 miles in the wrong direction. We met a soldier & he directed us home, but the whole trip was like a movie comic. The girls were swell scouts & now it all seems funny but at the time it was most serious. Capt. Butler was one of the four. Think my shopping will be nil until I leave Ellis—cause the transportation problem is like none I've ever experienced.

Suppose there isn't any use in asking how our war is progressing. Darling I think about you constantly & keep praying over & over that it isn't as hard this time. Hope your family decides to come to see you dear & I'm so glad you aren't going up there, at least not right now. Have courage sweetheart, just remember to take God's hand & He will help.

How is the weather down there now? The fellows are all wearing O.D. & look so nice. Will you wear them soon.

Be a good scrunchy, keep happy, the chin up & remember I love you more than anything in the world.

Your baby

Wed Eve (4 Oct?)

My dear baby,

This seems to be a pretty good time to get your letter written each day, my last free hour before the rat race.

Slept quite well today til 2:00. Suddenly it seemed like it was time to go to Bopsy's house & wait for him to come home. Instead I got dressed & went to the mailbox for that sweet letter. Found all the smacks & scruntches enclosed & that wee little mousy in one corner. Good baby, good.

Wrote to Dick this p.m. giving the details of my present plans, etc., tonight. I will write Chaplain Schwartz asking him to introduce me via letter to Rabbi Isserman. Hope nothing happens to spoil my plans for the 17th & 18th. Am a bit skeptical though because of the nursing situation here.

Bopsy last night was really awful. My poor legs were numb this morning. There just isn't any satisfaction in doing a job in that manner, it's a physical impossibility. Certainly neither of we nurses could be blamed for anything wrong that happened. Guess there isn't anything to do but keep going & let come what may. Capt. Butler is sick about the whole set up, but Chicago refuses to send any help so what can she do.

Hope Irving gets home safe & sound, imagine his letters read like a good exciting book. Am glad to know he is another who approves of us.

Did you hear the 1st game of the World Series dear. I heard the last half & know the Browns won. Yee imagine me telling you anything about baseball—but my Bops got me interested didn't he? Let's go to a big game some day darling & eat popcorn & peanuts & yell & holler—huh? Yes dear baby I too dream of all the things we have to do—places we want to go. We will sweetheart just have faith & courage.

Darling how's our twinkly star these days—does she still look in your window & does she still sparkle like a diamond in the sky? Tell her to watch over my darling cause I love him so.

Anxiously awaiting your call Friday afternoon.

I love you baby dear,
Miss Boo

Thur. Eve

My dear darling,

How is this for luck? Mrs. Farrington the librarian who lives next door to me has a portable and has offered me the use of it. Now I can run off a note to you in no time flat. I am a little late tonight for we gals have been sitting around chewing the fat, and Capt Butler gave us a drink. We are really quite the chummy kids, she is just one of the gang and it is so nice to have run across someone like that.

What a rainy old day it has been, and foggy, just like London, but darling when your letter came it made the sun shine. They are always such cute letters and I always exclaim sort of out loud, "what a sweetheart that Edward of mine is." Bops this is one spoiled old gal you love but I feel like a million dollars because I am so fortunate.

Honest darling this is the funniest Army post I have ever been on, am really quite happy though, there are no inspections, the ward men do all the work and pass all the medicines, do the charting, take care of the patients etc., they really have to because as of today we have exactly 9 nurses to take care of the whole place, seems so odd, and about all we gals can do is supervising and dispensing narcotics. It is really rather pathetic though, for it doesn't give us a chance to do any nursing. Think the 6th service command is going to pot, it amazes all of us why they keep Ellis open, which is by far the most poorly equipped post, and then close up a lovely place like McCoy. Funny things they do in war time.

Thank you dear for sending Dick's address, Capt Butler says I should not worry about taking my day off, but just to say when I want time off regardless of whether or not there are any nurses left to take care of the patients so expect I will ask for it during the first or second week of October. Chaplain Schwartz will write or call the Rabbi in St. Louis when I am ready and then I will also write Dick and his wife and tell them I'm coming. Think I shan't try to see Pudgy until all my business is taken care of, that can come later.

Last night Capt Butler, Mrs. Farrington and myself plodded through the rain to see "Kismet." It was really quite a fairytale, and I especially enjoyed the costumes and the color. We were sure soaked when we got home. Tomorrow night we are going to play bridge. Gee darling do you suppose I have forgotten all that you tried to teach me, what a dumb old thing that gun-boat is. You sure will have to find another partner when it comes to *that game darling cause I'm afraid if I were your wife you would probably beat me, huh? Oh darling it's so much fun dreaming and thinking about our future, please God keep being good to Bops and me.*

Just think by the time this letter arrives you will have talked to me again, can hardly wait until Saturday, it's almost like a real date except—oh well, you know what. Darling you are so good to your Bopsy aren't you?

Well sweet thing it's getting late and I should drop mom a note, always hate to seal you up inside that envelope though, but it has to be, with bushels of smacks there too.

Just love you more each day scruntchy, and cause you have been a good Bopsy, can I sneek in a little mousy? Geeeeee.

Good night darling,
Your baby.

Dear Gretchen,

I am sure that there is no reason for making excuses in my delay in writing, but this has been the very first time that I can call my soul my own. I know you will be as delighted as I am in knowing that little Wally passed the course with flying colors. It was a tough fight all the way, but on my final exam, I really outdid myself. Graduation is Wednesday morning and Friday morning I will be back in Florida talking to that lovable guy of yours. Honest Gretchen, if it wasn't for Ed, I would dread going back, but the thought of seeing him, makes me very happy. It is amazing to realize that I know him only 4 months. Yet in that short time, it is amazing to think how close I feel toward him.

Ed perhaps wrote and told you how my leave was cancelled, and although I was very angry at the whole darn Army, I think it was a break in a way. Elaine came here Saturday and she left this morning. As my train does not leave Richmond until 9:05 p.m. Thursday, and graduation exercises end around 10:30 a.m. Wednesday, I am going to dash into New York and be with my wife for a few hours.

Gretchen, don't ever think for a moment that anything or anyone can come between you and Edward. Such thoughts should never be in your mind. It's now past the point of thinking of others. Edward realizes this, and your future love and happiness as Mrs. Siegel is assured.

Please believe me that I am not saying this to allay your fears. It is because I know the trend of Ed's mind. He is cool and knows how the situation lies. Just keep that pretty chin of yours up and I'll be giving you a "Mazeltov" and a kiss at your wedding day.

I, too, was tickled to hear about your change in orders. Oh, Gretchen, can't you see that God has willed it that you should be near each other? With His ever loving guiding hand, your only tears should be tears of happiness and never of sorrow and despair. And for whatever tears you have shed in despair, will dry into glorious rainbows of joy and contentment.

I know that never for a moment will you ever regret the wonderful step you have taken in enfolding Judaism. It is, as you say, a simple and grand belief. If only more people, and I mean of the Jewish race themselves, would realize how wonderful it is, there would be so much less heartache and grief. But they too shall realize the error of their ways and atone for their mistakes.

Please write again real soon. Your letters are a deep source of happiness to me and always be assured that whatever is in my power to assist in your future happiness, is yours to command. Don't worry about Edward. His outlook is marvelous and whatever boost he needs, I am right there to give it to him.

Love to you from Elaine & myself

More than just fondly,
Wally

p.s. Write to me at Blanding

My dear darling,

Heh—what goes on Bops. I work all night trying to put a few pennies in our sock & you take women out to dinner, married ones at that. Well o.k. I had a letter from Wally today so there. Fun huh?

Am glad you took Col. out darling, never believe for a minute that all that chatter just said is serious, but we gotta kid each other a little don't we baby? Tell me what she had to say & Bopsy I don't want you to leave the States, please don't.

This sleeping is a problem. Two flies were playing golf on my face today, I got so darned mad—got up & killed them both—murder she says. Guess the reason I can't sleep is cause it isn't in my Bopsy's bed.

Had a tough night just past, not enough to do without having to call the A.O.D. to discipline a bunch of bad boys who were playing moo cow at 10:30. That ward is a mess. My blood pressure was 195—you should have heard me <u>order</u> one of those boys back to bed. You know that stinky little temper of mine that sneaks out—don't you darling.

The night really flies Bops. My knee isn't liking all this walking though, but I'll watch it. Bet it's a 20 mile hike every night.

Got up in time to hear the last half of the game—gee—even I was excited dear, eleven innings & 3 to 2. Wonder what will happen tomorrow.

Received my receipt for your Fortune Magazine. You will get it for 20 months. Isn't that nice?

Was so pleased to hear that Wally had passed his course. His letter was very nice. He and Elaine had been together regardless of no leave. He said the only thing good about returning to Blanding was seeing <u>you</u> dear baby.

Darling I will wait a few days before calling Dick, cause he will receive my letter with my plans & perhaps he will answer promptly. As things look now my plans will go through o.k.

Am kinda stupid right now. My tummy is howling & it's hungry time so have to go take care of that little matter.

I'm proud of your bridge dear. He's just an old whiz bang that's all. Tomorrow!! Yummy.

I love you my baby dear.
Miss Boo

My dear darling,

Sit back, cause this promises to be a lengthy letter as I have a million things to talk about and to tell you, you will just have to read and read.

My darling it's needless to tell you that my every moment is spent in thought of you and your trip home, I dread it with all my heart and soul for you to go up there and take another beating. That's the reason it's futile for you to tell me not to worry because I am so terribly concerned. Yes darling I know your mind is made up as to what the outcome is going to be and for that I can only thank God and pray that you have the strength and the courage to carry you through. It makes my heart ache to think that your parents are settled on their decision and refuse to let you have a mind of your own. I know they will say that this is the thanks they get for giving you everything, but darling I am not saying this to be cruel, and I know you will agree with me, that they have made it so pronounced in their giving you every material thing you have ever wanted that now you have been placed in the position of being extremely obligated. They are wonderful people darling of that I am sure because they have sacrificed for you but it is all wrong that they should rule you to the extent that they are removing the privilege of your being able to use your own mind and use your own judgment. Believe me darling when I tell you that it still hasn't made me feel bitter and because of the great barrier they are placing, I will try to my dying day to make them happy and be forgiving for their not understanding. Darling the only way left for us to do is to go ahead and prove to them by our extreme happiness that they were wrong. It won't seem nearly as bad if we once make our plans and go through with them. I am fully aware that they will be heartbroken for awhile, but it will pass away, it has happened over and over in so many cases. Another thing we need not fear is that we won't have to go back to Poughkeepsie for at least another year or two because you won't be out of the Army before that, and that will give us a chance to get our own four feet on the ground and to go directly there. Sweetheart, don't believe me to be forcing you into anything, but I know that this has got to work out for us and we have got to be strong enough to go ahead in spite of all that seems impossible to stand.

My heart almost stopped Sunday night when I heard your voice, my poor baby had been crying, how unfair it is of them to frighten you and make you believe that you are going to be the cause of deaths, etc. Darling that won't *happen believe me, it's only a defense mechanism. We had to call you back as we were all so upset, the second time you sounded like my Edward. That is the reason I called Wally yesterday instead of you, thought too that you might have left. Just be brave dear heart, take God's hand as he has taken mine in the last few days especially and all will be well. You probably will be surprised at the strength and courage you will have, I just know that this will be the greatest knowledge of God being with you that you have ever felt.*

Dear baby, at last I am a Jewess, it hardly seems possible, but it is true. I took my conversion under one of the four greatest and best known Rabbis in the United States. He was wonderful to me and will write you in the next few days. Darling I can't tell you what went through me when I stood before that altar in the Temple before the public and two witnesses, denouncing my faith and joining in the faith of Israel. At first I was very nervous and frightened, and then like a great wave of power the feeling of knowing that I was doing right and believed in it surged through my body and I stood with my eyes uplifted to Rabbi Isserman saying I do and I will. It was very simple and beautiful and every word I spoke, every prayer I said was followed with I am doing this because I love Edward. Now my name is Gretchen Ruth and I know darling that you are proud and happy for me. The preparedness has taken a great deal of effort on my part but my determination saw me through to the grand and glorious end.

Saw Rabbi Isserman in the morning in fact I attended the Sukkuth services. He was quite surprised was ready at that time to be converted, but after quite a long talk with him and he discovered what my knowledge of Judaism was, he didn't hesitate in the least. He is an extremely busy and noted man, but took time out to give me every consideration. He is the Rabbi that made the world tour with the Army and the Red Cross, he is a noted writer, in fact he autographed and gave me one of his books. The events that lead up to all this are almost unbelievable darling, our guardian angel in our twinkly star was watching over every event. In the first place it is odd that Chaplain Schwartz should send me to him for he is a personal friend of Dick's, in fact Dick has filled his pulpit several times. It is odd that I should have gone when I did, as he left last night right after my conversion and a dinner to go to Kansas City to speak to a crowd of 20,000. Had I gone to anyone else or at any other time none of this would have happened. He is sending my certificate of confirmation in a day or so. I will write him today expressing my gratitude and will enclose a check for the temple.

Darling I can't tell you how wonderful Dick and Sally were to me, I felt I had known them all my lives and they were perfectly dear, sweet and understanding and darling Dick and Sally both said that you have every right to fight for me, I really believe that they thought your old Bops quite the girl. Sally is just the sweetest thing in the world and Dick says, "Gretchen don't ever give Edward up, you were made for each other." It was wonderful hearing things like that. It was Dick's suggestion that we call Sunday night. We had some wonderful meals at their home and Monday afternoon, Sally planned our whole wedding. They want us to be married right there and they both said that they would take care of every detail for us. I could hardly believe that there were such people in the world, and darling that is where I would like to be married. What do you think of it? Am sure mother and daddy could get down there and I would like to have Rabbi Isserman perform the ceremony. You see it would be almost impossible to go home because there isn't a Rabbi anywhere except in the cities and then neither of us would know him. Darling I hope that I am not dreaming too far ahead, but I am sure that we will be married that is why I have done so. Darling I sincerely believe the sooner we are married the better it will be, for if we wait so many things can happen including you being sent away, darling and I couldn't let you go unless you were mine first. Guess I am selfish, or am I proposing? Ha.

Left St. Louis last night at 9:30 and got into camp at 3 this morning. I am exhausted, suppose the mental strain has a lot to do with it, but darling I accomplished almost the impossible and I am so very proud and happy in my heart.

Hadn't written you for three days but there was so much going on and my being on night duty that it was neglected, know you understand. This afternoon you will be leaving for home, I hardly know what I shall do with myself for consolation until your call or letter. Put a call through anytime darling and I will try in some way to talk to you.

Baby, baby I do want to come to Blanding, perhaps it could be arranged if the chief nurse there wrote to 6 Service Command, I have got to be near you soon. Darling our day of peace and happiness in its completeness is near, let's both be strong and see it through. God will help us dear heart.

Must write to Dick and Sally and also to the Rabbi so had better stop and tell you again that I love you Edward with the greatest love any human can know.

I love you my precious
Gretchen Ruth

Tuesday Eve (Oct. 10)

My dear darling,

Can you stand another letter, which makes two in one day, but even after that huge one I wrote this noon there are things that I forgot to tell you. Anyway I'm just lonesome for my baby and thinking of you every minute because I know that about now you are getting near home. God only knows what you will find, but sweetheart my prayers are with you like none I've ever said before because now darling we are alike in every way.

Have written a lot of letters today, thank you notes, etc., wrote to Wally tonight and I just know he thinks I am the biggest worrywart in the world.

Meant to tell you what Dick said about a position in the new program. He said the places are all filled for the ear program but that the eye hospital is getting underway and wondered if you would be interested in that. Darling I told him that I thought you would be more interested in the eye work than in anything else. He said that the staff for this hospital hadn't been picked and that if you were chosen you would have a definite status and wouldn't be running the risk of being sent out. So perhaps something fine will break yet.

Darling I owe you a dollar on the ball game, so here it is, now you can't say that I don't pay my debts, so there. I was sorry to hear that the Cards won, not just because we had a bet either, but think it would have been nice for the underdogs to have come through. Truthful though, about Monday I wasn't much interested in the ball game, there was so much on my mind and I had to study for my conversion for that eve.

Dear baby I feel so good inside now, what a wonderful step it was that I have just taken, know down deep in my heart that I shall never be sorry for it. To be like my Bopsy is the greatest thing that could ever happen to a girl. God is with us dear darling and I hope you have remembered to take your problems to Him and have taken His hand during these hard and trying days.

Am going to bed in a little bit, will say my prayers for my dear Edward who is fighting for our love. Remember always that I love you sweetheart.

Your baby

October 12, 1944

Capt. Edward Siegel, M.C.
Regional Hospital
Camp Blanding, Fla.

Dear Capt. Siegel:

Lieutenant Gretchen Boody was converted to the Jewish faith on
the altar of Temple Israel in St. Louis, Missouri on October 9th.
The following were witnesses to the ceremony:

Mrs. David Kriegshaber, Dr. Richard S. Silverman, Mrs. Maude
Heyman, and Mrs. Joseph Kohn.

I gave Lieutenant Boody the name of Ruth as a symbol of her
acceptance of Judaism.

With all good wishes, I remain,

Sincerely yours,

FMI:LS

CC: Lt. Gretchen R. Boody,
Station Hospital
1624 S.U.
Camp Ellis, Ill.

[handwritten note:] Your check & letter just came.
I shall use the former for a
worthy cause — the witnesses &
I were touched by the sincerity
of your conversion & wish
you happiness
Wasserman

POST HEADQUARTERS CHAPEL

CAMP McCOY, WISCONSIN

16 October 1944

Lt. Gretchen Boody, ANC
Station Hospital
Camp Ellis, Ill

My dear Gretchen Ruth:

Your letter of October 10 thrilled me beyond
words. It is really more than a letter - it's a docu-
ment, which I shall value for all time.

Rabbi Isserman

I am glad that you found my colleague, so fine
and understanding. I talked with him about you over the
telephone on the Sunday you left for St.Louis.

Now I am very anxious to know how Edward's
visit turned out. In any event I hope he will permit
nothing to stand in the way. I am writing him today.

of gene hopkins

Please let me hear from you by return mail.

With fond regards and every good wish, I am

Faithfully yours,

William B Schwartz

William B Schwartz
Chaplain,USA

WBS/iel

My dear darling,

Two days have passed since that unbelievable nightmare I had. Darling it wasn't true was it? It has left me so completely bewildered & with a feeling stranger than any normally felt by one who has been told tragic news. Darling the pit of my tummy is bottomless. I feel nothing—just numb & empty.

Perhaps it is wrong for me to write again, but I just can't stop, for you have become such a part of my daily life that I can't seem to sever it. Darling please tell me it isn't true, & that I may go on loving & waiting for you & that you said all you did because you were sad & confused. Don't give up baby when the going is tough. Think what it is doing to us & the rest of our lives, especially yours.

Edward I'm desperately sorry your mother is so ill, but should anything happen to her do you mean to say you would continue to be a martyr where the men in your family are concerned? Of course I don't want them hurt, but have they thought of how they are hurting you?

Bopsy I can't possibly believe after all your determination & vowing that you would make them see it our way, that you would weaken & continue to take all that they gave to hurt you more & more. It can't end this way darling. I just won't let it for your sake. You have a lifetime ahead & if you haven't courage & strength now, how do you think future years are going to be?

Believe me dear Edward if we went ahead as we had planned & prayed for, the results wouldn't be bad, in fact thinking about it is worse than the actual results.

You say darling that you will never let me down, but what am I to believe now. Do you really feel that the reward for all our waiting, my conversion, our trips & letters should end like nothing ever happened? It isn't your fault darling that things are this way, it's just God testing your strength. Right now you don't believe there is any way out but to give in to your family, but you're so wrong Edward. All our friends & even some of your relatives think we are brave & strong & shouldn't wait, how can two people be right & everyone else wrong? Please dear baby let's prove it to them.

As I said before Edward, nothing can change my blood, but darling I have changed to become a Jewess for you—and I am one now—no one can change that, not even your family.

Know your trip back to Blanding is going to be heartbreaking. You will return wondering how it all could have happened. Now you know what my return trip from Florida was like. It's awful darling, isn't it?

Darling will you please do one thing for me—will you let me wait a little longer—oh please Bopsy—so much can happen in the next few months. Bopsy I love you—you can't ask me to give up now. What would happen to your family were you to go overseas again. Do they realize there is a possibility? Would you go darling leaving me behind to worry & to wonder & not be able to have you as my own? I refuse to believe dear heart that your decision made over the phone was final. I asked for it by calling, but that message got the best of me.

Last night I called Wally—just couldn't get hold of myself. He was stunned at what you told me. I had to ask him what to do—because it was so unbelievable. Your mind was made up darling before you left Florida—but hysteria on the part of your family again seems to be the hand that guides you. Darling, you mustn't let it—it will wreck your life.

Do you down deep in your heart feel you can go back to Poughkeepsie & practice medicine feeling this way. It's an utter impossibility & you know it is too.

Perhaps I'm pleading my case, but I have every right to, because it's your life darling & you are the one I love. It's not a question of being stubborn or persistent, but a question of either of us being strong. Apparently it has to be me. Sometimes I wonder where it comes from, but the only answer is from God. He gave me strength to go through my conversion which was not as easy as you may believe & He still is giving me strength to hang on to life & to make me believe that you may need help & I'm the one to help you. Bopsy, Bopsy, please, please don't give in just yet. I promise to wait & pray & hope. The next time we try it will come true & we will be happy.

Perhaps this is making it hard for you darling, but not nearly as hard as future years might be if we stop fighting now. Yes darling you are a Jew & I am one now too so don't ever say I'm different. It won't work.

I love you darling more than life itself.

Gretchen Ruth

My darling,

Our phone call yesterday Bops, seems like a bad dream to me and as if it never happened. Our lips said all sorts of words which our hearts were constantly denying and fighting to overcome. Even now it's so hard to believe that everything seems so hopeless. But, here we are darling, back where we started from.

It's so funny baby, people in love always think of the other person all the time. My thoughts are only for you and I know yours are only for me. Of one thing you must be certain darling, and that is that I am and will be strong. You must never worry about me and how I am taking this. That you must believe because it is true and I have never lied to you, have I? As for you baby, I can't find words to tell you how ashamed of myself I am that twice I have taken you to the heights only to let you drop sickeningly to the depths but as you say, I did my best baby, you must believe me! Only one person stood us off and it had to be my own Mother. How paradoxical and ironical that a Mother should stand in the way of what a child wants but yet there it is. Darling, you and I both know that we could be the happiest people in the whole world. You and I know that the family is so wrong, but in view of the situation as it now stands our hands are tied. There are so many things we have to do in this world that are meaningless, that are wrong, but yet there are responsibilities which we must meet. I am not soft-hearted baby, as you think, I could do anything in the world but when I came home and saw for myself I knew what the answer had to be. Darling, don't try to understand anything, just accept this. Even I, knowing the family and being so close to them and knowing how I feel and how they feel have given up trying to understand this. Some people go through life getting all they want the easy way. Others have to fight and work and everything seems so wrong.

You want to wait for me, I know darling, but I wouldn't do that to you baby. Imagine you and I waiting for my Mother to pass away. It's cruel, but that's the sum and substance of it all. What a burden for you and I to carry, my darling. It's easy to say but just think of what it would mean. Still writing letters, calling each other, what is there to look forward to? One week, one month, one year, then years, who knows how long these things can go on. Even a great love can't stand the punishment of time unless there is some immediate fruit, some tangible something to hold on to. Even you darling know that we can't do that to each other. The world goes on darling, people laugh, life is a continual change and we must compensate and compromise throughout.

But, I am not writing this letter in a lonesome or depressing mood, my baby. It's hard to describe just how I feel. I just can't feel that I am losing everything when you have given me so much. There is no sense of loss or a blackened future for me because you're in my heart so deeply that even if we never see each other again, you shall always be close and dear and beloved to me. I know that I shall never feel toward anyone the feelings we have for each other. I know that I shall never expect to find anyone like you. Therefore, I am happy in a sort of way that we are as we are.

My faith in God and His Will still is with me Baby. There must be some reason that things are turning out as they are. I know that if God wants us together He will do it in his own way. Please continue to believe in God darling and He will look after us. Baby, I believe and you must to, that things are never as black as they look. We are all in a plan and scheme of things and all we can do is the best we can and see what happens. What I am trying to do baby, is pull you up by your boot straps and help you realize that we must be grateful for everything we have had. I won't go into talking about our time together. We both know what our two years together did for us. Oh darling, I treasure them so. They mean so much to me. We mustn't live in the past but we can think of that time together as ours and only ours.

Do you feel a little better, now darling? You must be my strong old, Gunboat. We both have a job to do darling and we must do it. Brooding, worrying, rationalizing,—these things we must never do. I'll go to work and you'll go to work and we shall find just what God has in store for us. I want to feel that I never have to worry about you in the days to come and when I wonder how that old Bops is it won't be wonder but rather I want to feel that you are all-right. I know that you will always love me darling because I shall always love you. I know that if I want you or need you all I have to do is call out but baby, you just mustn't wait and wait and wait until I get married. Marriage to me right now is so terrible a thought. Right now I find it impossible to think of even thinking of loving someone else ever, but you and I must go out and be with people, meet them and give them a chance. Baby, you and I know that there are so many people in positions just like ours who go through life living in the past and never giving themselves a chance for happiness, perhaps not that total complete happiness we would have but a very safe, dependable happiness of mutual respect and comradeship. Very, few people in the world have had the love we share darling. For that reason we are so lucky to have had it and as you, I feel no regrets, only the regrets of anguish I have brought to your heart. You will deny me all blame baby, but I still am responsible especially after all you have done and your conversion and everything. For that, I feel so badly darling, but that too can be remedied. Just go back to what you were baby. But, you and I are and always will be the same no matter what label they hang on us.

I think Capt Butler is right in not letting you go home. It is much better that you stay and work. Dick must think me an awful sissy, and a cad for doing what I have but I know he understands. His problem was so different. He went away from home, his family was so old. But, God will forgive me and punish me for all I have done.

Baby, you know that you can always call on me for anything. Those words seem so cruel and practical but nevertheless there they are. You can write to Wally, and I want you to if anything important happens. I still can't feel that this is a goodbye. It seems more like some interlude in a plan of some sort. I don't mean that there is any hope of this thing working out and someday we shall be together. I don't know how to express it but you're so much a part of me baby, that although we won't write or see each other I know that we are welded by unbreakable ties. To all acts, deeds, and events there is a pattern and what ours will be I don't know. All I know is that although the words on the paper say "so long," although my lips say the words, I am so happy for so many things you have given me. Your courage, your beauty, your love are all a part of me baby and I shall thank God the rest of my days for knowing you and being loved by you. I'm the luckiest guy in the world come to think of it. How many people have ever known and held a love such as yours. Thank you darling, thank you from the bottom of my heart.

Just remember baby, Life is what we make it! We can either make ourselves strong or we can turn into a couple of sniveling idiots. I know we are going to be strong.

Always be happy, my beloved, and God Bless you!

I love you, baby, I love you.

Mr Bops

One more thing darling, please don't go putting in for foreign service. Running away won't help you or anyone.

Sunday 15 Oct. 1944

My dear darling,

Forgive me if I must write this last letter, just a reassurance that your Bopsy is being a big lady, and taking this tragedy as "God's will be done."

It is futile to tell you my darling what it has been because we are one and part of each other and my feelings are your feelings. That means my dear baby that wherever we go whatever we do we will be with each other forever & ever. Our love shall never die.

Since I've become a Jewess my darling all the study of our people and the sorrows & tragedies have been brought to me because you know my sufferings. I shall always be true to our faith dear heart, its beauty & simplicity & belief in one God has & will carry me through.

Dear darling you must know that I have no regrets over these three wonderful years with you. We have shared all: sorrow, joy, heartache, and happiness & you have imparted things to me darling that have made me a woman, fearless, unafraid, & strong. God bless you my baby & keep you always mine as we close this beautiful chapter of our lives.

If dear heart in years to come, you need me for anything & fate enters into our lives, please know my love for you shall never have grown dim & that our twinkly star will guide you to me.

May God keep you strong and brave, not embittered by circumstances that no one but our Father knows the reason for.

When you grow lonesome and discouraged remember your Bopsy is pecking at you and scolding.

I love you dear heart. There are no words to express the beatings of my heart & to thank you for being my whole life.

Gretchen Ruth

15 Oct. 1944

Dearest Gretchen,

My one wish is that I could be with you at this present moment instead of having to write on paper this insignificant letter.

It is needless to explain to you how every ounce of effort was put forth in your behalf and Edward's when I felt that the situation was hopeful and held the traces of sunshine. But as I fought then to preserve the beautiful love, so now must I try and convince you of the utter hopelessness of the situation.

As I told you over the phone, it is not up to us any longer to question what is right or wrong. You must accept the situation as it is and try in your very brave and courageous way not to question the righteousness of it. Gretchen dear, you say that you would wait no matter how long. But what would you be waiting for? You would be waiting for a person to die. It is a horrible fact, but a true one nevertheless. Do you think that you could attain happiness under those circumstances? Can you picture a life with the thought that your happiness depended on the death of Ed's mother? It is too much to expect that you or Edward could achieve the great joy with such a barrier hanging over your heads. As I have said many times, and repeat now, I have never known a person so fine, strong and wonderful a person as yourself. I need not repeat that this is not idle flattery, because I am not one given to undeserved praise. At a time like this, I know that no matter how much your heart is broken, you will see the light. You have always sympathized with the way Edward has been buffeted from pillar to post, and so it has been. But as your thoughts have only been of his health and safety, so has his thoughts been of you. It is not an easy matter for him to say, "Gretchen, this is the end." But if he is to live with his conscience and feel that he was not the cause of his Mother's death, then he must say just that. But the way you are to take this statement also depends on his peace of mind. It is not an easy thing for him to do, but only too well you must realize, knowing full well that it is wrong, that this is the only way.

For the past few years, you have lived in happiness and fear. Certainly terrible doubt must have assailed your mind. Even at the most precious of moments when you were with your loved one, you knew that nothing was certain. That all depended upon the acceptance of his family. But when you blame yourself for the things you brought on Edward, you are wrong. Every moment spent with you and every thought about you when you were gone, were glorious moments of happiness for Edward. But even he was torn between doubt as to the outcome. When he returned yesterday, I saw a picture of a determined man. The picture he had seen at home made him realize the course of action to be taken. To one who is an unbiased standby, I could see that he was right. And certainly I would not call myself an unbiased standby. With all that I had fought with and with the thoughts of how wrong it may be, I was swept away by the fact that the answer was clear.

It may be so much wasted words if I were to tell you that your course to forget is the only right thing to do. To carry a burden and for any wishful thinking on your part would be a mistake. Writing each other for even a week now, would only subject the both of you to untold agony. It is far less painful to cut it off completely, than to tear at it piece by piece. Were I less frank than I am, I would perhaps tell you to have patience and hope for the best, but this I will not do. I realize it is not easy for me to tell you to completely forget Edward . . . the beautiful happiness you had and the plans for the future, but I must do it. If you are to think of your own health, and you definitely must, you must cast out all things held close to you.

No matter what I have said, and I hope you do not hate me for it, I want you to know that if you will allow me, I want to be your friend. I have treasured this wonderful friendship and hope that you will allow me to continue this bond of friendship. If ever you want to write to me and I do want to hear from you, remember that I will be here at your beck and call. Try to believe that what I have written has been from my heart with the view of what the future had in store for the both of you had a mistaken step been taken.

There is little else that I can say. The pressure that you have borne for the past couple of years is over with. I am sure that time will heal all wounds. Many times in the past have I seen people broken by a word or deed, but it has never failed that time itself has healed those heartaches.

There should be a consolation that at last the climax has arisen. And although it may be a heartbreaking thing, you will find that no longer is there the dread of a phone call or the fear of opening a letter. This may be a lefthanded way of appearing optimistic, but in the days to come I know you will understand what I mean.

Be brave my darling and God bless you. Fate has strange ways, and perhaps it is all for the best. We must believe in His judgment and know that He is guiding us in the right path to happiness.

Lovingly,
Wally

Wed. Eve (Oct 18?)

Dear Wally,

I'm sitting here so numb & bewildered. Hardly know whether I'm alive or not. Edward's wire from home arrived & frightened me so, I had to call. It was like that call last April Wally & it's needless to say what he told me.

I'm writing you now because—what shall I do? My whole life is nothing but blackness—which way does one turn?

Am sure Edward was frightened at my response to the future. It can't turn out this way Wally. It's so awful & unbelievable.

If I were brave & strong I would write him & give him courage, but having none myself guess you will have to do it for me. Just take care of Edward, Wally. It's the last thing I shall ask of you. Keep him brave & tell him I'll never stop loving him. Don't know whether I can ever write him again, but you must tell me what to do.

It has all been my fault. I never should have encouraged him & especially the last & final thing which I just did will never let him have peace in his mind. Guess my love was just too strong for one human—will he ever forgive me Wally?

I pray for my dear Edward & that He gives me strength to carry on. Please help me Wally.

Love,
Gretchen

Our dear little broken hearted girl:

I just felt blue all day Sun. thinking of you, because you had not called, I just said, no doubt Edward had sent you bad news. Well my dear little girl, we do feel for you, and only God knows your grief, and put your faith in him and all will be well. As he is the one who cares for us all, and will help us over our troubles and cares.

I know you are a brave girl you have had some hard things to fight; but we know you will be better for it all some day. I say it is God's will not ours, and I think you are both very wonderful to give up what we hoped would have been a comfortable life together, to share one life. But oh how could a human being be so selfish I cannot understand such a person, and if that is what she is, for my part I am glad you do not have to put up with her.

I am sorry you are so far away, and have no one to turn to, get out your Bible and read some of the Psalms, there are so many comforting chapters in them.

Mother will pray as usual for your comforts, and that some day you will be happy, in a home of your own when peace and happiness will be forever.

I feel as you do, that she and others who were bitter, will some day be paid for their acting this way. I just cannot see why people who have a heart at all can act that way.

Poor Edward, it has been doubly hard on him, hope he can take it all. I shall write him a note and then to top it all off we had to write you about our farm trouble. But I guess we are still not bad off when we read and hear of the terrible things this old war is causing, and it looks like it will go on for months yet.

We do hope & pray you will be left in the country, some place will need a good steady nurse and you will get the position.

Our grand weather still continues. Got the barn whitewashed today and it looks grand. I must get out and help dad put things aright in the barn after the mess.

He joins with me in hoping your broken heart will soon be healed by the grace of God.

And the sooner you can forget all of this and get out and try and have a good time, (that is easy for me to say I know), but my dear don't worry over it, and get sick. There never was a man worth all of that, and there are lots of others, we hope, just as good.

Poor May who was married last Feb is a widow, so there are others who have trouble too. Poor Jean had to bid Gen by-by today too, so cheer up you are not the only one who has trouble.

God bless you and keep you my dear baby.

Kisses with tears my dear,
Mother & Dad

10/18/44

Capt Edward,
Dear Friend:

The news from our poor broken hearted little girl came today, and I feel so sorry for both of you.

It just seems it was not to be and it is too bad you were so deeply in love, what a grand happy home I know she could have had.

But I guess God knows best and I look at it that way, if it was for the best, this is the way it had to be.

I tried to tell her in March to just forget it all, and maybe some day things would work out for the best. It was too bad it caused your mother to be ill.

I am glad we did not stand in the way, and I always say the young people who think they can be married and be happy all well and good, they have their lives to live. Why should I bother.

So we are indeed sorry we did not get to meet you, as all the wonderful things you have done for Gretchen we appreciate and you have our sympathy in this tragic ending of such a wonderful companionship in the past three years.

I am sorry she is so far away so we cannot comfort her at this time. But she can pray to the God above who cares for us all, and I am sure He will comfort her, and give her peace of mind thru it all.

Wishing you the best of luck in your work and hope you will be returned to your parents some day.

Sincerely,
Mr & Mrs R. Boody

My dearest Gretchen Ruth,

If you ever stop writing to me and looking to me for comfort then I will consider that I have failed in my mission of being your very good friend. Please write always, because I want to know how you are and be able to tell you things that may be a source of comfort to you.

Darling, the more I get to know you, the more I realize that the reams of praise I have so justly set upon your fair being, is indeed insignificant. I honestly have no right to tell you certain things, because it is so totally unfair in view of what has gone on in the past week, but this is one case where discretion is not the better part of valor. Gretchen dear, perhaps I am a fool for saying this, and I know that it is unfair to build up any false hopes, but I cannot be convinced that all is ended between Edward and yourself. You have been so strong, faithful and wonderful in this affair. I need not tell you to continue your newly founded faith. I still am firmly convinced that God will not let so great a love fall by the wayside. Even as you so rightly stated, I am not telling you to wait with any sort of high hopes for a bright future, but then I cannot help but tell you not to despair. This all may sound contrary, but in my own poor way, I find it so difficult to tell you to forget, but still not to forget. It all must sound so confusing, but I know that you understand my meaning.

Gretchen dear, do not worry about Edward. It is all so confusing and wrong to him, but you and I can see how torn he is between conflicting emotions. That his love for you is stronger than ever is beyond any doubt. That he will love no one but you, is quite evident. I know that he would want you to write to him whenever you want to, or whenever you are in need of any help. Please do not bear the pain alone. It is very difficult for a person to carry the weight of their troubles without unburdening it to someone. Please let me be that someone.

Darling, my courtship with Elaine was not an easy one, although I would not compare it with the heartaches involved in yours and Edward's. Ours was filled with bitterness, anguish and despair, but all this made the culmination of our hearts so much more beautiful and appreciative. Although Elaine does not know the entire story, she knows enough to realize what you are going through, and feels that eventually happiness and joy will wend its way into your hearts. And wrong as it may seem to others, I too can only see Edward's happiness being with you, and yours with Edward's.

We are now waiting for a hurricane to hit this place. All officers have been restricted to their wards and quarters in the event that the awaited hurricane hits here. At the present moment, it is raining and blowing something fierce. It may bypass us, but they are ready for any emergency that may arrive.

Take good care of yourself, dear, and don't forget that I want to be your friend for always. Love from Elaine.

Your devoted and faithful friend,
Wally

My darling,

I know I am doing wrong, baby, in writing you—but I find it impossible to just cast off all relationships with you as if this love of ours had suddenly run off a cliff. I received your letter yesterday darling and your courage and strength were just wonderful & terrible to behold! I'm really writing, my beloved, to try & discuss with you just what our present status is. In spite of our phone call, in spite of our parting letters, I walk around in an aura of unbelief that this is happening to us—or rather has happened. I know just what goes on in your mind, baby, because it goes on in mine also. I'm still thinking that there must be some way, somewhere, somehow ; sometime to all of this—but I just can't find it anywhere.

I just want to tell you all about the trip home. I should have told you before but—the entire hopelessness of the situation made me just want to end it once and for all. Baby, when I went home I saw the family as I would see a patient. I saw them all objectively, not as a member of the family but I saw an example of to what lengths background, custom and *(illegible)* could do to a family. I saw also how pride could blind 3 wonderful people to such an extent that they would do the things they had. The whole matter came to a head darling, when this woman from home talked to Mother and tried to help us. Then this woman evidently told someone else & before a day had passed several women had come into the store and started telling Mother, "I'm sorry, Mrs. Siegel, etc. etc." So you see, baby how it has accumulated. People, people, people. Instead of Mother, holding her head up high and sticking up for us, her son, etc., it had the exact opposite effect. And so Mother had to go home & she went to bed. When I got back home, she was in bed & she had periods of being rational & then irrational. I examined her and her pressure was high. Darling, Mother is the sort of person who never forgets a thing. She carries things within her for years and years. After the first night home & she saw me and I promised her everything under the sun, she was a little better. Her pride was so affected darling that they told me they would have to sell the store and move to save face. You see, darling, they have built up their little world for themselves, *(illegible)* they sure made no provision for anything that may alter their plans. They just can't see how this would happen in there and after it has happened they still can't accept the change. This, my darling, is how people go crazy. They come across a situation that they can't meet & try to figure out rationally & try to see it *(illegible)* instead of meeting it & *(illegible)* they collapse into self-pity and misunderstanding. What the present thing amounts to now darling, is that you & I are the stronger of the two factions and we are the ones who are intelligent and can accept this as it is. Wow, baby, you and I know that our immediate responsibility is to see that Mother gets well and overcomes her present condition. We can't be like the family—selfish and unyielding because there must be no selfishness or bitterness in us. It all boils down to the fact darling, that Mother is one of those people who can just kill themselves with grief because *(illegible)* she wants to without realizing all why some worry & how selfish it is. There are people like that—so what can be done about it?

Wow baby, we . . . ? What shall we do? Under the circumstances, what alternatives do we have? Am I justified in having you wait for me? Am I justified in consoling the family into a false sense of security that they have & then in the future hit them with this again? Would we just trust in faith that "if this is to be" something will bring us together somehow, somewhere, someday? My only thoughts darling, are of what is best for you! I don't want you to feel darling that I think I owe you anything. I'm selfish in that respect in that I know I need you to look after me. I'm selfish baby because I know you could make me happy. You know us so well—you know me as I am. And you know also, that I can help you, I can look after you & take care of you. That is true baby, we love and think only of each other but the reason we love is because of mutual deference & sacrifice. I'm trying baby to bring everything in the open—for us to realize consciously what we are up against & what we can do about the future.

Now I come to the present. They called me from Hdqts. Monday for me to take an overseas physical. 4th S.C. telegraphed for an EENT man and I took the physical and my name was sent in. I may get orders in a day or 2 or I may not get them for 2-3 weeks or I may not get them at all. In all probability, I will probably get them. To be straight with you darling, I'm happy to get them. I want to go "over again." 3 of *(illegible)* left yesterday for Camp Ellis & I left thinking, suppose I was sent there and put in the same unit—what then? But we mustn't be swept away by wishful thinking!

If this were peacetime darling, I wouldn't have written but I know you want to know where I am & what I'm doing because a drowning man grasps at all straws.

Knowing you as I do baby, I know just what your conversion means to you and that you are sincere and so wonderful. The thoughts of the terrible predicament I have placed you in stifles and *(illegible)* me but I know you won't blame me for this—it's so like you!

It's so insane darling that if we sat down & read this story in a book, we would think it almost unbelievable. "Earth and High Heaven" was a breeze compared to this, wasn't it baby?

Your letter was so beautiful baby—I like the way you said, "Another beautiful chapter has closed in our lives." How will the book end though, darling?

I shouldn't be writing this letter darling and keep fanning the flame. I shouldn't be writing and giving you hope but perhaps some dim ray of intelligence will persuade Mother's reasoning that she is so wrong. But suddenly, I feel a little more brave & I am readily returned to earth and the actual facts.

Darling, you must promise me that you will always turn to me for help of any sort. If you feel you must write me for any reason, do it darling, please. Only I don't want you in the position of waiting, waiting, waiting.

There must never be any despondency darling or bitterness.

I know there will never be another Bopsy—I love you with my very fiber and muscle and bone in my body, and as you cry with every heartbeat.

Forgive me darling for writing this I felt I had more to say and more you should know.

I love you, love you,
Mr Bops

p.s. Wally doesn't know I've written.

22 Oct. 1944

My blessed baby,

Could hardly believe my eyes when your letter was handed to me this noon. I've read it over & over like a priceless masterpiece one would cherish. Darling you were both right & wrong, as I am in writing, but by some sign you & I must know that there is a reason for our hearts to tell us to do this.

Baby neither of us has lived these past terrible days—to me it's been like existing only because my heart hadn't stopped beating. I've walked miles, ridden horseback at a wild pace, anything to keep me from thinking, it's been like nothing neither of us has ever experienced. It's needless to subjugate you to my feelings for you know every minute, every hour of disbelief because you have experienced the same thing. Darling to make a confession about my innermost feelings as to this being the end would only make you doubt my sincerity in realizing what the situation is. Let it suffice to say my baby that not for a moment have I fully believed our love could be totally severed. Not our love, for Edward dear it's an example of something so strong & deep people wouldn't believe were they told.

About our present darling; you know full well I've accepted the situation as impossible for the present. I've felt it was for you that I was doing it & that's why it was possible. Neither of us could live with ourselves or each other were we to think of no one but ourselves. Your mother comes first baby & your family but my dear darling you have told me about time healing & changing things. Don't know why I say these things but here it is. Something will cause your family to realize the world & all its cruelty will change their way of thinking too. They have told us we must not live in a world of unreality—right darling, we mustn't, but neither can they. Yes perhaps for a time but not for always.

Now darling about our future. Perhaps it has taken all this to make me stop dreaming & becoming a true fatalist in a sense. I fully believe now what is to be is to be. Perhaps you will come here, perhaps not, but Bopsy something tells me (perhaps it is God, for I have been closer to our Maker than ever before) that our paths shall cross in some peculiar way. Maybe it will be the same unit, it isn't impossible—nothing is these days. Another thing is that I don't believe you will ever go into practice in Poughkeepsie. So your family would never have to fulfill all the black thoughts of shame & pride. I know you will think I am dreaming again & perhaps doing a lot of wishful thinking, but it isn't that darling, too much has happened to us through peculiar circumstances to make me think that way any more.

You are not placing me in a position of waiting darling, for I'm not, but I fully believe fate will enter, somehow, somewhere, some day.

Darling because I love you so deeply, do you think for a moment if you came here that I could not see you? If you come darling you must be with me every free moment, regardless of all our past goodbyes. The only thing we would have to promise each other is not to have self pity, to make plans or talk of all the unfairness. All we would do would be to love, be together, love every moment to the fullest. It's impossible to put all I want to on paper dear, but you must understand, for I know you can read my thoughts. Darling I can't & won't believe it's the end, but if need be I can make myself do in actions anything you want me to.

Darling I've not written any of our friends about us. Again fate because something told me not to & beside my heart has been so broken I didn't have the courage.

Dear baby my conversion means everything to me & please please dear baby don't feel hurt & to blame. I did it & remember long ago I said no matter what happened I would go through with it & that you didn't say "Do this if you love me or because I love you."

Let's not plan anything or dream any dreams darling Edward, just keep it deep in your heart that I love you & we love each other, & let's see what happens. In the meantime Bopsy have courage & hope & pray as we have for three years. God hasn't forgotten us nor your family & we must believe in His wisdom.

We shall not write often darling that we mustn't do—but please please let me know what happens, where you go, about your work, etc. I've not asked this before because I felt you wouldn't want me to know, but that is what hurt so much to think my baby was someplace & I couldn't find him.

Keep strong darling, be brave, & remember your Bopsy's love has never & will never change regardless of time & eternity.

I love you baby with every heart beat.
Gretchen Ruth

23 Oct. 1944

Dear Mrs. Boody,

Letters are such a poor substitute for our emotions and perhaps it is just as well that they are. Words about Gretchen and myself, our love, our trouble, just don't seem available to express the apparent hopelessness of this situation.

I know it is so hard for someone to understand just why Mother feels the way she does and it would be difficult to try and explain it to you. As is so common in many Jewish families, parents have build their dreams of their children's lives according to their plan. They think that life goes its merry way and if something happens to mar that plan, they just can't understand it and to them it is all wrong. I thought that the folks had enough confidence in me to accept what I thought was best and that they would at least make an effort to meet Gretchen and see why I feel the way I do. Needless to say, I think Gretchen is the finest girl in the world, merits the best in life and I wanted to give everything to her. I'd do anything in the world for her. I know that we would be the happiest people on earth if just given the chance and - know the folks would love her to if they knew her as I do. I can't just believe that God would let Gretchen and I fall in love just to snatch it away from us and I still can't accept the idea of Gretchen and myself not being to-gether someday. I know that people in love always think their case is different, that this is the one case that is different, but all our friends, some of my relatives, practically the whole world approve of Gretchen and myself but my own family. Seems so ironical that this should be the case. I too believe in God and his will, but I just can't accept this as God's will, because wasn't it also God's will that we met, that we loved? It's all so unfair, so unjust, so confusing. But, what can a man do? Speaking for myself, I know that I can never feel toward anyone as I do toward Gretchen. The things I feel for her are so deep, so sincere that looking at someone else leaves me cold. We are not children anymore. When one is 20-21 it is easy to forget but not at our age. I've written Gretchen that it is all over, that the situation is hopeless, that there is no chance. I'm so ashamed of myself that I have twice taken her to the heights of hoping, only to drop us both back to grim reality. I want to look after her and take care of her aslong as I live because I feel it is my place in life to do so. But, I just can't have her wait and wait and wait. I keep saying there must be someone, somewhere, somehow, who can invade that wall of sheer misunderstanding on the families part and show them how wonderful and fine Gretchen really is. Perhaps, that day will come, but when I don't know.

As far as Mother is concerned, she is one of those people who can brood and carry things with them forever. She is so sincerely convinced that we could never be happy but she doesn't realize that she can make and insure our happiness if she wanted to. All my arguments, my reasoning, have fallen on deaf ears. Seems so paradoxical that Mother being so concerned for my happiness is having just the opposite effect.

My fine office home, all my material earnings, my profession seem so empty without Gretchen. She has become so much a part of me. I know that we both can go through life and compromise with Fate but nothing will seem the same. After the war is over, I'll go home and practise but I dread going back alone because people can be alone in the midst of plenty of people.

I shall probably be going overseas again, as I just took another physical and perhaps there I may find an answer to all this.

You have been wonderful to me Mrs. Boody, I was hoping that it might be Mother Boody someday and that we could all meet in happiness and understanding. I would love to hear from you any time you care to write and I feel that I may write to. Please don't judge Mother too harshly because of the way she feels. I know she is doing what she thinks is best. I would marry Gretchen in a minute if it weren't for the danger of what Mother might have happen to her. If anything happened to her neither Gretchen or myself would ever forgive ourselves.

As they say in baseball, the game isn't over until the last man is out, so I feel that in my heart I know that Gretchen and I belong to each other and that no matter how black things seem there is always hope. I can't write and tell her to keep on waiting but the issue is far from settled in my heart and mind and as long as there is the God above who brought us to-gether so I shall continue to believe that if he wants us to-gether again, He will do it.

Thanks again for writing. Please remember me to Mr. Boody.

Edmund

Return Road

My dear darling

Tonite I have to write you just like nothing ever happened. It was only a bad dream darling I know & besides writing you will help chase away this terrible chill & hurt in my body. You too are so lonesome baby. If we could only be in each other's arms & forget everything & everyone but us. Several weeks ago you made me promise that Gretchen would be a big lady & not a baby any longer. Oh darling, how hard it is. The strain has been so terrific, trying not to let people know & no one to turn to. Am so glad Wally is with my baby because he needs someone to help get things straight.

Am working very hard. It's the worst set up I've ever been in. Can I come to Blanding baby to be with you? Darling regardless of people & circumstances nothing can ever keep us apart. God won't let it be that way.

Bopsy I'm almost sure another overseas assignment is coming up. Col. Clemonts is making rounds again—sending girls regardless of L.S. overseas. This time it means going for sure. How my heart aches when I know how Bopsy said he would never let me go. Darling you know all though so won't go into that. Regardless of my health I shan't refuse or try again to get out. Perhaps it will find us in the same unit, for I know you don't care anymore & just waiting for time to pass & for fate to bring us together.

Sweetheart please don't write to anyone yet of our troubles. It's not over or ended just another struggle that is bound to turn out alright. Let's keep on being brave, someday we will make that trip to N.Y. & be two happy people just being together. If I were only out of the Army, I would go to see your family—but it's impossible now. Don't you see darling why we can't give in, for things will be alright if we just wait long enough. I need your scruntches & hugs baby & to pat my Bopsy's head & brush the cares away. It looks like we will be in the Army for a long time so let's just forget about your practice in Poughkeepsie. Time that day comes we will be together.

Darling I'm a bad girl for continuing to worry you—but I'll never never stop fighting for something that is right. You will come to me some day darling & say as you have, "Bopsy how did you know?"

Tomorrow night when you call darling, your voice will be happy again for now you are determined to wait as long as need be, because sweetheart Bops wants it that way. Please don't think about the fairness for that no longer matters. Who has been fair & unfair & what is in this wicked old world.

I'll pray for you each night dear heart. May God bless & keep you & make you strong & happy for our future. Darling I'll always need you.

This afternoon I scolded a little didn't I? But it's for you darling as you are my only concern.

I love you my precious for ever & ever.
Your baby

My darling,

Thought I'd better sit down and write that Gunboaty Old Thing a letter to let her know I'm still around. I enjoyed your letter so much baby, and you must have known that I was going to write again. I know there are so many things you want to know about and what is happening that I see no reason why we can't be a couple of sensible adults and let each other know what's going on, you know what I mean baby, don't you?

Before I tell you anything about what's been happening around here and about my orders, etc, which I haven't received as yet, I want you to know darling that we are both a couple of grown-up people and not a couple of emotional idiots and there is no reason in the world why this present situation should cause us to forget that there is a world we are living in, that the world goes on in spite of all, that we have taken everything it has thrown at us and we can take anything more it has to offer. I know the hours are hard, that you are trying to keep yourself so busy that you cannot think, or rather to keep from thinking. But, that is all wrong, my sweetheart. We can never run away from life, its facts, its implications and its apparently unending tragedies, etc. It's best to meet a situation head-on, tackle it, come to a conclusion and make the best of things. There is no reason in the world why either you or I should become depressed, let our work slide, feel self-pity or anything. I won't have us go down that way. You and I, my beloved, can take it and we'll go along living our lives as God lets us. I want you to be strong and brave because I am darling and from me gather and use my strength. O.K. Baby? You rascal!

Now, I still haven't received any orders as yet. Wally had a letter from Yvonne who is with the 115th Evac at Shelby now that a friend of hers saw my name on the roster of the 139th Evac which hasn't been totally activated as yet. That may or may not be true. If it is well I shall probably be getting some orders any day now. I hope it is because you know I've been wanting to be with an Evac ever since I've been in the army so I can do some work and be up there in the thick of it. As soon as I hear definitely where I am going and to what outfit I shall wire you darling, you may rest assured that you will always know where I am and what I'm doing, so there! I spoke to Col. Maley who just left for the Chief Nurses Office in Washington. She will be there on temp. duty until she flies to the

CBI* Theatre. She told me that if she knew I was going out that way she would ask to take you with her but inasmuch as I don't know where

I'll be going, she didn't want to take the chance of taking you along and then having me end up in France somewhere, see? If I go to this outfit at Shelby, Bops, and you want me to I'll try and get the Chief Nurse to ask for you and maybe we can try and be together. I don't care about the future darling, if I can fix it for you and I to be together for a couple of years more, I'm selfish enough to want it and I think you do too. I've quit worrying about the future and I'm just going along as you are seeing what each day brings us. You must believe me baby, when I say it isn't fair to either of us to sit back and brood, worry, fuss and fret. We must do our respective jobs in this world, see what happens and let the world know that Miss Boo and Mr Bops are right on the ball and not a couple of old Futzes!

I must know darling, that you are strong, that you are going ahead being the same, splendid, angel you always have been. I must know and believe that you are eating, taking care of yourself and being sensible. You must believe yourself that I am well and am not going to let this lick me or change me. Wally showed me your letter about the date with Frank, etc., and I was fit to be tied I was so mad. Dates are o.k. baby, and you must go out and not be a stay-at-home. I go out once in a while and although the time is wasted, yet it's something we have to do once in awhile. The thought of someone pawing you baby, is enough to make me kill.

Mother got out of bed last week and is slowly getting back on her feet. The trouble with you and I darling is that we are too good for our own sakes. You and I both know and you were so right in your letter that I must make Mother well and strong. I must do that for not only her sake but yours as well. Our love would be a worthless thing if it destroyed something so that it may go on. I'm so proud of you darling. I'm so lucky to be loved by someone as you.

Mother is reconciled to the fact that I am going over again, and I know she is going to worry and worry about me.

I received a lovely letter from your Mother and I answered her. She is such a grand person Bops, that I know where you get your loveliness from now.

The only people I have written about us is Dick, Aaron, Father Laws and Chaplain Schwartz. I thought they should know. I haven't heard from

---

* China-Burma-India

any of them as yet. I'm enclosing Father Laws letter after he had seen the folks in N.Y. and you can read for yourself what happened. He was impartial and you can see how they affected him, so you can see darling what I'm up against when I meet up with the family.

Enough for now darling. Just go ahead, keep your head high, do your work and please my darling, for my sake and our love, please take care of yourself physically, it's very important not only for yourself and me but for your family. Promise?

I'd be interested in knowing what Capt. Butler thinks of your chances of getting sent to my unit if and when I know.

Be a big girl darling, and I still say my prayers with you in my heart and mind. As you say, in this day and age anything can happen and as long as there is a war on we never know. I know that if it is humanly possible I shall see you before I leave the country.

I love you
Mr Bops

From Father Laws   16 October 1944

Dear Ed:

I met two grand persons in New York, your Mother and Father, and it was regrettable that this meeting had to take place when their minds and mine too were troubled.

I went into that meeting, Ed, ready to give them the "one-two" and keel them over with the logic of my side of the story. I'm sorry to say however that they had me groggy before I got out of my corner. They impressed me so much with their sincerity (plus tears) that I almost agreed with them. As a result I had to sympathize with them and seeing how certain and opinionated they were I gave up. I did however impress them with the fact that you did not look well and that I was concerned of your health.

Here are my impressions to date. Your Dad and Mother, tho grieving, seem to be <u>inalterably armored</u> against marriage. Their concern about you is grave, paradoxical as it may seem, and not withstanding that they are most adamant. In my opinion Ed, that leaves you only a choice, Gretch or the Family. Choose the Family and you don't get Gretchen and infinitive and all that entails. Choose Gretchen and you definitely (in my opinion) lose the Family. For how long is in the hands of God. Consider the loss on both sides Ed and then choose.

Frankly Ed, my emotions are too unstable to aid you in such a choice. Logically and reasonably my opinion concurs with yours. On the other hand I hate to see the Family suffer.

Your Dad asked me to see if I could help in getting you nearer home in order to absorb some "atmosphere." Feeling that professionally you would be better off, I made such an attempt but as yet there is no definite progress. Do you mind?

Please keep in touch with me Ed. You are constantly in my prayers.

Fr. Jim

Edward's Tape states:

My duty at Camp Blanding, Florida was part of an examination team for all inductees, and I must admit it was a very, very uninteresting assignment, sitting on a chair, checking the eyes, ears, nose and throat of the recruits as they came through the line. It was hardly a challenging professional project. I was considerably dissatisfied with my appointment and my present duties and as a result, this reflected itself in my attitude which caused my being transferred to Fort McClellan.

31 Oct. 1944

My darling,

I just got orders assigning me to the Regional Hospital at Fort McClellan, Alabama. They were all set to send me to this Evacuation Hospital when they changed the orders sending me to McClellan. I don't know what it means as yet baby, perhaps it's a break, at least it will probably mean staying in the States a little while longer, I don't know. Anyway, it puts me a lot closer to that old Gunboat, as a matter of fact 400 miles closer. This may mean getting a break in my specialty and staying in the States. As soon as I get there I'll be able to know more. Perhaps I'll be able to call you up the early part of next week baby, and let you know more about it.

Wally is a sick puppy to see me leave baby, and I'm really sorry to leave him but there's not much can be done about it. Maybe if I see the job is more or less permanent I can get that old Gunboat reassigned down there. You know nothing is impossible these days.

I'm leaving Thursday morning and will probably pull into McClellan Friday afternoon. Take it easy darling, be a sweet baby, and I'll try and call you early next week.

I love you,
Mr Bops

NOVEMBER, 1944

My darling,

Gosh, Bops, the past few days have sure been hectic for me. My orders were actually made out for this Evac at Shelby and at the last moment they were changed and I was sent here. I guess that twinkly star of ours is still in there pitching or else I would have been on my way. I stopped off at 4th SC headquarters and saw a few brass hats and they told me that I was sent here because they needed an Eye Ear Nose and Throat (EENT) man very badly. They told me that my job here would be as permanent as anything can be in the Army, so who knows but I have a feeling that I shall be here for a while anyway. I met the CO who seems a very nice old fellow. The clinic here is the busiest place I've ever seen. The officer in charge is a Lt. Col who does Ear, Nose & Throat (ENT) but hasn't done any bronchoscopies so I shall do all of them. There is a Major who does only Eye and then there is poor, little me who will do anything and everything he can get his hands on. If I stay here long enough but who knows these days about anything. The quarters here are much nicer than in Blanding. We are 100 miles from Atlanta and 65 miles from Birmingham, 120 miles from Chattanooga and what is most important 425 miles closer to Camp Ellis which is about 685 from here. At last I'm going to be busy and working and I'm telling you sweetheart I'm looking forward to working again.

Poor Wally was sure upset when I left and I know I shall miss him, he sure is a swell friend we have Bops and you should write him when you care to about anything.

I want you to know darling that I'm going to spend my next leave with you. It may be before Christmas or just after depending on the set-up here in the clinic and who wants to go, so you just think about it and decide whether you want to take leave and we can spend it together or if you want me to come to Ellis. I just want to see you baby and love you and hold you in my arms and have fun and to hell with planning, wondering, thinking, etc. If you don't want to and think we shouldn't see each other darling just tell me and I'll do whatever you want. I was thinking that St. Louis might be a good spot but we can talk about it later when I hear about what you think.

I spoke to Daisy Flowers and she said the policy here was that girls who have been overseas don't have to go and they always have more than enough volunteers too. I still don't want you going away baby. I made a contact in the Surgeon General's office and if you want me to darling I'll try and get you stationed here. I don't know if I can do it or not but I could at least try. What do you think? There is so much I have to tell you about that has accumulated in the past couple of weeks that I don't know where to begin but I'm such a bad boy, baby, not writing and then starting to write like this again. But, I just have to tell you so many things, don't I Bops?

Gosh, just think Bops, I was practically snatched from the Port of Embarkation (POE) and here I am doing a lot of work and I'm going to work hard so you'll be proud of me.

Tell me exactly how you feel darling. No more despondency, baby, please. We both must go ahead and as you say see what happens. I've had a lot of dates darling in the past two weeks, but being with other women only makes me realize that there is only one Bops in this world. Be a strong, healthy Baby, darling because I want you to and I promise I shall be too.

I love you,
Mr Bops

My dear darling,

How is my sweet Bopsy after another trip & a new post? Know you will be awfully lonesome for awhile & will need my letters won't you darling? We know things happen for the best dear heart, so please be happy there & I do hope McClellan has something fine in store.

Bopsy, Bopsy if you only knew what that wonderful letter did for Miss Boo. It performed a miracle really. All that gaunt, lost feeling that has haunted me is gone. Just to know we are big people & can take this with all the rest is so unbelievable dear. Regardless of all our fine resolutions, we now both find they can be tempered with being sensible. Believe baby the one big thing that hurt was the fact that I wasn't supposed to write. Golly there is no use explaining cause you know. Our love has taken a terrific beating but baby we both should be so proud to have come through without bitterness & hate, that's why it is so different from others. Darling all I want now is to know where you are, if you are well & then if at all possible to be with you somewhere, somehow, even for a little. While I too feel so strongly about the future, in that it has utterly ceased to exist in my thoughts. All will be as God wants it sweetheart. Yes & regardless of what happens, we must live today. Yes we are two selfish old things & want our happiness too but baby we shan't worry cause we'll have it I betcha.

Darling if things look at all promising at your new post for an extended stay, please pull all the strings possible & at this end all will be well. We have got to work together though to make it so don't we? So far Bopsy, crazy coincidences have occurred & who knows what comes next.

Sweet baby please don't worry about my health. I have to admit your Miss Boo tried to be a cowardly escapist but it couldn't continue, cause there was that old Bopsy saying shame, shame & not very proud of his old thing. I took your strength dear & now it's so much easier. My prayers were answered darling & my Bopsy's were too I know.

It will be like a dream to talk to you again, dear, I shall not move from the house till you call. Must know all about everything & then too to say, "I love you." It seems centuries doesn't it?

Was so relieved to hear your mommy is better Edward. Can you possibly know how deep it has hurt to think I've been the cause of her ill health. Some day darling I shall go see her if for no other reason than to tell her or show her I'm not a wicked, reckless bad girl who plays with people's lives.

Wally has been so grand about writing. I've really taken advantage of a fine friendship, but it has been a great comfort to talk to him & then too to know he was watching my Bopsy.

Have you heard from Dick & Sally—what do they have to say? Know they are with us in whatever happens dear, cause I feel sure they liked me a little. Am rather planning to go to St. Louis Nov. 11 to see Pudgy—will try to see them too.

Darling no one knows our status, that is our close friends except those few, let's just keep it that way. It seems dear that neither of us will give up, not completely as long as there is life. We just will know that no plans can be made won't we?

Did you know sweetheart that I crawled into my snuggly corner & Bopsy's big strong arms have been holding me so tight. It's so yummy—heaven darling.

I'm being a big girl, yes, your angel as you say—so keep smiling dear & say your prayers with me at night.

For I'll eternally love my baby

Your Miss Boo

Sunday a.m. (Nov. 5?)

My dear darling:

Golly Bops it is so wonderful to be able to sit down and write to my sweet thing if I want to. How much better things seem since we began to be sensible old guys.

Was so relieved to get your wire dear telling me of your safe arrival, I followed and thought about you all day Thur. and Fri. knowing how hard it was for you to leave Wally and going off again by yourself. Am sure it won't take long to make and find new friends dear, you are so fortunate in that respect, because everyone likes my Bops so very much, and that makes me proud you know.

Am so anxious for your call, crazy old me sat around last night and sort of hoped that it might come through last night just cause it was Saturday, but baby I am so excited about hearing that old sweet voice again.

Capt. Butler had a call from Chicago yesterday and we General Service gals have all got to have another physical, so haven't the slightest idea what is going to happen, one never ceases to wonder. There are some more General Hospitals being activated here so we hear. Darling if I should get in one of those would you be interested or not. Am not too anxious for a General Hospital again, but time will tell what happens.

Baby dear how are you feeling, are the spirits better and how much do you weigh? There are a million questions I could ask if we could be together. It isn't odd darling that I shall never stop wondering and worrying about you always, it's just something inside that will never stop no matter what happens. Bopsy I do think we are two unusual people, who else could go through all we have and yet come up smiling and not have our love marred by all the heartache. I still say its cause we trust in God.

Mother was so pleased with your letter, darling. I'm sure that deep in her heart she believes there is an answer for us somewhere, someday and she is perfectly amazed at our stamina. Yes dear she is a sweet and understanding mother, but all mothers are wonderful anyway, that's why you and I have done the things we have, because of our love for them.

Four hundred miles closer, golly Bops that really sounds close doesn't it. What do you think of Alabama and the post in general? Your letter hasn't arrived as yet, but imagine it will answer all these questions.

My dear precious old sweet thing you, did you know that your Bops still loves you and darling I dare not think of those smacks I think I would be happy if it was just one little peck for baby I am so overwhelmingly thankful for even a tiny spark of your love.

Must get busy as I am alone this Sunday, we are not working too hard though, only 357 patients.

I love you darling
Gretchen Ruth

My dear darling,

Honest baby I could hardly believe it was you tonight. Are you sure it wasn't just a dream.

Bopsy sounded awfully lonesome though, guess maybe it's sort of tough being away from Wally and all old acquaintances. New posts are just that way. Anyway Bopsy needs his Miss Boo doesn't he? My poor lonesome disappointed baby.

Darling I hope my actions weren't too previous, but things are happening so fast & some day soon we are all going to get our orders & if this transfer doesn't go through it will surely be with a unit. Just had to take a chance & if our twinkly star watches over us it will go through. Just think baby that we should be together some way or somehow. You aren't sorry are you darling that I want to come to be with you? Sort of thought you sounded a bit skeptical or was it the fact that you felt the way should have been paved first.

Edward our plans for a leave together sound so perfect. Just imagine being free and happy & together. Of course I want to be with you darling, it would be the most perfect thing in the world. My plans at present naturally can't be made in advance, but something will break won't it dear?

St. Louis sounds fine Bops, then maybe we could run up home for a day or so & into Chicago. All are so close together. I do want mother & dad to know you darling, of course that part is up to you—but it would be quiet & peaceful there & a good rest—whatever you say darling. How do you think of such wonderful things dear, please never feel you owe me anything cause that would spoil it all.

Edward don't scold yourself for writing & trying to keep us together. Often times I wonder how either of us could go through so much & come back for more, but now it's quite different, not that it has changed either of us except we are now living only for our present happiness.

About my weight sweetheart, you see I was 117¼ at the time of all our troubles then zoom down I went to 108 but this past week & since a little courage was talked into me my appetite & disposition just skyrocketed. Remember how I told you what that one letter & one from Wally did for me. Am really proud to tell you dear that your Miss Boo took herself by the bootstraps with your help & got busy on being a sensible person. But baby I've been awfully worried about you. Darling you aren't well are you. Father Laws's letter gave it away. First you're smoking far too much, & not sleeping

well isn't that right? Don't keep anything from me dear. All this worry &
trouble hasn't been good for my Bops, but soon I'll make my darling happy
& take care of everything so all those old troubles will just have to scamper.

What is McClellan like darling. Do the girls wear seersuckers & can they
wear formals? Who is the Chief Nurse & is she nice. Daisy Flowers is a good
gal isn't she?

It's really getting cold here Bops, but still isn't as bad as McCoy. That
place is breaking up fast, most everyone is gone.

Well sweetheart it's really bedtime. Capt Butler & I have had a long talk.
She's really a lonesome gal too.

Goodnight baby dear. Here is a wee mousy cause you're such a good
good Bopsy & I love you.

Miss Boo.

My darling,

It was super-deluxe talking with you to-night and you sounded so strong and wonderful that I was so proud I almost popped a panty button. Rascal!

This is a quickie—

I just wrote to a Miss Grace Hoyt who is the Chief Clerk in the SGO office in Washington. I told her that you had put in a letter through channels requesting transfer to McClellan, etc. Now what I think you ought to do Bops is write immediately to your friend

Major Ames, I believe it is, and tell her exactly what you have done, etc. I think it may help and it certainly won't do any harm to tell her all about what you want to do. O.K.?

Be a good girl, eat, be happy and always remember that

I love you,
Mr Bops

Thursday Eve (Nov. 9?)

My dear darling

Your quickie arrived today dear so will get an answer off immediately to let you know what has developed this week.

First of all darling how are you and how goes the new job and the new post? Am anxious to hear just what your work consists of, who your new friends are, how the social life is, and most of all how my scruntchy baby is. Bopsy, Bopsy this having you so far away is not good for me at all and anyway I really think something should be done about it, cause Miss Boo is really a sad sack with no smacks and no hugs for all this long time.

Darling my transfer request was returned and didn't even get by Col. Jacobson, insufficient reason and besides I am General Service, so that takes care of that little issue, was afraid that would happen but nothing can be done about it. One of the nurses here, a 1st Lt. with whom I work, wrote to a couple of friends of hers, told them the story and perhaps something will develop yet. These officers are brass hats, one of them is right in 4th Service Command headquarters and she has known him since she was a little girl so perhaps he will be able to do a good deed for her.

Am trying to remember how your voice sounded Monday, baby my heart was beating so fast that it was almost impossible to speak, why do you do such things to me, is it still that old love of ours. Gee darling when our vacation comes, I wish it would last forever, but we will be two awfully happy people for awhile anyway won't we? Am planning on it so strongly and do you think there is still a chance of your getting off the first of December? What will happen if your family finds out that you have leave and didn't come home?

We girls have acquired a little black puppy which takes up all our spare time and drives the loneliness out of the house. She is so cute but has been sick for the past two days, the Vet said probably beginning distemper, so last night I specialed her and gave Sulfdiazine q 4 h what do you think of that? Frustrated mother instinct I guess Bops.

Baby there isn't much happening here, very boring to say the least and anyway all I want is for time to pass for me to either be transferred with my Bops and for our vacation to start.

I love you darling oh so much.

Miss Boo

My darling,

I've been busy before but never have I been as busy as I've been since coming to this place. I've been on the go from 8 until 5 and sometimes I've been working on the Ward at night catching up. I guess my loafing days are over and I'm really grateful. There is nothing like keeping busy. Comes bedtime I'm just too tired out to even think and off I go to sleep. I've been doing nothing but ENT but perhaps it's just as well to do that and let the eye go because I was losing all interest in ENT and now I am becoming more interested in it because I have to do it. I'm getting children to take care of too. I've done 8 tonsils, three on children since being here and I do all the bronchoscopy and esphagoscopy because the Chief hasn't had any training in it and lets me do it. So at last I'm working and really enjoying it.

Mother seems to be better Bops, but her pressure is still high and she has those anginal pains in her chest, so that's the way it is.

I got a letter from Chaplain Schwartz who is at Camp Reynolds, Pa waiting to go overseas and he sure was mad at me Bops, but I had it coming to me. He criticized me severely for letting you go ahead and then not going ahead with marrying you and he didn't pull any punches. But, he is of course right and I have no comeback outside of being terribly ashamed of myself as you know I am, but that's that!

I wrote to this person in Washington about your transfer but haven't heard anything as yet. At least we will try darling to get it through but it's a very difficult thing to do. I wrote you that Daisy is 2nd in command. The Chief Nurse here is very nice so I'm sure they will do all they can when the time comes if you get released from the 6th SC.

Wally is lonesome as hell and there may be a chance that we can get him transferred up here. It sure would be something if it could be arranged but it's bad to build all these dreams and then be let down.

I heard from Aaron and he is very upset about you and me and he wishes so that he could be with both of us now. He's a grand guy and he writes that he still wants to meet and know you some day.

I'm really quite all-right darling and putting on some weight. I am smoking too much but what the hell, I have to do something and there's not a drop of whiskey to be had around these parts. I have every third week-end off and next week-end I'm going up to Chattanooga with a few of the boys and take in this Look-out Mountain which they say is very beautiful. I live in some pretty nice quarters with a bunch of dentists and we play poker and shoot dice most of the time and have some fun. I'm about $50 ahead for the past week so it isn't bad. Played poker last night and I was losing $27 and in about ½ hour I won it all back and $23 besides so that old Bops must have been looking over my shoulder.

My social life is practically merely a word. I took some gal to the club dance last Saturday night and we both ended up telling each other about our respective girlfriend and boyfriend. Sure is funny Bops, but everyone has a story to tell and plenty of heartache in their lives nowadays. The nurse here in the clinic came in the other day and she had just been notified that her husband was killed in action and so this lousy world wends its merry way, so perhaps we should be grateful for what we have.

Going up to your home sounds swell, but perhaps we better see what happens to your request or if you can get leave before you hear, let me know as I can see what I can get.

Be a good girl darling, don't worry, eat a lot, be happy 'cause

I love you,
Mr Bops

12 Nov. 1944

My darling,

I anticipated that your request wouldn't get very far because of insufficient reasons. But perhaps it's just as well that Col Clement doesn't get wind of it or she would probably get her dander up and send you out right away. For you to get sent here requires the best laid plans or else you may find yourself transferred to the 4th SC and further away than we are now. So we'll see what my Washington friend has to say and see what happens.

As for the leave I was thinking that perhaps it would be better for me to get leave and come up and see you so that I wouldn't be taking any time away from you so you could get home. I don't know just when I can get it but I should put in for it right away so as to know just when I'll get it. You didn't tell me if and when you can get leave. I think it best if I see when I can get it and then perhaps Capt. Butler can give you a few days off and we can spend some of it somewhere. As far as the family goes I'll just tell them I'm on DS* somewhere.

The connections are pretty good to St. Louis from here. The train leaves Birmingham at 9:30 at night and gets in St. Louis at noon the next day, not bad, eh? I am only 65 miles from Birmingham and can drive there.

Stay well, darling and soon we'll be seeing each other.

I love you,
Mr Bops

---

*   Direct Support

STATEMENT OF MISS GRETCHEN
RUTH BOODY ON THE OCCASION OF
HER CONVERSION TO JUDAISM
ON MONDAY EVENING, OCTOBER 9, 1944

I, Gretchen Ruth Boody, do herewith declare in the presence of God and the witnesses and rabbi here assembled, that I, of my own free will, seek the fellowship of Israel and that I fully accept the faith of Israel.

I believe that God is one, Almighty, Allwise and Most Holy.

I believe that Man is created in the image of God; that it is his duty to imitate the holiness of God; that he is a free-will agent, responsible to God for his actions; and that he is destined to everlasting life.

I believe that Israel is God's priest-people, the world's teacher in religion and righteousness as expressed in our Bible and interpreted in the spirit of Jewish traditions.

I believe that God ruleth the world with justice and love and in the fullness of time His Kingdom will be established on earth.

I promise that I shall endeavor to live, as far as it is in my power, in accordance with the ideals of Jewish life.

I further promise, that should I ever be blessed with children, I shall rear them in conformity with the Jewish religion. May God strengthen me in these resolutions. Most fervently, therefore, do I herewith pronounce the Jewish confession of faith:

"Shema Yisroel Adonoy Elohenu Adonoy Echod. Hear, O Israel: The Lord our God, the Lord is One."

Praised be His name whose glorious kingdom is for ever and ever.

Thou shalt love the Lord, thy God, with all thy heart, and with all thy soul, and with all thy might. And these words, which I command thee this day, shall be upon thy heart. Thou shalt teach them diligently unto thy children, and shalt speak of them when thou sittest in thy house, when thou walkest by the way, when thou liest down, and when thou risest up. And thou shalt bind them for a sign upon thy eyes. And thou shalt write them upon the doorposts of thy house, and upon thy gates:

To the end that ye may remember and do all My commandments, and be holy unto your God. I am the Lord your God.

RABBI _J. M. Doerman_

WITNESS _Mrs. David Kriegshaber_

WITNESS _Mrs. Joseph Kohn_

WITNESS _Mrs. Maud O. Heyman_

Mon. Eve (Nov. 13?)

My dear darling

Was so disappointed to return to camp & still no mail from my Bops. Did you forget Miss Boo darling, aren't you well, are you too busy or what? Perhaps my letter about my transfer hasn't reached you yet.

Took Capt. Butler to St. Louis with me, we really had fun. Pudgy is still the same old gal & could you have seen us you would have said gee that's the Bopsy I fell in love with, honest dear I felt more like myself than I have for months. We had fun talking about our spending our leave in St. Louis. She is anxious to meet you dear. How do things look down there for our plans to progress?

Sat eve we talked for hours, had a few drinks & a good dinner which Pudge & I cooked—it seemed like old times. Sunday we went out to Forest Park to the zoo etc. It was so gorgeous out, called Sally & Dick. They too were thrilled about the possibility of our visit. Dick is very busy. Said he had your letter & will write soon.

Crazy things go on here all the time, our unit nurses have left but we got replacements which we are all glad for. This three week business of closing & moving doesn't seem to be progressing so well. I have my doubts dear. Darn I want to come to McClellan so badly. Am just keeping my fingers crossed. What next do you think I should do Bops?

Am enclosing my letter of conversion, pledge, etc., just thought you might like to see what it was, just received it today. Please return it darling. I'm so very proud of it.

Had a letter from Wally today he sure is lonesome for Edward, it's a shame he had to be left behind, for it made me feel more comfortable as long as you had such a good companion.

Write soon darling. I get so awfully lonesome, but am being your big girl honest.

Take care of my Bopsy won't you & keep well.

All my love forever & ever,
Miss Boo

17 Nov 1944

My darling,

So good speaking with you last night baby. It always is and makes us both feel so much better to be able to say hello and 'Que Pasa.' I was going to call you myself to-night but you beat me to it and saved me some money, that's good!

No kidding, Bops, I'm really working hard. So far I've had to work not only all day, but through part of the night as well. Every six weeks all the infantry boys have to be examined, etc., and that must be done at night so you see the time is well taken. Again last night, someone got the bright idea to run the Station Complement the same way so that was about 1,000 more. At least I don't have to examine each one but am the EENT consultant and see only about 1 in 10. I have also been appointed a Medical Witness for the Army Retirement Board here for Officers and Nurses. I examine the patient and give an opinion as to whether they are fit or not for further duty. I'm getting to be quite the busy little bee, and I'm grateful for it, really I am. You've no idea how much better it is to be working and not have all the hours hang heavy. Now, I have much less time to think and when the day is over, I'm so exhausted I don't have any trouble sleeping, although I'm never too tired to say my prayers for both of us and dream of you, baby.

Mother is definitely on the upgrade as far as her emotional upset is concerned and I've been writing her trying to convince her that her boy has returned to the straight and narrow. I don't have to kid you darling, that it isn't an easy job to try and keep them all happy, to tell them that all is well, and in other words to write letters that come merely from my fingers and not a bit from my heart. It's an almost impossible position to be in, one that requires all the courage I can muster and I'm doing a good job I think. There are no secrets between us darling, there never will be. I love you so much darling. It's unbelievable how one person can so become so attached to another. Love is an amazing thing. I firmly believe that it is the most powerful influence on earth. Your certificates of conversion I have and I'm keeping them for a little while because I like to look at them because to me they symbolize all the heartaches, tears, anguish that you have gone through for this old thing! I wish there were words that I could describe you darling, your sincerity is something out of this world. Only a person knowing you and understanding you could ever realize that there are people such as you who have taken all that you have and are not bitter, angry, vicious. I try so many times to analyze why this happened to us, baby. Here we are, you and I. I can honestly say that I don't think that we have done anything that should now come back to haunt us. I know you have never hurt anyone in your whole life and I haven't. Just like when I first met you darling and after a short week I explained the whole thing to you, I was trying even then to not hurt you, to try and tell you why this and why that, but loving each other the way we did, we just hung on as we are doing now—loving each other more and more if that is possible, helping each other through these trying times, trying to make the load a little bit easier and yet I know what it is like, don't I, Bops. Aaron wrote me last week, and his concluding paragraph as very interesting. He said, "Every time you take one on the chin, it makes your chin a little tougher." He sure is right baby, and I bet that between us we have the toughest chins in the world. But, on we go, each never giving up, each praying, each hoping, that in the end Right will Triumph over Ignorance, and that is what it really amounts to. That old Bops writes me she isn't hoping or waiting and yet you are, you rascal. I don't know how I got into this long harangue but I just happened to be thinking along those lines.

I think I'll be at Chattanooga for the week-end. I'm going up with one of the dental officers and we have a hotel room and will have a couple of good meals and just take it easy.

Your trip to St. Louis sounded swell darling and I'm so glad you managed to see Pudge. She sounds like so much fun and I sure would love to meet her. Perhaps in January we can both get away for a few days and have a swell time ourselves. I didn't put in for my leave as I was going to because it's really silly as you say, for me to come up and not be able to be with you for any length of time. There is a lovely place here to stay—the Officer's Club has a guest house and people may stay for one week.

These nurses here, many of them want to go overseas and there just isn't any call for them and they don't send them if they don't want to go. All the chief nurses I have spoken with and they tell me that they never send anyone who doesn't want to go and I know you won't be sent even if you get orders and tell them you don't want to go. I haven't heard from Washington yet as to what goes on about you and how we may swing it but as soon as I do I'll let you know. The Chief Nurse here is a nice gal and Daisy told me she would help all she can if and when the time comes. It all depends on getting you out of the 6th SC and how we will manage that I don't know.

Wally is home on leave now, I guess and I hope he is having a nice time. He writes he has to catch up on a lot of homework, the rascal!

They had a beer party up here at the Nurses Rec Hall. The nurses have a beautiful hall here given to them by the people of Alabama and it's all theirs and they run around up there with slacks, cook a lot of their own meals, and have a fine time. The nurses are also permitted to dress formal for the dances here Saturday night and they really love it. They say it makes them feel human once in awhile. Daisy is really a swell person, but I guess it's because we talk about you a lot, so there!

Hey Bops, someone dragged me out on a blind date the other night with some civilian gal from the local town here. I spoke to her for awhile and got her life's history. Why do people always tell me their troubles? Anyway, she's 24 and was married when she was 14, has two daughters, 9 and 4, and got divorced last year. Holy smokes, I thought that was really something, but they tell me the usual marrying age down here in the South is around 15. Some stuff? Dates and me are very funny Bops. I just don't know what to say or do and I don't give much of a damn one way or the other about them. When you get used to someone, JUST LIKE AN OLD SHOE, you know how it is, eh Bops?

This has really been a long one Bops, so I guess it's about time I signed off and took my shoes over to the repairman for a little repair job.

Be a good little sweetheart, don't worry about your old Bops and he won't worry about you.

I love you,
Mr Bops

Friday Eve

My dear darling

Baby if our love weren't so deep & we didn't know each other so well, these crazy premonitions & this mental telepathy wouldn't happen. Suddenly last night it was as if you had spoken the very words "Bopsy I want to talk to you." That flash of something came through me & I couldn't wait long enough to even let you finish your dinner. Baby don't you know how Miss Boo can read between the lines of your letters. Such a big brave old darling trying to cover up that deep hurt & unhappiness but just a little boy wanting his Bopsy to feel the same. My precious sweetheart I know, honest I do, but certainly after all this nothing can ever tear us completely apart. It's just fate or whatever they call it, undoubtedly God's will.

It was so wonderful hearing your voice darling—if my humble words could only express what it does to me. I hate being a sentimental old thing but we both know it isn't that don't we.

Darling I hated so to hear you had received another reprimand, but we just must face so much it seems. Just believe profoundly that they weren't my words & that regardless of others, nothing matters except I love you & never will I change or go back to the religion I gave up because of that love. Let your mind be at ease dear baby & don't say, "It's my fault," for in my heart I wouldn't want it any other way.

Am so dreadfully sorry about our leave, but it's one of those things. I talked to Capt. Butler again & she said, "If you were being married I'd give you any time you wanted." At that statement I was completely at a loss, so didn't explain or anything. We will just have to wait apparently & hope & pray.

Bopsy will you call Wed. or Thur. on accounta I have to serve food at a party for our enlisted men on Tues. eve. Didn't know that yesterday. Were you to call early I might be in but one of the girls goes on leave & it necessitates my working til 7. Call Wed or Thur. after 7 p.m. dear. I shall be so anxious.

Played bridge tonight with Lt. & Mrs. Isley & Whit (one of the nurses). We are behind 2500 pts. My goodness, but feel pretty good on accounta I bid a little slam & made it. Really feel I'm improving. We play a lot. Baby how's my old gambler—hope you're still winning. Just be careful & don't lose the panties. My salary is big but I don't know your size—so golly—are you gaining weight?

Awful sleepy sweetheart so better go to dreamland so we can be together.

I love you darling—but you know that & how much.
Your own Miss Boo

The Read House, Chattanooga, Tennessee   Nov. 18-19, 1944
Handwritten

My darling—

    Chattanooga is a red-hot, wide-open town with about 10 women for every man. Ft. Oglethorpe, the WAC's training camp is about 2 miles from here and every week-end there are hundreds of WAC's running around and if you so much as smile at them, you're surrounded.

    This dental officer and myself drove up yesterday & we had a swell meal & then went to some dance in town. Just got up—it's 11:30 and this is the first morning I've had any sleep in a long while.

    I managed to get a good supply of liquor. Alabama is pretty dry & it is rationed—one bottle a month.

    I'm driving back this p.m.

    Just reporting, baby, what your rascal is up to.

I love you,
Mr Bops

Sunday P.M. (Nov. 19?)

My dear darling:

This is really a gloomy old day and I have to work this afternoon, and as you can see it isn't going to be very hard. The best part of all is that I have some time to have a wee chat with my baby.

Guess what Bops, it snowed a little this morning, the first that I have seen in four years, golly I was excited, and honest I like the north and the cold brisk weather now that I have gotten over my Panama spell.

What's new darling and how are things going, keep thinking and how disappointed you must be not to be encouraged in taking your leave and coming up here, but honest dear it would be a bad set up, you really would hate it, because there isn't any place or anything to do at all especially if we didn't have a car. It's just impossible to get out of this place and I haven't the slightest idea what you would do with yourself all the time I was on duty. Hated so to tell you not to come but am sure it is the best way. Now there are a lot of things that can happen in the meantime, and one of them for sure and that is that I have to go on night duty the 27th of this month. Think that if all goes well and these other girls get their leaves over with I will be able to get some time right after the first of the year, but darling I do want to spend it with you regardless of where we go. Feel I should go up home for a couple of days and thought perhaps you would enjoy it too, the folks are so understanding and I am sure you wouldn't feel at all uncomfortable, in fact mother wants you to come if you get some time off, it's just because they love us both so much. Is there any possible chance of your postponing that leave until January, see what you can do about it dear. Fate will play a hand again and our twinkly star will look after us so that is why I am not awfully disappointed for the postponement at the present time. Perhaps too you will hear something from Washington before then.

Darling I am enclosing some service stripes, think they are really pretty and when I got some for myself, of course I had to think of my Bopsy, wish I could be there to sew them on for you dear, perhaps you have gotten some for yourself by this time, but hope not.

Sweetheart I have been racking my brain to think of something to give you for Hanukkah, but as yet my thoughts haven't been very productive, please don't write back and say, "don't get me anything Bops, I don't need anything," but I do want some suggestions, please Bops.

What an evening we spent last night, I have gotten to be a regular old bridge fiend darling and honest injun I am improving if I do say so, bid six spades last night doubled and redoubled and made it, wow, isn't that something, I was so excited. Darling I am sure you would be beaming if you could see this old Bops of yours these days, everything seems alright just because we love each other and are writing and not worrying, inside I'm happy darling because I am so proud of we two old things. Haven't had a date for weeks and weeks, and never even think about it; the date I want is with my baby sometime, someplace and in the meantime those telephone calls are so wonderful.

The latest news around here is that they are forming five new general hospitals, some of the personnel are arriving, and I am just as curious as can be to know what the next few weeks will bring forth, gee Bops maybe they will reassign you who knows. Every day I look for familiar faces to appear around here because such strange things happen, and I have seen so many that were with the 210th.

Golly the way I jabber on and on, it's terrific isn't it, but baby it is so beautiful, beautiful, just to talk with you when I feel like it.

Be a good darling, don't work too hard, have fun and remember that your Miss Boo loves you more than anything in the world.

I love you
Miss Boo

My darling,

Received your sweet letter this morning darling and it is so good hearing from you. Thanks a million for the very gilty stripes but you forget that I am entitled to wear five, you rascal so if you get another one send it along. They sure are pretty.

I received a letter from Dick and he sure must be busier than a one-arm paper hanger with the 7 years itch. He sure is some guy and doing a wonderful job. He would like to have us there for our leaves and perhaps it may come about that way. I know one thing Baby, and that is if and when you do get leave you must get home to see your Daddy and Mother. I would never think of depriving you and them of each other.

I don't know just how all that travelling will work out but everywhere is so far away and the time is so short. If this war were only over, then people could go when and where they please, but golly Bops, the damn thing just seems to drag on and on. But we shall see what happens.

I received a lovely letter from Aunt Sally in which she told me how sorry she is that things are the way they are but that her hands are tied and she just hopes and prays that someday something turns up for us. She is a grand person.

I was very interested in Capt Butler's reaction to your request for leave now and I would feel the same way if I were her. She probably thinks that I'm a first class heel for wishy-washying all over the place and she just doesn't want you to have anything to do with me unless it is to get married. She is of course so right in her way of thinking and I must present a very unlovely spectacle to a lot of people. Guess I sure am a bad boy, aren't I baby?

As for the Chanukah present, I already have something for you darling. I have had it for quite awhile now. I won't tell you what it is but when we see each other, I'll give it to you then and don't go pestering me with questions, you rascal. As for what I want, our wishes are mutual as far as that goes. I want just what you have always wanted darling. I'd just like to hold you close and know that all our heartaches are over, through and done with. But perhaps God above will someday give us that in his own due time and as he sees fit. Your love is enough for me baby, to know that you love me is present enough and if the rest is not to be, so be it. Prayers are prayers and I still pray baby for you and all the rest of the world. I shall be calling to-night and saying hello to you darling and I know it will be wonderful hearing your voice.

I love you,
Mr Bops

Thursday P.M. (23 November, Thanksgiving)

My dear darling,

Golly how hard I thought of you this noon when I was eating that turkey it surely brought back wonderful memories of another Thanksgiving when we were together and just having fun. Remember the eggnog at Murphy's—golly. Our dinner was very good, but we had cocktails at the Officer's Club at 12:30 which made it seem better I guess. Everyone and his brother was there and some of the Drs. really were feeling no pain. I helped serve and we had either martinis or eggnog. Naturally I had to be a good girl because I am on duty this P.M. Capt Butler was really feeling alright, but it was good for her, she really is a swell person and lots of fun, we get along just perfectly both at work and at play.

There I go rambling on before telling you darling what a wonderful treat it was speaking with you last night. Bopsy, Bopsy, just to hear you laugh is worth all the money in the world. Aren't we two amazing people though sweetheart? Honest baby, what's the matter with the finances, gee whiz, you don't have Bopsy to take to the movies anymore, must be you found another gold-digger, huh? Maybe you ought to stop one of the bonds for the next month or so, so you can catch up. I will call you next week, so there, but baby you are such a spoiled old thing, but it's fun to spoil you, only I don't have enough real good chances do I? Do you really need some money, baby?

Darling I don't want you to feel uncomfortable about my asking you to go up home with me, but if you really don't want to I can take my leave at least part of it a little earlier and meet you in St. Louis the last five days. You probably would get enough in that time, I mean of seeing your old thing. Think mother and daddy would be terribly disappointed if I didn't come up and I certainly owe them a little time don't you think? We could have a glorious time in five or six days don't you think baby, just laughing and loving and being the old guys we used to be?

Bopsy you never in the world will guess what you are getting for Hanukkah, so there, but I will give you three guesses. If there is something, I mean one thing that you would like please give me a suggestion otherwise I have in mind several little things darling. Anyway whatever it is I am giving it because I want to and with all the love in the world for my baby.

It is about time for me to make my rounds, write and tell me what you did to celebrate Thanksgiving won't you dear. I have been thinking of you every minute and wishing so hard that you were here. Yes, darling this love is the most mystifying and grand thing in the world, but there is one thing that I want you to stop and that is fear that your family will find out about us again. Darling you are a man, not a little child and if they won't let us marry they certainly can't stop us from loving and being together once in awhile. I know baby that I have no malice in my heart, but I do know that I have your happiness in my heart, and if this is what you want then I do to, anyway I guess maybe I want it most or something, just an old selfish thing or something huh?

Bea good baby and work hard, cause that is best.

I love you darling,
Miss Boo

24 Nov 1944

My darling,

I sure had a wonderful talk with you the other night darling and it's, oh, so good to hear your voice and laughter these days. Just makes me forget all the troubles and those few minutes are wonderful indeed. If you insist on calling me, you rascal, my extension at the quarters is 1306 and how about next Wednesday night? I just never know when I'll be having any night work but I'll try and be there for sure after 7.

Yesterday we had a swell Thanksgiving dinner and after it was over I went home and got that picture we had taken of us and looked at it for so long. Those were really the good old days, darling, and I don't know if we appreciated them or not. I sure do now. There really is nothing like an old shoe darling, is there? You put it on and it's so comfortable and warm and the longer you wear it the better it feels and you just can't get yourself to throw it away ever, can you?

Bops, what's the difference in delivery between free and air mail? I was just wondering whether there was a great difference or not.

No kidding, Bops, I actually have to find time to write letters these days. I'm not writing half as many as I used to.

Be a happy baby and I bet you look so wonderful darling with that 114 pounds. Boy, what scruntchin'—!

I love you,
Mr Bops

Officers' Club; Peoria, Illinois Sun. Eve (26 Nov.?)

My dear darling—

 Guess what, just a little vacation, all by myself. Gee Bopsy, it's so nice here & all that's missing is my baby—so there.

 To-morrow is my day off going to get a permanent in the a.m. & do some shopping so came down to Peoria this p.m. because of a ride. It's awfully good to get away for overnight.

 Just returned from "And Now To-morrow," it's almost ten, am going up to bed as soon as I've said good-nite to you dear.

 Stopped in at the Club cause there is a radio & am having a Coke. It's very quiet, no one but me, but a cute cozy little club. Here is a picture of it. The Pere Marquette is a lovely hotel, & my room is nice too. Capt. Butler is coming down to-morrow p.m. to shop so we will go home together. Must finish my Christmas shopping for the family. This will probably be my last free day until late Dec.

 Darling your letter which was written the 24th arrived to-day. It was such a sweet letter. You know I always read them over & over & over. Yes our call was super & I will call Wed. eve. Go on nite duty Tues. but will call before going on duty since you are an hour ahead of our time.

 Bopsy, Bopsy you rascal, how come you have my present already. Now I know why you are broke—huh—bad boy. Sweetheart if you weren't so priceless I probably wouldn't hang on till my teeth fall out.

 About my leave dear. Will get it the first part of January, seven days is all I get, so I must go home for part of it. What would you say if we or 4 days together. Do you think the trip would be too hard for that short a time darling? Mom & Dad will understand so don't worry about that part. About Capt. Butler's attitude dear, she doesn't think such a thing as you say. She just wonders what's best for me, but darling, no one's ideas or opinions mean a thing as long as I love my Edward, & he loves me & somehow, some place we can be together & be happy. Nothing or no one matters to me except that baby, believe me.

 Gee whiz. I forgot about my Veteran needing five stripes. Will get you a new set & you may return the four & I will use them on my other suit—o.k.?

 Next letter try "free" dear it probably will come just as fast. Promise to let you know, but unless there is something special we may as well take advantage of not having to lick stamps.

It's bed time darling. How good it will be to not have to get up at six. Will dream of us Edward, those dreams have never faded, neither have my prayers been forgotten.

Miss you so terribly, especially when things happen that we might enjoy to-gether.

Good night my beloved.

Your Miss Boo

My darling,

Your wonderful letter to hand darling, and am so happy you are feeling well and puttering about in your usual manner.

I'm enclosing a letter I just received from the gal that wrote "Earth and High Heaven." It sure was swell of her writing as she did and you can see that we have an invitation to visit her some day. That old Bops is right on the ball, right? Save the letter Bops.

I got a letter from Dad the other day and he says he is coming down to see me right after Christmas. Just when that will be I don't know. I'm going to try and get him to bring Mother down too so that I shall be able to have seen them both and can take my leave in St. Louis. I hope it works out all-right. I shall probably know more about it later on but the time being that's the way it is. You <u>must</u> go home and see your folks, baby, when you get your leave. I absolutely insist upon that. We must think of them I know how badly they want to see you, you rascally thing, you.

I'm working so very, very hard darling, and you are right about work helping a lot. The days go by so quickly when I work and before I know it the week is over and another one is here.

I haven't heard a word from these people in Washington. I guess the connection wasn't as good as I thought it was but I'm still hoping. I wish I knew just how long I would be around here. You no sooner get settled in one place and then something comes along and you get changed. Just thinking the other day that in a couple of months it will be a whole year darling since you've been back. The time really goes fast, doesn't it? I was looking at the snag of letters you have written me in all that time and it's funny, I just pick up one at random and I know the letters so well, it seems as if it were written only the day before. But that's the way it goes and will always go.

I heard from Aaron to-day. He is completely upset about you and I of course and feels so badly about the torment we are having. He feels that we are just going on making things worse for ourselves and that if we can't be married we should break clean. Funny how people just can say things so easily. He feels that we are both too fine and wonderful to go on being apart, going on waiting and waiting, missing everything that way. But, he really knows down deep that it just isn't that way. Funny, the sequence of things Bops. Last June Dad visited me and then you did. Now he is coming down again and we shall probably meet after he has gone. It's a vicious cycle.

This present business is really getting me curious. Just what it is I haven't the slightest idea but I bet it's something only that old Bops could think of. Right?

I'll be waiting for that call any day now baby, and oh yes, I dropped Capt Butler a note the other day expressing a little thanks for you and her being such good friends. I hope you don't mind.

I love you,

Mr Bops

My dear darling,

Was so disappointed not to be able to get the call through to-night, but I tried from six to seven (our time) and there were no free lines and again from nine to ten, for you to see I had to go on duty. Am going to try again to-night dear and one of these times other people will stop talking long enough for us to say hello.

The second night is just about gone, and that makes only seven left, it sure tuckers this old Bops out as you know, wish they never had invented such a thing. Now does that sound natural to hear me fuss about night duty. Will be off the morning of the eighth and have the eighth and ninth off sure wish it were possible to get up home and back but the train connections are so awful just can't do it, its almost six hundred miles up there from here.

Did I tell you the latest news on the leave situation, seven days sure isn't much but that is all any of the girls are getting because of the nurse shortage here. Wonder just what we should do dear. It provokes me no end when I have so many days accumulated and then can't take it.

We had a beautiful snow storm this eve Bops, it sure is nice and brisk around the edges, but makes us all have lots of pep. How is the weather down there?

Bops what's my present, just tell me one little wee thing won't you, please, I can't wait honest. Ha ha I bet you think you are getting a pair of gloves, but you aren't so there.

Certainly this is a dead old place, just nothing happening, but Col. Clemont is coming the 15th of Dec. and I suppose she will have plenty of changes to make. Would you mind being in another General Hospital Bops. It's a funny thing, I want to go and yet I don't. Crazy kids aren't we. The old U.S. looks pretty good to me yet, but if you go out darling then I sure don't want to stay behind and that's that.

How is your work dear, are they still running the little old fanny off my Bops. Baby I am so proud that you are getting to do something worthwhile and also that you are doing things that others don't know how to do. My Bops is a smart old thing and pretty soon they will get that promotion for you dear, I feel sure.

Just an old jabber face that's me, better quit so you won't grow weary. Darling you have never said for a long time that you need some smacks, do you?

I love you baby
Miss Boo

DECEMBER, 1944

My dear darling,

Don't know how it can be, but those telephone calls of ours get better and better don't they dear? It seems impossible that you are so far away when your voice is so very close. Gee darling how I want to reach right out and give you a great big hug, I do in my thoughts though so that will have to substitute until our day comes along.

The old night duty is rolling right along baby, just five more left, sure wish I could scoot right down to Alabama and see my Bops for those two days I have off. Would you let me get a little snooze though on accounta I fear I would be a little sleepy. Wonder if we could figure out a way to meet some place sorta half way, there I go dreaming, but golly darling I am getting so anxious.

Hope you are successful in getting your mom to come down to see you. It would do her good to get away dear. Perhaps if she were well and away from home environment she would realize a little better that this old Army life isn't all a bed of roses and that my Bopsy would like a little happiness too. It's a funny thing dear, but I can't seem to get it out of my crazy head, that one fine day I may win them over. Probably overconfidence or something, but am afraid they haven't heard the last of Miss Boo.

Whatever comes darling neither of us must worry any more and I feel that God will hear our prayers some day, cause we sure have been old bothers for Him, haven't we? Am so proud of my Judaism dear and only wish that we could go to services together. We will on our vacation, won't we Bops, want you to see Temple Israel if we go to St. Louis.

Say Scruntchy I am still waiting for one little inkling as to what my present is, why do you always have to get a thing so far ahead of time so that I have to puzzle and puzzle? Is it big or little? What's it made of? How is it used? Now there are my three questions. Wish you would tell me what you want dear so I wouldn't be having such a time. Will send your package down in another week, although you have to promise not to open it until Hanukkah so there.

Was so pleased over the letter from Miss Graham, she must have had an experience darling, maybe not personal but a friend perhaps. Liked her invitation to bring your Erica to Montreal, Bops, wasn't that nice? Guess maybe we will have to take a trip someday darling in that big Buick you are going to get, and we will visit all our friends and see all that we want to see. One thing we will do is visit your aunt and uncle in Philadelphia, won't we?

Am so concerned about Aaron's statement dear, it sounds so easy doesn't it, but when I hear or read those words, "break it up," I nearly have a convulsion, it gives me cold duck bumps and a great big ache in the middle of my tummy. Darling I don't think anyone can ever do that with a love like ours. I've learned more about how love affects you since all our troubles began than anyone could ever have told me, haven't you dear! It is extremely powerful if it is the right thing darling and there can never be a doubt in our minds about it. Bopsy dear do you know perhaps it's silly but I am happy just knowing that you are mine, perhaps not officially but just this way, it really is all that matters. Feel so empty sometimes that we can't have our dreams fulfilled right now but darling I don't believe I'll ever completely give up until you take me out and drown me in the lake.

Funny you haven't heard anything from Washington, but then I have been thinking that it might happen that about the time I were transferred, your orders might come through again. Just bet that we will go out again dear, and if either of us gets an assignment, we must try to get together. If it were an overseas unit, there shouldn't be any trouble getting in, do you think? Baby, we are the craziest things in the world aren't we? But in spite of it all, I think we are two very wonderful people and just all right. Especially my baby. And I always get mad when you say he's a bad boy. Nobody can say that, not even you, Bops, so there.

It's awfully cold up here, but the ramps are quite warm, so it isn't too bad, don't feel like walking to-night though and it's at least five miles I'm sure around this place. Just stayed in the old bed to-day until five o'clock. Every time I am on night duty I think about Bopsy's bed and how I used to pound the old pillow until you came home. Yummy.

Darling I thought you had probably thrown my letters away a long time ago. Guess both of us do things alike though, for I have never destroyed even a wee note of yours. They are priceless to me and I read one out of the stack every once in awhile especially when I get lonesome, they seem to help so much.

Bops, you remember that fellow that I told you about who has been waiting for me all these years, the boy from home, with the bad heart. Mother wrote that he was married awhile back, sure was surprised, but am glad he finally gave up, for there surely has never been any feeling there for years and years.

Golly this is a lot of jabbering, but it's wonderful fun to sit down and have a good old talk with that sweet thing of mine. Darling I love you so much geeeeeeee.

Be a good boy and keep the wolfessess away just on accounta.

I love you
Your Miss Boo

My darling,

So wonderful talking with you the other night baby and hearing your voice. Just makes up for all the time we haven't seen each other somehow. Those calls are really so close, it makes you feel sort of silly not being able to just hang up the phone and run over for a few personalized scruntches and smacks. Yes, baby, I do need a million smacks, so there!

Bops, the more I think of the leave business, the more exasperating it seems that you only get 7 days. I don't understand it—if a gal can be spared for 7 days, then she certainly can be spared for 10. If you are that busy then how can you be spared at all. Sort of silly, but I guess that's the way it is. How in the world are you going to get up to Hudson, see the family for a few days, then jump into a train to St. Louis and then get back to Ellis all in 7 days is quite a job and I'm afraid that old gunboat will be worn to a frazzle. Perhaps it would be better if I could get to Chicago instead of St. Louis and then I could meet you there and save all that time. We could then be to-gether in Chicago for a few days and then I could take you back to Ellis or something like that. The train connections from Chicago here are pretty good they say. Our plans will have to be letter-perfect so it will work out. I just don't see how you can get to St. Louis, etc. in a week. So we'll have to see just how it works out and make some plans. The family's visit will have to be decided upon too and I'll have to know just when they're coming and if I can get leave right after that. Gosh, wish the damn war would get over with so people could be human once again and know how, when, and where they will be from one day to the next.

I won't give you even the slightest hint about your Chanukah present, so there. You'll never guess this Bops in a thousand years. As for what I'm getting, I haven't the slightest idea, you rascal.

Did a general tonsil this morning on a 10 year old kid and really had quite a tussle. The kid just bled and bled but it finally stopped. Some of these GI instruments are enough to turn what little hair I have left gray.

Hope the clinic isn't busy so I can listen to the Army-Navy game this afternoon. Take it easy on that old night duty baby and don't work too hard and you haven't kept me posted on your weight.

We have a whole bunch of Dictaphones now in the hospital. Do you have them? If you do—I'll talk into one for you and send it through the mail so you can hear the maestro's voice. They are really wonderful, when you learn to use them.

I love you,
Mr Bops

My darling,

Just received your long two page letter and it was swell hearing from you.

I've been scratching myself trying to think of some sort of plan that will get us to-gether for the coming week-end but it's just too far Bops. If the planes were running and I knew I could get a seat I could fly to St. Louis but I need a priority and I'm liable to be left being AWOL. I guess we're just a little too far apart. Too bad I wasn't assigned somewhere in Missouri or Illinois but there we go again.

I repeat you can't have one solitary inkling about your present so just sweat it out and wait, you rascal.

Just had to run over to the O.R. and do an Incision and Drainage on a kid with an infected sebaceous cyst of the left ear. Remember those we used to do, Bops.

Well, I spoke with Dad the other night and he's trying to get the place for me, buy the home, equipment, records, etc. It's a lovely home Bops and sure would be a wonderful place to live. I asked him what about my office I already have and Dad felt this would still be better. I tried to sound interested and told him to buy it if he wanted to but that one of these days I'd like to buy something with money I had made myself. Money, money, money, everything but what we really want. Nuts! SNAFU! EGAD and other sundry remarks! Hah! Hah!

Instead of our usual week-end party after you come off night duty Bops, how about me calling you Friday afternoon around 5 or a little earlier. If you go somewhere just let me know and I'll call some other time.

I love you,
Mr Bops

My dear darling

Golly it's good to have the old night duty over. Am waiting now for Uncle Ben & family to arrive. Haven't seen them in about seven years, so it will be rather a strained meeting. They will stay overnight.

Baby you will have to use the good telephone next time, sorry you couldn't hear me so well, your voice sounded just as good as ever, but I sure had to yell didn't I? Didn't go to bed in the a.m. & another girl & I did some shopping in Macomb. Wanted to be back in time for your call, but was so tired had to go to sleep while waiting. It's sure funny how we can tell all about each other by just hearing each other's voices. You could tell I had been asleep & I know you had a cold. Darling please be careful at that game today & don't catch anymore or you will have to be sent to bed, so there. Bops should be there to give you fluids & make you rest, shouldn't she?

Have got to give a little lecture on this new purchase your daddy is making—always something for me to fuss about, but darling I hate to have you spoiled in that manner. I feel you should be left to make a few investments of your own & as you see fit. Honest baby you would appreciate them so much more especially if it were something you had worked for & earned. Yes darling, there is nothing I want more than to see you spoiled & have things, but not entirely in that manner—but then I suppose it's not my business. It's too bad baby that your daddy feels he can buy you happiness, isn't it.

Got the stripes yesterday dear, only these are so much nicer. Sew them on carefully so they will look especially nice. The material in the background of these will be much better on your O.D.'s.*

Gee Whiz, something to wear, that could be most anything. Will you tell me if it's any of these, a robe, riding boots or breeches—all right. I'll give up, but Bops do I have to wait till January. I know, you just want to see my eyes sparkle—huh? Shall I keep yours till then too?

Will put in for my leave the 15th or better still the 12th. Go home the p.m. of the 11th, meet you in St. Louis the 15th. If I have 7 days that would mean I wouldn't have to be back here until midnite the 18th. If we get a new chief nurse (this is what I was trying to tell you) she may give me two days. Capt. Butler is being relieved this next week-end or a few days thereafter. I agree with you fully on the reasoning. Just don't know what will happen to me dear,

---

*   Non-formal Army Service Uniform

am pretty sure there will be lots of changes made after Jan. 1st but we won't cross that bridge yet.

Had a nice letter from Wally & he said he had just heard from you. Suppose he has written about his nice leave. He is still plugging for us baby.

Better stop this gabbing. We will talk more about our leave as the days go by. Perhaps you can figure out a schedule, want to be home four days & with my 7 day leave I get one day travel. Can go to St. Louis from St. Paul late p.m. of my 4th day home. So get busy guy.

I love you darling & your call was so good.

Did you like my big smack?
Miss Boo

My darling,

I'm a bad boy for not having written in the past few days darling, but the old one-arm paper hanger has nothing on me these days. I've been working quite hard lately and the Col who has charge of the clinic here made me take yesterday off. As a result I went over to Atlanta and saw the football game. I wasn't going because I had some sick chickens on the ward but I went anyway and I really enjoyed the ball game.

That old Bops hasn't changed a bit and she sure is a sleepy old thing when she gets up in the morning, aren't you baby. I could just picture you standing there with those sleepy eyes of yours.

Heard from Wally the other day and I'm happy that he is writing you as you are him. He's a peach Bops and I really miss him. We sure have some wonderful friends, Bops. I think I have the most wonderful friends in the world. I don't think there is anyone who has so many of them got a letter from the Chief Nurse who was at Blanding with me and she is now in India and is about to take off on her rounds which will take her over 30,000 miles by air. Should be very interesting. I hope some day you will meet her Bops. You'll really like her as much as I do.

I'm sorry to hear Capt Butler is leaving and I wonder whether she has any brainstorms about taking you with her. Perhaps she has. I wonder what you'll do Bops if she wants to take you with her. I'd want you to go because you could be with someone you know and like and then again, I wouldn't. Golly, baby, when will it all end?

I guess I told you about me getting the best ward in the hospital, didn't I?

I'm going to put in for 10 days leave beginning on or about the 29th of Jan and I'll see that Gunboat come hell or high water because it's just about time and I don't know how much longer we can wait. I hope I get it and perhaps that time you will be able to get more than 7 days.

I have made reservations for the family to stay here at the club on the 8th of Jan and they will probably stay about a week. What I'm going to do with them I don't know because there is absolutely nothing to do but I'll manage. I shall really be the great actor Bops when they come down. It's a tough job baby, trying to be 2 people at once but I'm getting to be pretty good at it. How long I can keep it up I don't know but I'm right in there pitching. You are of course Baby, my one worry, outside of the family. I wonder just how long it can be kept up and somehow or other I seem to get courage from just looking at your picture. You old Gunboaty thing!

I'm looking forward to that package one of these days and I can hardly wait. Poor Bops will have to wait until the last part of January because I'm too selfish to send it through the mail. I want to see your face when you open it. So there!

Oh yes, I am on the same time that you are—Central War Time. So we are the same time and there is no hour interval.

Be happy darling, or at least a reasonable facsimile, you're an angel with and without wings and I think of you as much as you think of me.

I love you,
Mr Bops

Edward's Tape describing his stay at Fort McClellan which lasted November-December, 1944:

McClellan was the WAC Center, WAC's being the female component of the Army. On my arrival at Fort McClellan, I looked at the duty sheet and found I was to report to a certain Quonset Hut on Monday morning at 8:00. When I got to the Quonset hut, I was met by an Army nurse who acquainted me with what my duties were to be. For all the people who are not familiar with Army life, the well-known "short arm inspection," was usually confined to men—enlisted men—and consisted of a visual inspection of the genital parts of the men soldiers. The purpose of this was to ascertain any gonorrhea or syphilis. This was bad enough for an ophthalmologist to consider as his duty, but when I walked into the Quonset hut and found a series of 40 tables, lined up row after row, in which females were lying on their backs in a Trendelenburg position, and covered only by a sheet. What I am saying it was my duty to do a short arm genital inspection on female Army personnel. It is one thing for a bachelor—or any male officer—to visualize a bunch of beautiful women lying down on their backs in Trendelenburg position. For the unprofessionals, this might seem a rather bizarre, erotic journey into voyeurism. However, to have the genital parts of 50 or 60 women exposed to one's examination, is hardly a romantic interlude, and one which immediately disenfranchised me to the point that I hightailed it to the Commanding Officer of our Hospital and requested an immediate transfer to anything but this type of duty. The net result was that I was transferred to the 375th Station Hospital stationed at Camp Ellis, Illinois . . .

Editors' Note: His dictated tape ends at this point, and it is curious that this story is not described in any of the letters.

From Gretchen's journal December 1944

One day Ed called and said that he would soon be in Camp Ellis as he had been assigned to the 375th hospital which was its staging area and that his commanding officer was a medical officer we had both served with in Panama. What good and bad news for he would be going overseas again but without me. On his arrival he came to see me at once and brought a most beautiful emerald cut diamond which he wanted me to have as a friendship ring. My heart fell and I refused to accept it, for I knew he had not bought it for that purpose, but told him I would keep it safe til his return. Be it God's will, fate, or that I was at this post when the 375th was looking for a Chief nurse, through some maneuvering, I was appointed and my world had taken on a new look, for I would again be near the man I loved. We couldn't believe this happening. I was promoted to Captain & Chief Nurse of the 375th.

Editors' Note: The 375th Hospital was being deployed to Okinawa.

JANUARY, 1945

My dear darling,

You told me not to bother about writing, but I can't stand it any longer and besides your little letter just came which makes me ashamed for not having sent just a hello anyway.

Bopsy, I certainly feel that you should have your promotion and probably nothing would happen on it until we were all set to go, then too there is this problem about promotions being frozen, don't know how it affects overseas units but so want you to be a Major and it's only right that you have some reward for your faithfulness and hard work. Doesn't the T.C. call for a Major in charge of EENT?

Sent my request over for my T.R. for the 18th Bops, so that means I shall leave here the morning of the 18th, get into St. Louis at 5:30 P.M., leave there at 11:05 and get into Louisville the morning of the 19th at about 7 A.M. That is a day early and Lt. Gray thinks that I should be there by then. It's only a week away baby and that isn't too long for us to wait. Golly I get all goosebumps and a little jittery, and really I think that I should die if anything happened that you were taken out of the unit. As far as the Major is concerned dear he will never let you go it it's at all possible cause as I told you he thinks he has a jewel in you and I told him, "Indeed you have Major."

My packing is almost completed, have everything in order I believe. Went over to the Judge Advocate yesterday and had a will made out, thought it best and Larry Hall who is the J.A. is an old acquaintance of mine from Madison so he drew up a nice one for me, not the old form that most people use. The family is getting very excited dear about their trip, they will leave home the morning of the 20th, honestly they are like two kids.* Mom feels a little badly about my going, but both of them feel very comforted to think that we are going to-gether.

Had a nice letter from Wally yesterday and I wrote him about all our excitement and the wonderful break we are getting, he will be thrilled to pieces for us. Have you written him or have you been too busy.

Darling how are the boys doing in their training? Do you have the complete list of the nurses that are going? I am inclined to think that my

---

*   Gretchen's parents had sold the farm in Hudson, Wisconsin and were permanently moving to California

*appointment came because of your trip to Washington, what do you think?**

Baby dear I am really kinda lonesome, keep thinking how glorious it will be to be with you all the time, can't seem to realize that it is really going to be. Darling I think that if it weren't for you I'd be an awful coward, for your great strength morally and mentally will be what will carry me on. All I pray for is that we are kept to-gether and that we both can do a good job.

What do you hear from your folks, darling, are they all well?

Am sorta looking for a call baby, such a spoiled thing as I am huh? If you have any suggestions as to what I should do in preparing for these girls, please let me know. I have quite a few things lined up such as interviews, etc.

Keep the chin up dear Bopsy and soon there will be lots of days for us together. Yummy, yummy

I love you,
Miss Boo

---

* Edward made a trip to the Pentagon to request Gretchen's assignment.

6 February 1945

Dear Ed:

It looks as if the clan is gathering at Nichols General Hospital. All you need now for a decent Hospital unit is Lefky and myself.

I got personal warning orders from the Chief of Personnel in Washington. It will be in February, he says. Where I dunno and don't care. May we meet again for further service. You know there are a lot of suckers for poker games running around and I'd like to take advantage of it.

Sincerely I am glad to hear that Gretch is with you. There's such a thing as getting married by a Chaplain you know. I'm told it is done regularly. What are you waiting for? You've given this 10 months trial. You should have reached a conclusion by now. Act. I wish I were with you Ed.

About calling me before you go Ed. You know I'm never in one place long enough for that. I live off the Post ($75 extra per month) but I'm never in till midnight. It is basketball, poker & bridge at B.O.Q.* or the Club. Incidentally this scribble may not reach you before you go.

God bless you both.
Fr. Jim

---

* Bachelor Officer's Quarters

Gretchen was transferred to Louisville, Kentucky in January, 1945 and departed there May, 1945 for Seattle.

Her Journal entry:

We awaited supplies for the hospital but left shortly thereafter to pick up our newly recruited nurses in Louisville, Kentucky. These nurses had been on duty in the Army hospital there and got their first experience with the casualties of war. I found them fresh and willing & ready for overseas duty . . . One must walk a fine line when they are in charge, but I tried to be fair and they were willing to take orders. We went by troop train to Ft. Lewis, Washington, and saw beautiful scenery in the Rockies. After a few days briefing, we boarded ship. It was void of any luxuries, no furniture except in the mess and in sleeping quarters. Our first port after days at sea was Eniwetok to refuel. The brave ones went down the side of the ship on rope netting just to get on the ground and to visit the PX there. Now we were on our way to Okinawa in the Ryukyus near Japan.

Editors' Note: The ship spent two weeks at Eniwetok Atoll and an additional two weeks at Ulithi, a large secret Navy base 360 miles southwest of Guam.

OKINAWA, 1945

From Gretchen's Journal

The kamikazes from Japan had been very active and when it was safe, we docked in Naha. There was no city anymore, the island had been bombed to bits, hardly a tree was left standing. Shuri Castle was near the abandoned air field where we were to set up our tent hospital. The castle was a shell but some G.I.'s went there and looked through the rubble and brought me back a complete sake set.

While the hospital was being readied, my duty was to disperse the nurses to various field hospitals. One morning right after my girls left, I had been violently ill during the night and was awaiting transportation to go to a hospital when there was a terrific explosion which filled my tent with dust and debris. Knowing I wanted to escape to safety but in a semi-delirium, I left my cot, but knowing it was hopeless, I returned to my cot, but found it with an unexploded shell there which could have been me. My time had not come!

After a week with bacillary dysentery, I recovered & returned to duty. Ed was very worried but visited me every day.

Our hospital did not have many patients for it seemed the Japanese were almost ready to surrender. So patients were being evacuated from the island as fast as possible. Rumor started the beginning of "False V.J. Day," and anyone that had a gun was shooting off live ammunition and the sky was filled with tracer bullets. It was very frightening, but fortunately, we had no casualties. A few days thereafter, the Japanese signed the peace treaty on Sept. 2, 1945.

Our next task was to dismantle the hospital, but before it could be accomplished, a most severe typhoon struck the island and what was left of the hospital was completely destroyed. One tent was left and all personnel stood shoulder to shoulder hanging on to the tent to protect patients that were there. Many of our ships in Buckner Bay were badly crippled. Now everyone was awaiting orders to return home, we had no duties and it was an anxious time.

Rosh Hashana Services Okinawa 1945

Sake cups found on Okinawa. Gift to Gretchen from anonymous G.I.

Edward describes the same experiences on tape

When we landed on Okinawa, there was absolutely nothing on the island. Only thing standing was a small part of Shuri Castle in Naha which was the capital, and this was tilted on the side. It almost looked like the Leaning Tower of Pisa. The rest of the island was absolutely decimated by gunfire, explosions, bombings, and so forth. There was no water, no facilities, no electricity, absolutely nothing. We set up our hospital compound trying to get it ready to receive patients, but there was considerable amount of time on our hands because of the inability to get things organized. We finally got our hospital in working order, getting ready to receive patients, and we did have a couple, when the first typhoon struck us. A typhoon is an interesting phenomenon of nature, and one which almost defies description unless one has been through it. The best way I can describe a typhoon is that when it rains, it doesn't rain down; it rains up because the wind is blowing so hard. We had one big hospital tent and one or two patients at the time. It was all we could do to keep the thing from blowing away completely. There were two typhoons while I was on the island. Gretchen was in the first one; I think she had gone back by the time the second one came. Both typhoons took a terrible toll, mostly physical on the island, and the Navy took the brunt of the beating. There were many beached ships and those who survived had put out to sea on the first warning. While waiting to receive patients, there was a considerable amount of time on our hands of all personnel and most of us spent time reading and doing various vocational things such as writing letters, or modeling airplanes, or conversation. At one time Johnny Tice, head of our dental department, and I were sitting in a modified slit trench. I was reading "Forever Amber," a novel many of my generation will probably remember, by Kathleen Windsor, and Johnny was modeling an airplane with some sandpaper, when all of a sudden, the world around us became one of sound and fury, and wind and dirt, and so forth. What had happened was a Japanese ammunition dump had been blown up by sniper fire. During the midst of the noise and the confusion and the dust, something plopped in front of us which turned out to be a red-hot, unexploded, three-inch naval shell. John looked at me and I looked at John, and as if motivated by the same thought, we said, "You know it wouldn't be a bad idea if we sort of moved from here." We didn't panic, I dog-eared the page which I was reading, and John put his model airplane in the little plastic box which it had come in, and we promptly proceeded to leave the area, not running or anything. It was only after we had left the area for about 5 or 10 minutes, that we suddenly developed these secondary shakes and realized what we had just been through, and how lucky we were, but the shaking finally stopped.

At the same time, Gretchen had been having a bout of bacillary dysentery in which she had high fever and was sometimes a little, not irrational, but unoriented, due to the high temperature. She got up from her cot in which she was sleeping and decided to take a little walk. Fortunately for her she did because almost two minutes after she left her cot, the explosion occurred, and when she got back to it, it was ripped completely into shreds by flying shrapnel. Some sort of fate must have intervened in our lives because we both survived what is an interesting experience to recall.

Life at our station hospital with only a limited amount of patients, was not a very fruitful one from a professional point of view. After the typhoon, there were no patients, and we tried to put our hospital together, but by this time the immediate threat of the war was continuing to subside, and many of us were starting to get orders to go back home. Life at this time consisted of Rosie *(Norm Rosenberg)* taking rides around the island in the Jeep which I had gotten from the Seabees, and which almost proved disastrous for him, because it turned over one day, and here was this six-foot-five giant of a man crawling out from under an overturned Jeep, and how he survived, we don't know to this day. Our commanding officer, Col. Hanna, had gotten himself into a little difficulty by sending a bunch of our people over to a storage depot in order to appropriate a reefer. Reefers were giant ice boxes supported by their own generator. And the reason we did this was because it was sitting there idle, and it sure would be nice to have a whole bunch of ice for our hospital. Well anyway, we procured it, but the Marines raised hell, as a result of which Ed Hanna was relieved of his command. I was appointed as investigating officer to see what the facts in the case were. My investigation took me to Ie Shima Island where Ernie Pyle was buried, and this provided a very interesting time to see his grave. Ernie Pyle, as many of you know, was a remarkable correspondent who contributed so much toward the understanding of the Pacific War to the people of the United States. At any rate, my recommendation about Col. Hanna as investigating officer was, inasmuch as no personal profit had been obtained, and the reefer was being used for good purposes for our own Armed Forces, that there was indeed no cause for charges to be levied against Col. Hanna. As a result, he was relieved of his command

and sent back to the States, which was really a great benefit rather than a punishment. Col. Hanna was replaced by some farmer from Iowa. He made such an impression on me, that I do not even remember his name to this day. One interesting event took place around August at which time there was false rumors of Armistice having been signed with Japan. This was known as false V-J Day. As many of you know, the medical corps in the Pacific, especially on duty in Okinawa, was armed. This was unusual, but in view of the fact that there were reported atrocities, and so forth it was thought that all soldiers should be armed, this included the medical profession and the enlisted men, half of whom wouldn't have known how to handle a gun if Billy the Kid was there to instruct them. At any rate, it was announced over Armed Forces Radio that peace had been obtained with Japan, a false V-J Day; and immediately all the troops on the island started shooting tracers into the air, firing their weapons which 90% of them, and the medical corps especially, had not been qualified to use. To set the record straight, there were between 10 and 15 deaths due to what we call "friendly fire" on Okinawa in what we now call "False V-J Day." At the peak of this, guns going off, tracers lighting the sky, guns being fired, my commanding officer turned to me and said, "Siegel, go out there and get those men to stop firing." I said, "Sir, with all due respect, you go out and get them to stop firing," and I promptly dove under one of the floor boards of one of the nurses' quarters. You can imagine that my response certainly did not endear me with my Commanding Officer. At any rate, we survived False V-J Day.

THE WEDDING

SEPTEMBER 25, 1945

Edward described the wedding on tape

One day Gretchen was notified that she had received her orders to go back to the States, and would leave within one week's time. This created an immediate crisis between the two of us because we both knew that if Gretchen went back to the States, without a commitment from me or not being married, that in all probability, we would not get together again, because I would be, once again, submitted to the objections of my family to this marriage. I remember the night clearly that Gretchen and I discussed this on one of the beaches of Okinawa, which incidentally is one of the most beautiful in the world, and I finally realized that it was really my decision to make, that unless we were married before she went back, we wouldn't probably even see each other, or at least not in a marital situation.

We decided to get married before Gretchen went back to the States, and this unleashed a period of activity which has probably never been equaled in all of mankind: getting ready for a marriage, getting an adequate dress, getting a ring, getting permission from the military to get married, and a whole host of problems. We immediately went into an emergency session with all interested parties, which included Gretchen's old chief nurse *(Captain Johnny Butler)*, and Norm Rosenberg, who was to be my best man.

One of the first problems we faced was Gretchen's wedding gown which was solved when her nurses got together and made her a hand-made, made-to-order bridal gown made out of a white nylon parachute from one of the fly-boys. The ring situation was solved by the Dental Corps who supplied gold teeth which were melted down from Jap survivors and which formed my wedding band, and Gretchen's wedding ring amounted to removal of the sterling silver bomb site insert in a Norden bomb sight. This is what you call ingenuity at its best: a wedding gown and two wedding rings.

The next problem was getting permission to get married. As you know, weddings are not official anywhere, unless they are performed with the acknowledgement being made of existing civil authority. There was no civil authority on the island of Okinawa. There was no military government, there was nothing. So we did go to the Jewish Chaplain, Rabbi Hershel Lyman, who said, "Ed and Gretchen, I'd be very happy to marry you two, but you must remember when you go back to the States, to make it all official. In event of any legal problems, you get married again in the States with adequate existing government permission and licensure."

The next problem came as to who is going to give the bride away. From my recent remarks about my commanding officer, you knew damn well, that he wasn't going to give Gretchen away. Norm Rosenberg, our best man, popped up with a suggestion: General Stillwell, good ol' Vinegar Joe had just returned from the China-Burma-India Theater and was the Commanding General of the Tenth Army Corps taken over in Okinawa. Rosie says, "Why don't we have General Stillwell give the bride away?" So everyone thought that would never happen, so at any rate, he called General Stillwell's headquarters and spoke to his Adjutant. The Adjutant said, "Let us get back to you in 24 hours and see what the General thinks." Well, anyway the Adjutant got back to us in 24 hours with the great news, "General Stillwell will be absolutely delighted to give the bride away." You can imagine the ecstasy and the excitement at our little hospital in Okinawa.

Once it was known that General Stillwell was coming over to our side of the island to give the bride away, like magic and for all interested people, Gretchen and I believe that we had more people at our wedding than at any wedding in history. There were 5,000-7,000 GI's, sailors, stragglers, non-combatants, prisoners of war assembled. This got out as the first real social event that this island had ever seen.

The Marines had built a Chapel of Peace on Okinawa consisting of all home-grown rocks which they had put together and formed a wishing well, a chapel, a non-sectarian chapel. Anyway this is where the wedding took place, at the Chapel of Peace.

I still had my Army beige uniform which I had gotten before we had gone overseas, at which time I weighed 198-almost 200 pounds. I never realized I was in such good shape. I was playing baseball with the enlisted men, playing first base, having a great time, and so forth. At any rate, if you've seen the wedding pictures, I look like a sack of bones.

General Stillwell arrived and he was absolutely the kindest, most gracious gentleman that Gretchen and I had ever seen. He was keenly interested in our well-being, in who we were, in what we were doing, and in what our plans were. In fact, as an aside, when we got back to the States, we went to see General Stillwell's widow in Carmel, and she showed us the letter that he had written about how he was going to give the bride away at the wedding of this young American couple.

Our wedding reception was held that afternoon and our Commanding Officer showed up anyway, complaining that the enlisted men were drinking with the nurses, were drinking with the Officers, at which time we told him that if he had any complaints, he should complain to General Stillwell, which shut him up immediately.

Gretchen was due to go back to the States the following morning, and our honeymoon was to be spent at MacArthur's headquarters about 40 miles north of where we were married. MacArthur's headquarters consisted of several Quonset huts and the only flush toilet on the whole island. Anyway, we received General Stillwell's permission to go up there to spend the nuptial evening. Gretchen and I, thoroughly exhausted by this time, got into a Jeep, and travelled 35-40 miles over roads that were almost impassable and impossible even for an American Jeep. It took us several hours to get there, and we arrived there at about 8:00 or 9:00 at night, knowing full well that we had to leave there by 5 or 6 in the morning to get Gretchen down to Naha to get her ship to get her back to the States.

The wedding boudoir was something to imagine. Picture a Quonset hut which is about 150 to 200 feet long and about 40 feet wide which was set up for various things. We walked into the hut. There in this Quonset hut which was absolutely bare except for two hospital beds which were set up in the middle, touching each other, covered with mosquito netting. We took one look at this and we started laughing so much we didn't know what to do. To this day I have no details about the consummation of the wedding night, except we were both so exhausted, I'm sure we fell promptly asleep, and were awakened in the morning by this raucous loud speaker system. The men at MacArthur's headquarters knew that we were coming, so to wake us up in time so we could get Gretchen back to the ship, they did not have any copy of Lohengrin's (Mendelsson's? whatever the hell it was) Wedding March, so we were awakened in the morning by the loudspeaker blaring, "Happy Birthday." I suppose in this way it was the birth day of a great marriage.

The Army guys wanted to bake us a cake, but they decided they were not going to bake a cake out of canned eggs. So they took their beer ration out to a Navy ship anchored in the harbor, and swapped their beer for several dozen fresh eggs. That to me was a sign of true admiration, and to this day, we appreciate it. At any rate, here we were having our wedding cake made of fresh eggs—almost unheard of—course you know the Navy is still the greatest service, and they had everything except liquor. Anyway the Army swapped their liquor for the eggs, and Gretchen and I had our wedding cake.

After the wedding cake, in which the enlisted men participated, and we finally got them to turn off the damn birthday song, we got back in the Jeep and back-tracked our way to the port from which Gretchen was to leave. We got to the point of debarkation barely one-half hour before the ship was to sail, and I promptly started up the gangplank to see her off, when I was stopped by some Major asking me where I was going, and I said, "Well, I'm just about to see my wife off for her return trip to the States." As soon as he heard we were the married couple for whom General Stillwell gave the bride away, his attitude completely changed, and it was, "Yes, Sir, No Sir, and Anything we can do for you Sir," until Gretchen finally sailed. There's nothing like knowing the right people.

Gretchen describes the wedding in her journal

With encouragement from our friends, Ed & I planned our wedding for the 25th of Sept. at the Chapel of Peace, as my orders were to leave on the 26th of Sept. This was a major decision for we knew that the distance between his home & mine was great & that we dared not depend on Ed's family to accept me. My nurses were angels and by hand they made my wedding dress from a white discarded parachute. A former jeweler in our unit made our wedding bands from a silver bombsight and gold from extracted gold teeth. My maid of honor was a nurse I worked with at Camp Ellis (Johnny Butler) & had been stationed with on the northern part of the island in a field hospital. Ed's best man was our orthopedic surgeon, a good loyal friend, Norm Rosenberg from Seattle. When we learned that General Joe Stillwell had just returned from the Burma Road, the boys contacted his Aide and asked for the General to give me away & he was delighted to. Our wedding was beautiful & simple. All of our unit's G.I's attending and many others who were curious and with nothing to do, grouped around the outside of the Chapel. We had a reception in the mess tent, cake & all, gaiety reigned. We had been invited to General MacArthur's Headquarters for our honeymoon so after a 2 hour jeep ride on badly rutted roads, we arrived and were escorted to our tent. The G.I's had set up two cots covered with netting in a huge empty Quonset hut. We were exhausted and seemed to have just gone to bed, when we heard reveille, which was a "Happy Birthday" recording blasting from Hqs. We had breakfast of eggs and wedding cake & rushed back to port as my ship left at 7 a.m. Ed & I parted with tears & laughter for he would return to the States shortly thereafter.

Mr. and Mrs. Reuben Henry Boody

announce the marriage of their daughter

Captain Gretchen Boody

United States Army Nurse Corps

to

Captain Edward Siegel

Medical Corps, United States Army

on Tuesday, September twenty-fifth

Nineteen hundred and forty-five

Chapel of Peace

Okinawa

**Chapel of Peace, Okinawa
Wedding Location**

General Stillwell en route to wedding

General Stillwell escorts Gretchen down the aisle.

Bestman Norm Rosenberg, Maid-of-Honor Johnny Butler, Gretchen and Edward

After returning from overseas Capt. and Mrs. Seigel visited friends here recently. They were enroute to Poughkeepsie where Capt. Seigel will return to his practice as an eye, ear, nose, and throat specialist. Capt. and Mrs. Seigel expect to be discharged from the Army in the near future.

Gen. Stilwell Gives Nurse in Marriage

A marriage of interest to many took place September 24 on Okinawa when Capt. Gretchen Boody, a graduate of the Methodist Hospital School of Nursing and the daughter of Mr. and Mrs. R. H. Boody of Van Nuys, Calif., became the bride of Capt. Edward Seigel, Poughkeepsie, N. Y., Army physician.

Chaplain Herschel Lyman of the 25th replacement depot performed the ceremony in the picturesque Chapel of Peace, the only real chapel on Okinawa. It was constructed by the 845th Aviation Engineer battalion in memory of their buddies who gave their lives in the service of their country.

Capt. Boody was given in marriage by Gen. Joseph W. "Vinegar Joe" Stilwell. She wore a gown and veil which three of her fellow nurses made for her from a white nylon parachute. She carried a satin-covered Bible.

A G. I. orchestra provided music for the reception which was held at the officer's club on the island. Capt. and Mrs. Seigel spent their honeymoon at Gen. Douglas MacArthur's home on Okinawa.

Mrs. Seigel did private duty work in Madison for several years after her graduation. She then served as an assistant to Dr. D. L. Williams and later to Dr. Burr McWilliams. She enlisted in the Army Nurses Corps before Pearl Harbor and was stationed in the Panama Canal Zone for some time.

Gen. Joe Stilwell Gives Away Bride, Local Girl, At Wedding on Okinawa

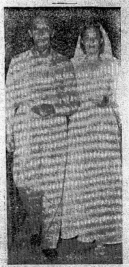

Above, General Joe Stilwell is shown escorting the bride, Capt. Gretchen Ruth Boody of Hudson, down the aisle of the beautiful Church of Peace on the Island of Okinawa, at the recent marriage of the Hudson nurse to Capt. Edward Seigel, 33, of 16 Narcard ave., Poughkeepsie, N. Y. General Stilwell gave the bride away at the ceremony. Mrs. Seigel is the daughter of Mr. and Mrs. Rueben Boody, formerly of Hudson but now of Van Nuys, Calif.

The bride, former chief of nurses at the 375th Station Hospital on Okinawa, wore a white nylon gown fashioned from a parachute by fellow-nurses in less than four days. With a sweetheart neckline trimmed with nylon thread loops from inside the 'chute, the gown had a very full skirt which gathered at the waist, and long fitted sleeves also trimmed with the intricate nylon cords. The skirt boasted a four-foot train, while the veil, complementing the bride's lovely blonde hair, was gathered from an improvised ruching. The bride carried a white Bible with nylon tassels.

The ceremony was performed by Chaplain Herschel Lymon of the 25th Replacement Depot. Capt. Jeanette Butler, of 55 Center St., Waterloo, N. Y., was bridesmaid and carried a bouquet of native flowers, red and pink hybiscus. Capt. Norman Rosenberg, 28, of 1792 SW Montgomery Drive, Portland, Ore., was best man.

The Church of Peace built by the 854th Aviation Engineers to furnish its men the finest place of worship in the Pacific, was the scene of the wedding, Okinawa's third. The structure was constructed of native-quarried stone found in many war-demolished villages on the island, and the resulting chapel has attracted visitors from all parts of the island.

Chaplain Herschel Lymon

Okinawa
7 October 1945

Dear Gretchen,

It took quite a few visits and a number of days
to finally see "Uncle Joe" at Tenth Army Headquarters,
but today we saw him, talked to him, and secured his
signature to the marriage certificate. It was tough,
but I am happy to report: "mission accomplished".

We saw Ed Saturday and he was on his way back to the
States, having cleared at the Personnel Center. Needless
to say, he was rarin' to get back home. Too bad you
couldn't have returned on the same ship, but then too
you won't have the satisfaction of a joyous reunion in
the good old U S A!

I want to take this opportunity of telling you how much
I enjoyed meeting you and knowing you and helping you
arrange for your wedding. It was one of the most moment-
ous and beautiful weddings I have ever seen or participated in -- and I was both happy and proud over the way
things turned out!

And now, a word about the bride: (and I shall try to speak
objectively) she looked both lovely and beautiful, and was
an exemplification of all the fine things everybody has been
saying about her. (P.S. I am talking about you.)

I know that your marriage will be successful, and that you
will achieve great happiness together. If I had any doubts
about that, I would not have cooperated with you so whole-
heartedly and eagerly...

My very best regards to you and Ed, and maybe I shall be seeing both of you very soon in the States. At least I hope so!

Yours as ever,

Herschel L.

Tell Ed that I am taking care of the photos, and that I'll
send them on to him.

'Vinegar Joe' Takes Part in Wisconsin Nurse's Wedding

Gen. Joseph Stilwell gave the bride away and Gen. Douglas MacArthur gave his home for the honeymoon when Gretchen

★ ★ ★ ★ ★

Boody, Hudson, Wis., married Maj. Edward Siegel, Poughkeepsie, N. Y., on Okinawa Sept. 25.

Sheer nerve prompted Capt.

★ ★ ★ ★ ★

Boody of the army nurse corps and then Capt. Siegel of the medical corps to invite "Vinegar Joe" to take part in their wedding, the only army marriage on Okinawa so far.

The bride in a wedding dress made from a parachute marched down the aisle of the Chapel of Peace, dedicated to the men who died fighting on Okinawa, at 6:30 p.m. on a Tuesday.

On Wednesday she sailed for San Francisco.

The happy ending came when Maj. Siegel also landed in San Francisco only a few days ago.

The couple met four years ago when both were en route to the Panama Canal zone for service. In the same unit, they served in Panama and returned to Louisville, Ky. Last May they sailed for Okinawa, still in the same unit, and working together, helped plan a hospital on the island.

But first a hurricane seriously damaged their hospital and then the typhoon which struck Oct. 9 completely demolished it. That ended their work in the Pacific.

The bride, daughter of Mr. and Mrs. R. H. Boody, now of Van Nuys, Calif., and sister of Mrs. Harold Gifford, Hudson, is expected in Hudson this week-end. She completed her nurse's training at Methodist hospital, Madison, Wis.

Gen. Stilwell

Associated Press Wirephoto

MAJ. AND MRS. EDWARD SIEGEL
Their photo album pictures the first army wedding on Okinawa

Gretchen shows wedding gown to actress Catherine McLeod

GOING HOME

OCTOBER, 1945

Gretchen departed September 26, 1945 on the U.S.S. Gen. D.E. Aultman. Excerpt from her journal:

This huge transport had some 3,000 aboard. I was in charge of the library. One of the entertainers was the youngest Marx Brother. We were carefully guided via the Aleutian Islands with a constant look out for mines. We embarked in Portland, and I was a guest of our best man's parents in Seattle & stayed with them. His mom helped me buy our wedding announcements and I shall never forget these wonderful people. After a few days, I was officially discharged from service and left for Van Nuys, California where my parents now lived.

Edward's Tape

Gretchen then went back to the States. I was left by myself contemplating my return and our eventual reunion. I was scheduled to go to Seoul, Korea with the Occupation troops, but before that happened, my orders came for me to go back to the States.

One interesting thing that happened to me, that before going back to the States, I was assigned as part of a medical inspection team to fly over Nagasaki and Hiroshima to see the effects of the atomic bomb. To this day, I cannot describe what we saw, and I will always remember that as one of complete devastation, probably like shots of the moon when the men landed there. It was a completely earth-shattering experience and one which I will never forget. Also as part of this team, we landed in Tokyo as part of the 12th Airborne Division which took over for about one hour, so I could at least say that I was in Tokyo. Then we came back to Okinawa from where we set sail back to the States.

Dearest Gretchen,

Mrs. Siegel!! How wonderful that sounds. Never in all my life have inadequate words been a fault of mine, but what mere words could express my joy and happiness over your marriage. People in the post office thought I was crazy because I hadn't even opened the letter and I had let out an exclamation of joy. The envelope spoke a million words of tears, heartaches and joy.

Somehow how my darling I knew that eventually a love as great as yours and Edward's could find only the happiness and blissfulness you both so richly deserve. Even now as I am writing this my heart is so full of gladness for you that it makes my mind all jumbled and confused. But only confused with my failure to be able to express what I really feel. What more can I say than to wish you all the beautiful years which I know you both will share. May God with His infinite goodness bless the both of you for all time.

Rated number 2 is the grand thought that both of you will be home soon. What I wouldn't give to see the both of you and to throw my arms around you.

I am sending your letter to Elaine. It would be very foolish on my part if I were to dare attempt to describe your glorious wedding unless I copied it word for word. I can imagine the thrill she will get out of it. Even though I probably will never meet any of those wonderful people who helped make your wedding such a tremendous success, I am more than deeply grateful to them. And although it would have remained a priceless treasure to me if I could have been there, I shall be amply repaid when I see you. After all, I consider myself far more fortunate than those people who attended your wedding. Most of them will only remember that lovely wedding, but I hope and pray that I shall be honored to know you for the rest of my life.

As of Monday I have been doing interview work at the Separation Center. It is very easy and time passes quickly.

Since I am only 5 miles from Columbia, I have joined the Town Theatre and at present am rehearsing "A Bell for Adano." I am taking the part of Sgt. Borth, which William Bendix portrayed in the movie version. Opening night is November 12th and it will run for one week. I am also doing radio drama for this group. They put on ½ hour dramatic skits every Thursday night at 10:00 P.M. over one of the better local stations. So you can see that while my discharge is not in the immediate offing, I manage to pass my time very pleasantly. However my one thought is to get out as quickly as possible and be with my darling Elaine.

I haven't heard from Edward in quite some time, but as soon as all the excitement passes, and I do not mean the excitement of being married to you, because that will be for a lifetime, I know he will write and tell me the wonderful news.

What more can I say in closing, than once again to tell you how happy you both have made me, Mrs. Siegel. God grant you joy and happiness.

All my love and love from Elaine.

Your very happy,
Wally

23 Oct. 1945

My dear darling,

    Yummy, yummy, what wonderful news to have my sweet thing back in the states. Oh darling I have worried so terribly about you but thank heavens you are back, safe and well. Now just hurry and get yourself down here fast cause you are in for the biggest lot of scruntching and hugging you have ever had. Oh sweetheart it's so good to know that at last we belong to each other and I will have you with me so very soon, it will be heavenly.

    Baby dear I have so much to tell you that I hardly know where to begin, but here is old jabber heels so bear with me and I will try to tell you all. Know that those few minutes over the phone are going to go so fast that we will probably just have time to say, "I love you," about half a dozen times and that is all. You know us.

    Lots of mail was awaiting me on my arrival here, just hearing from everyone and their happiness for us, it will take you a week to read all these wonderful messages. A letter from the Chaplain stating that you were leaving on the 8th or 9th which relieved my mind no end and by that I knew that you had evaded the storm, it kept me at ease until your letter came telling me how awful the typhoon was and that you were in it, made me just sick sweetheart, but then I was so thankful that you were safe and not hurt. To-day your letter telling me that you were leaving definitely arrived, so know I am just chewing my fingernails and trying to be patient. It's a tough job darling, but there has been a lot to keep my mind and body busy which has helped.

    Barbara and Don* are wonderful and we have been having a lot of fun, then Barb's mother is a dear, very modern and up to snuff and she has been so sweet to me.

    You should have seen your old baby on her shopping tours, have been having the time of my life and Bops when you see this Mrs. Astor I'm sure you will be thrilled and proud. My clothes, what few I have gotten are beautiful and practical, but I remembered all the things you told me so they were a bit expensive. Have only two outfits but have gotten accessories, blouses etc. to make all sorts of combinations with them, they are really beautiful. Darling you will never know this slick chick I betcha, but you just better had.

---

*   Gretchen's brother, Donald Boody and his wife, Barbara

Yesterday when we came home from our shopping, and by the way I didn't forget my sweet thing this time, have a surprise for you, here were mom and dad waiting for us. I so very surprised at how soon they arrived, since they didn't leave Wis. until Oct. 12th. Didn't expect them until the later part of this week. It was so good to see them, mom looks wonderful, but daddy had cracked a bone in his shoulder just the day before they left and hasn't been feeling too comfortable. They are so anxious to see you darling and they are giving us their car to use for a few days, so I have a few plans for us and hope you will be pleased with them, so listen closely. Want so to come up to Beale to get you, but think it is much too far for me to drive by myself, so thought it best for you to come into L.A. and I shall meet you there, then mom and dad think we should have a day or so to ourselves and will make reservations for us at some nice place and we can have another day or two of our honeymoon by ourselves before you meet the family. Think darling it would be far too hard on you to come into all this newness of in-laws etc after going through all you have these past few weeks, so want you to get a little rest all by ourselves first. How does that sound? After that we can make our plans to go east. We will have some trouble getting reservations I am afraid so while we are waiting for them we will have plenty of time to visit with the family.

Mom and Dad have been upset because the house they had planned on going in is a total mess and can't be lived in. Of course Don didn't tell them all that for fear they wouldn't come, so now we are having a few problems. Thought at first we had a lot for them and then they could build, but daddy is afraid to get something like that started with materials uncertain, etc., so to-day we have really been tearing around, because you see they just won't stay here and impose on Don and his little family, I agree it wouldn't be good. Well late to-day I think we discovered a gold mine. There is an estate close by that is looking for a couple. They have a five room house for them. Work for daddy would be excellent and then mom could be right there with him. We will know in the morning what the rest of the set up will be but we think it is a cinch, and they are thrilled to death. Of course mom gives me all the credit for being the go getter, but darling I just have to help them, you know me.

Baby I haven't gotten the message off from the Gen. as yet, but will do it in just a few days, because the Gen. is back you know, and it will be quite authentic, it's just that I haven't gotten into L.A. as all our shopping has been done on the outskirts. Yes I think it is a good idea, it ought to help.

Darling I called Martin, he was a little upset, but was all right to me, so don't worry on that score. You see apparently they hadn't received the cable, cause mom and dad didn't either, and your letter had only arrived that day so the shock was just new, so naturally I understood. As soon as I got here, a letter was waiting from Aaron in which he asked me to call him, but not to worry, that your dad was taking it fine and really nothing to worry about. I have tried to get him, but he was in Washington and will be back this week, so shall call in a day or so, by that time he will probably be able to tell me a little more. I haven't attempted to call the family again, for Martin said he would write to me and I haven't had a letter yet, so that is hanging fire. Sweet baby don't you fret now, but I do want you not to call the family until I can see you, just send them a wire and that will be enough, I only ask you to do this because I want you to know all the latest developments from the first, Aaron will have seen them again and will have talked or written to me etc. Just don't get upset because there really isn't anything besides this, it's just that I want to have you familiar with all the details first and not to be excited or worried over nothing. Darling you have done enough fretting and you mustn't because all will be well. I have prayed so hard for us, and God will listen and help, you just wait and see. All right darling? That's a dear.

Your baby is getting fat darling, just feel wonderful. And when you get here, we will have lots of good food, fruit, vegetables, and lots of orange juice. It's going to be so good to have you fat again darling.

That's right Baby, I'm glad you will be wearing the leaves*, it will help a lot I'm sure and I want you to do it, don't feel badly because it should have been that way long ago. I will be terribly proud of you too sweet thing so you just do it for me too.

Am so anxious to see you, touch you, and have you at my side darling, it will be heavenly and what fun. Just think we are almost old married people after a whole month, but I still feel like a brand new bride. Darling it is going to be a riot around here with these teases, honest they are terrible. I need you here for defense, what a razing and ribbing I have been taking. Can just see a mess of pranks being cooked up for our benefit.

Sweetheart I am going to quit and will write in another day or so. Have so much still to tell you but can't put it all in one letter.

---

*   Promoted to Major

Dear darling, I love you with all my heart and soul, be a good darling. Just don't forget to say your prayers and not worry, just trust in God dear heart and remember we are together for always.

Your own
Mrs. Bops

My darling,

 The days have just been whizzing by sweetheart & soon you will be here to be in my arms—baby, baby—hurry, hurry. Have tried so hard to keep real busy so time wouldn't drag, but each day that passes I find myself counting & calculating & wondering surely by the end of the week there will be that glorious telephone call.

 Nana (Barb's mom) & I just came out to the folks, while they are finishing their dinner, thought it a good chance to have a chat with my sweet thing. We want to take them to a movie this eve.

 Darling, this ranch they are on is lovely. We could have a wonderful time here for a day or so. You see Mr. Coe owns thoroughbred riding horses & has a lovely tennis court & wants us to spend a day just having fun—sounds nice doesn't it? The ponies are beautiful & daddy loves them. Am sure Mom & Dad have found a real home & I'm extremely thankful.

 It has been a dark dreary day & your baby has felt a little blue, the first time since my arrival. Just plain lonesome for her Bops. Can't stand it, being without you much longer dear heart. Life is so incomplete without you.

 Spent most of the afternoon writing letters. Most of them to the girls. Had many thank you's to say & I've really been negligent. Am packing a box of my Army clothes to send them. Fear they lost a great deal in the storm & someone may be able to wear mine. Also wrapped a nice pair of earrings for Johnny Butler.

 Yesterday Nana, Mrs. Siple & I went to Grauman's Chinese Theatre. The footprints were interesting & we saw two good movies, then we had dinner out. It was fun.

 Barb teases me constantly about my beautiful clothes & says Edward will never be able to stand it, his tongue will be hanging out. She is a dear Bops, and you will feel right at home. Carol is an adorable child, sweet & lovable, their second one is due in Feb. which was a surprise to me.

 Did a little shopping Friday, got an adorable dress you will like dear. I'm so surprised to step into a size 10 & have it fit like a glove. Am gaining, however, just filling my bones out. Weigh 116 & that is good isn't it sweet thing. Everyone says I look so wonderful since my rest & stay here. Darling they really feed me like everything. Gallons of orange juice, we just go out in the yard & pick the oranges off the trees. It's really fun. I think you will enjoy getting acquainted with Calif. Everyone is talking me into talking you to stay out west. They need Drs so badly & especially your type, EENT.

Haven't had any news from the East, so really don't know how things are going. I will call Aaron ina day or so. He should be back from Washington & doesn't report to Letterman General until the 9th of Nov. Martin said he would write but to date, nothing.

Haven't gotten your gifts for the Gen or Rosey. Think it would be good for you to help me.

Darling I really don't know what to do about reservations. Think we could fly to Chicago as cheap as by train. You won't mind terribly if we run up to see Dot on our way east will you. We don't know when we will be back that way & I must get my business taken care of, transfer accts, bonds, etc. What do you think darling? Know you will be anxious to get home, but that little rest & change will do you good before we go back & really settle down. Think we won't want to do any traveling for a long while & just live quietly with the exception of N.Y of course, ha.

Are you well baby dear. Just can't wait to get my hands on you. Watch out sweet thing. Will send all my hugs & kisses until we can have the REAL ones.

Darling my conscience bothers me about not coming to Beale to meet you, but you do understand I'm sure.

Oh sweetheart I love you so dearly. Hurry home to your lonesome Mrs. Bops.

Good nite dear, hear.
Gretchen

Edward's Tape

This story of Gretchen and our experiences would not be complete until I take you through our experience with our so-called second marriage. You recall that as I told you before, Rabbi Hershel Lyman said, "Look, Ed, you better get married so that there will be no question about the legality of this whole thing." Gretchen and I met in Glendale, California at which time we went to the County Courthouse and spoke to the Clerk and said, "My wife and I would like to get married again." He had this peculiar look on this face, and I tried to explain to him which I guess he completely didn't understand. At any rate, we were still in uniform, and I guess he still thinks this was one of those quick, hurry-up romances. At any rate, he agreed to have the service performed which was done by the county judge. It took place in this room which must have had room as a County Courthouse for 400-500 people. We filled out the forms and he went through the ceremony, and Gretchen and I almost couldn't contain ourselves when it came to the part which is "If there is anyone who objects to this marriage, speak now or forever hold your peace," and we looked around there were only 4 people in the whole damn room. I half expected people to come screaming out of the woodwork objecting to the marriage, but it didn't happen. And after a good burst of laughter which the performing judge didn't think was especially funny, we were finally married, this time legally.

Certificate of Marriage

I HEREBY CERTIFY THAT ON THE ___8th___ DAY OF ___November___, 19_45_

AT ___Glendale___ IN THE COUNTY OF

___Los Angeles___ STATE OF CALIFORNIA, UNDER AUTHORITY

OF A LICENSE ISSUED BY J. F. MORONEY, COUNTY CLERK OF LOS ANGELES COUNTY, I, THE UNDERSIGNED,

AS A ___Justice of the Peace___ JOINED IN MARRIAGE

___EDWARD SIEGEL___ AND ___GRETCHEN LOUISE BOODY___

IN THE PRESENCE OF ___Gertrude C. Beckett___ RESIDING AT ___Glendale___

CALIFORNIA, AND ___L. E. Ashby___ RESIDING AT ___Glendale___

CALIFORNIA, WHO WITNESSED THE CEREMONY. *I Further Certify That the Foregoing is a Copy of the Original Certificate of Marriage of the Parties Therein Named.*

Bert P Woodard

SIGNATURE OF PERSON SOLEMNIZING MARRIAGE

EPILOGUE

Edward's Narration

We ended up in Philadelphia with Uncle Murray and Aunt Sally who were so kind as to take us into their home while I was still experiencing difficulty with my family. Our stay with Uncle Murray and Aunt Sally was truly a delightful one. It was at this time my relationship with Cousin Irving and Cousin David came to maximum fruition. And I feel we have become much closer since this experience for all of us.

From Philadelphia I went to New York where I took some course at New York Eye and Ear Infirmary and where Gretchen started working.

This concludes the saga of Gretchen and Ed and we hope it will give our families the ability to share in our life to date which has been very interesting and one filled with great, great memories. If you have any questions about Mother and I after having heard these tapes, please feel free to ask. But of course the best part of our lives together has been the result of that marriage, our two children.

I know what my father meant to me and although he passed away on August the 8th, 1958, I must say that I think of him very often and that whatever decisions I have been called upon to make, I try to solve them within the context of how my father would have solved them. Having Janie and Andee around has been a great boon to me and if Mother wants to add something to this, I will certainly allow her to do so, but right now, I am just speaking as myself. You children are great, I love you dearly, and as I used to say to some of my student nurses when I was teaching, "If you have any further questions, please feel free to call upon me."

Gretchen's Journal

When Ed returned from Okinawa later, our plans for the future were uncertain. We were not welcomed to go to his family in Poughkeepsie, N.Y., but we called Aunt Sally and Uncle Murray Levine in Philadelphia who knew of our plight . . . They welcomed us with open arms when our train from California arrived in their city. Our stay there was about three weeks . . .

As the years went by, Ed's father visited us (secretly) and we would meet him half-way unbeknownst to his wife and other son. He adored meeting his granddaughters and always showered them with beautiful clothes as he owned a clothing store.

One day when the girls were 4 and 8, and we decided this alienation from their grandmother had gone on long enough, we packed and drove to Ed's home. When the door was opened by her, we just said, "We want you to meet your family." She looked so stunned but in a moment, she embraced all of us. Grandpa Siegel's face was one of relief and joy. We had a great visit. The girls were taken all through the big house at 16 Barnard Avenue, and they ran back to tell us about the secret places they had found. Grandmother could not do enough for those children. We had a lovely dinner and stayed overnight. Ed was so grateful and happy that at last we were all accepted.

Poem mom sent to dad.

Forever
By J. E. Yarborough

Deep in my heart I hold your love safeguarded.
And, holding it have little cause for tears.
With you beside me I shall go brave-hearted.
Down the bright aisle of years.
Knowing these things, I should not sorrow ever,
And yet sometimes I weep, half sick with grief,
For though I know our love will last forever,
Forever is so brief.

Obituary for Edward Siegel

Edward Siegel, MD, died September 30, 1998 at the age of 86 after a brief illness. Dr. Siegel retired to Sarasota, Florida in 1983 after being Executive Vice President of the New York State Medical Society (1973-1983). He was an ophthalmologist in medical practice in Plattsburgh, NY from 1948-1973 and was Chief of Staff at CV/PH Medical Center (1964-1971). Dr. Siegel received numerous community honors including Citizen of the Year (1964), Presidential Citation for Outstanding Community Service (1960) and was a Rotary Club Paul Harris Fellow. He held many leadership positions including Chairman, City Youth Commission and was past president of Plattsburgh Board of Education, Clinton County Medical Society, Temple Beth Israel, Rotary Club, YMCA, B'nai B'rith, and United Fund Drive. As a Colonel, US Army Reserves, he was buried with full military honors at Arlington National Cemetery.

Obituary for Gretchen Siegel

Gretchen Siegel, formerly of Plattsburgh, NY, passed away peacefully October 21, 2008 at the age of 95 following a brief illness. She was the widow of Edward Siegel, M.D. They resided in Plattsburgh from 1946-1974. Mrs. Siegel was appointed by Governor Rockefeller as a Trustee of the State University of New York. She was an active member of Temple Beth Israel and many other community organizations. She was very proud of her work with the early recycling program in Plattsburgh. Dr. and Mrs. Siegel moved to Sarasota, Florida after living for five years in Long Island. She is survived by two daughters, Jane (Siegel) Whitmore of Pittsburgh and Andrea (Siegel) Feinberg of Mill Neck, NY, and 3 grandchildren.

As a World War II veteran, Mrs. Siegel was interred with her husband at Arlington National Cemetery with full military honors.

As we read these letters and prepared this book, we heard our parents' unique voices in the phrases they used, not only in the letters, but throughout their lives. Many were likely colloquialisms of the era, therefore worth saving. They were also shaped by the movies they saw and the books they read. Here are some:

Mad as a hornet.

An awful snag of letters.

A whole snag of questions.

Nuff said.

So there!

They can't see beyond the ends of their noses.

It came by dog sled.

It's pokey.

It's beastly hot.

Dear heart.

Duck bumps.

Holy Cow!

Tom Foolery.

The thermometer chases up and down.

You're a scamp!

Whiz bang!

Get your head chopped off.

You rascal!

We'll talk til the cows come home.

I'm busier than a one-armed paper hanger.

Davenport.

Like a fly on a hot skillet.

Just sweat it out.

Make a mountain out of a molehill.

It was a scream.

I slept like sixty.

Every cloud has a silver lining.

I'm in a dither.

I feel like a million bucks.

It's colder than heck.

Blasted hot.

There's no place like New York.

Jeepers!

Gee whiz!

Tucker me out.

You're a brave soldier.

I'll have to hold my chin up with a crowbar.

A wee mousie.

Your fanny's getting fatter.

How the mighty have fallen!

Fit to be tied.

Sick as a dog.

Behind the 8 Ball.

Swell.

Punkins.

Movies They Saw

Up in Arms
Man from Down Under
Phantom Lady
Red Hot Riding Hood
Song of Russia
Madame Curie
Sensations of 1945
Mr. Skeffington
Kismet
Dearly Beloved
Eve of St. Mark
Going My Way
The Good Earth
Dragon Seed
The Impatient Years
Since You Went Away
And Now Tomorrow

Books

Graham, Gwethalyn. Earth and High Heaven
Rostand, Edmond. Cyrano de Bergerac
Wells, George Ross. The Art of Being a Person
Winsor, Kathleen. Forever Amber
Yutang, Lin. With Love and Irony

Other Media

Oklahoma by Rodgers and Hammerstein
Fortune
Coronet
Collier's
Hollywood Omnibook

Colgate commercial: "If it's kissin' that you're missin' and it's huggin' that you need, buy Colgate."
The Day After Forever. Song by Andy Russel.

Acknowledgements

We, as sisters, were not close growing up. Writing this book has bonded us in a unique way, and has facilitated a dialog that continues; we are missing the dialog we could have had with our parents. It is with deep gratitude that we honor them with this book.

We hope this inspires our readers to capture more stories before they are lost forever.

Special thanks to Patty Neiderhauser for her keen "Eagle Eye," to Jan Dominick for technical support, and to Nancy Fox for coaching.